The Writings

of

T. Austin-Sparks

Volume VII

A limited edition

Published by   The SeedSowers
               P.O. Box 3317 Jacksonville, FL 32206
               1-800-228-2665

Library of Congress Cataloging-in-Publication Data

Sparks, T. Austin
        Prayer / T. Austin-Sparks
        ISBN 0-940232-81-2
        1. Spiritual   1. Title

Times New Roman 12pt

PRAYER

by
T. Austin-Sparks

This volume contains
three of T. Austin-Sparks' books,
all on the subject of
Prayer.

Preface

T. Austin-Sparks is one of the great figures of the twentieth century who ministered outside of the organized church. For over forty years he held forth at Honor Oak in London, England. The conferences he spoke at, both in Europe and America, have had a profound influence on our time.

Brother Sparks published over one hundred books and pamphlets. The majority of them have ceased to be available to the Christian family. This has been a great loss, as the content of his message has placed him in the category of only a few men of the last one hundred years.

T. Austin-Sparks and Watchman Nee, more than any other men, have influenced the lives of believers who are outside traditional churches. We have felt very strongly that all of brother Sparks' books and pamphlets should be brought back into print if at all possible.

This is the seventh volume of a series that will ultimately contain all of his ministry that found its way into books.

Read T. Austin-Sparks. It is our hope that in republishing these works, his ministry will take wings again, and the influence of his word will spread across the English-speaking world. Hopefully this will give his message a greater influence than ever before.

We send these volumes forth with a prayer that what he ministered will become realities in the 21st century.

The SeedSowers

Discipline
Unto Prayer

Table Of Contents

Part One

Unmoved and Undismayed

And when Daniel knew that the writing was signed, he went into his house; (now his windows were open in his chamber toward Jerusalem;) and he kneeled upon his knees three times a day, and prayed, and gave thanks before his God, AS HE DID AFORETIME.

(Daniel 6:10).

There is something tremendously impressive about a man who is beset and attacked from every side, apparently overwhelmed, and who yet maintains a quiet, dignified persistence of faith and goes on with his God, unmoved and undismayed.

Daniel's troubles sprang from the fact that he had been marked out for advancement. "The king thought to set him over the whole realm" (v. 3). There were two presidents equal with him as well as many satraps under him. All these reacted violently to the decision about his promotion, so violently that they plotted to destroy him. At first they had a great deal of success. It seemed unlikely, or indeed impossible, that Daniel could ever obtain the supremacy planned for him. Yet he did! The evil scheme failed. The servant of God was delivered and placed over the kingdom. The means by which he was advanced must have seemed very strange. Yet they are in full harmony with all that the Word teaches us about spiritual progress. Especially is Daniel's experience in accord with what is shown in the case of the Lord Jesus, that the way to the throne is by death and resurrection.

"As He Did Aforetime"

The lions' den was a kind of grave. Daniel was not spared the grave; he had to go right down into it. Since, however, he was God's man and kept true to his God, he lost nothing and gained everything by that descent. His rivals went down into the same grave, and they stayed there. By the end of the chapter we find no more mention of presidents and satraps. They could not stand the test of the grave. Daniel, on the contrary, was given his place over the whole realm, not by any effort or planning of his, but simply by his maintained position of faith in God. The lesson is for us. We, too, in His amazing grace, have been marked out for advancement, chosen for the throne. This explains for us, as well as for Daniel, the peculiar bitterness of the conflict in which we are often involved. There are great issues in view; we need to know how to behave in the midst of it all, and what is the secret which will enable the Lord to fulfil His purpose in our case as He did in Daniel's.

We find that he came through wholly and solely on spiritual grounds. His own wisdom, his earthly authority, his influence among men, his experience, his friends—all these counted for nothing. As he was hurried away and thrown into the den, he must have been a picture of complete helplessness. There was nothing he could say, and nothing he could do. He did not try to wrestle with the lions; it would have been useless if he had. In a spiritual conflict—and ours is that—nothing but spiritual strength is of any use. For all his apparent helplessness, Daniel had a standing with God. The key to his emergence from the conflict in such complete triumph is found in our verse about his praying, and particularly in the last words, *"as he did aforetime"*.

He was steadfast in his faith. Yet it would not be enough to think of his having faith in a merely general way, or being a man who habitually prayed for all sorts of things. We can only understand the nature of his steadfastness if we realize that he was keeping true to a definite and God-given vision. He had understood the purpose of God with regard to His people. Moreover, he had adjusted his whole life to that vision, as the open window and the "three times a day" prayer-watch show. He knew what God wished and intended, and had given himself wholeheartedly for its fulfilment. Day in and day out, fair days and foul, he kept himself in God's direction and stood for God's will. No wonder that human jealously and spite were used by Satan in a determined effort to silence him! But he could not be silenced. He could not be made to close his windows. "Aforetime" he had persisted in his faith vigil; now that trouble was pending he refused to be turned aside from his set course with God. He had a spiritual 'routine', a holy habit, a steady heart purpose. When this brought him into the cross-currents of conflict, and the writing was signed against him, he seemed to take no notice at all, but calmly continued in his watch with the Lord—*"as he did aforetime"*.

We may be tempted to wish that we were that kind of man, calm, steady, unmoved—wrongly imagining that this was a matter of Daniel's temperament. If so, it is good for us to remember the kind of man he could be. "I was affrighted, and fell on my face . . ." (8:17); "I Daniel fainted . . ." (8:27); "Then said he unto me, 'Fear not, Daniel . . .' " (10:12). This was no man of steel, but one very like most of us, with all our inward quakings, our timidity and our tendency to faint. Yet he was undismayed. In the midst of plots for his destruction, in spite of tremendous pressure to panic or compromise, without any show of strain and in quiet dignity of faith he went straight on with the Lord. And so must we. Perhaps it will help us if we try to discover some of Daniel's secrets.

The Largeness of His Vision

The first reason why Daniel was able to proceed so calmly, as though nothing had happened, was found in the largeness of his vision. If we have a vision that is chiefly concerned with ourselves, our circumstances or our ministry, we shall be puzzled or offended when things begin to go wrong with us. We need, indeed we have, a vision of God's universal and eternal purpose in His Son, and this alone will save us from being overwhelmed in the hour of spiritual conflict.

Daniel looked back, far beyond his own time. The open windows looked out on an original purpose for the people of God, who had had their origin long before his own generation. The Jerusalem which he remembered was a poor affair compared with the true glory of Zion. Most of us are apt to dwell with regret on things as we once knew them, and to sigh for the days of the past. But it is vain, and altogether inadequate so to limit our vision. We have been called for something much bigger than that. We have a part in the Divine purpose which was conceived in eternity and realized in Christ by His Cross. If we set our hearts only on what we have known or experienced, on the limited sphere of our own past, we shall get into confusion when for the time being everything seems to be going wrong. Our natural vision is limited to the immediate, to the present experiences or to the tiny span of our own lives. We need to be saved from ourselves, and this will be by receiving spiritual vision as to the vast range of the Divine purpose in Christ. Like Daniel, if we look back far enough we shall be kept steady by the reminder of God's original intentions.

Daniel also looked forward. We are told that he not only prayed, but also "gave thanks before his God". Of course there was much cause for thanksgiving in Israel's past history, but to the man of faith, the man of vision, the real motive for praise lies in the future. He had received assurance that there was to be a future for Jerusalem, a future even more glorious than the past. He knew that God would realize His end. It mattered little to him, therefore, if all the fury of hell raged around him for the present; it was of very small importance if he, Daniel, were swept off the face of the earth. Nothing could prevent the fulfilment of the purposes of God. Whatever else happened, the Lord would go marching triumphantly on to His goal. With this conviction, and his windows opened in this direction, Daniel could afford to ignore his enemies, and to treat all the decrees of men with dignified contempt. "And when Daniel knew that the writing was signed, he ... prayed, and gave thanks before his God, *as he did aforetime.*"

The little calamities of the present time are contemptible in the light of the certain glories that are to be. We are meant to be people of eternity; we are called to view all present problems and difficulties in their larger setting. It may be true that we, like Daniel, seem to be involved in disaster, that for us the writing is signed which makes our own future quite hopeless. Our vision is not a personal one, nor is our ministry personal, so we must never allow ourselves to be overwhelmed by what is only personal. In Christ we have become closely associated with God's eternal purpose for the greatness of His Son. This is the largeness that will lift us out of our own natural pettiness.

Daniel saw far beyond his own surroundings. He had gone to his house and entered his own chamber. It may well have been a large room, as rooms go, but in any case it was bounded by the four walls of what was essentially his. He did not look at the things around him, but away through the open windows towards the city of his God. How important it was at that critical moment that he should not look around to what was merely local, to the unpromising circumstances in which he himself was found, but should keep well in view the Divine prospect of the God-filled glory of Jerusalem. Only the eye of faith could see that city then, but Daniel had the eye of faith. Surely it was this vision that kept him steadfast.

There is a sense in which men who are under great pressure to capitulate or compromise can only resist the temptation by remembering that their 'cause' is much greater than themselves. They are kept true by the realization that, provided they do not despair, the cause with which they are associated will ultimately triumph in spite of anything which may happen to them. How much more is this the case with those whose 'cause' is spiritual! Had Daniel's main preoccupation been about his own survival he could not have behaved as he did. If he had been thinking chiefly of how he himself could be preserved, he would probably have made terms with his enemies or in some way capitulated. To him, however, the vision was so great that his biggest concern was, not as to whether he could survive, but as to whether he could remain faithful. He felt that he had to be faithful because of the very importance and vastness of the issue.

This constraint to be faithful was noticeable in every part of Daniel's life. It was true, not only in the prayer chamber when he was on his knees, but also in every feature of his ordinary daily life, that "he was faithful" (v. 4). There can be nothing mean or insignificant in the life of a man who finds himself associated with a great Divine purpose: he realizes that this association demands a very high standard in every aspect of his daily life. Few of us can be placed in such difficult circumstances as Daniel was in Babylon. And very few indeed have kept as faithful as he did in the many tests and temptations which came his way. Perhaps it was because he had so learned faithfulness in the smaller matters that he triumphed so completely in this supreme testing.

If Daniel had considered it most important that he

himself should survive, it would have been very simple for him to have refrained either from praying, or from kneeling to do so, or from leaving the windows open for all to see. After all, he was no slave in Babylon, but a man of great importance. He was no enemy of Darius, but his good friend. Had he wished he could have kept his personal safety, and no doubt he could think of many very good reasons why he should try to do so. But then what would happen to Jerusalem? What would happen to the purposes of God for His people? To Daniel it was the vision that mattered, not his own personal good. And in this very way he found his own deliverance. The man who remains true to the God-given vision can afford to leave the question of his own fate in the hands of the Giver of that vision.

This, then, is the challenge which comes to so many of us, the call to be faithful to the vision. Daniel reminds us of how important it is that one man should remain steadfast to the Lord. None of us knows how much of great Divine purposes may be served by our simple faithfulness. In a sense we do not matter at all. It is not important for us to avoid the den of lions, to be saved from difficulties, to justify ourselves or fight for our own position. But in another sense it matters supremely that we should be true to the Lord. In order that we may do so, we need to keep in view the largeness of the vision.

The Greatness of His God

To Daniel God was greater than all. It was as simple as that. He had many visions, concerned with all sorts of people, places and events, but he had one transcendent vision, and that was the vision of his Lord. None of the historical or prophetic allusions can be without significance, for the Word of God is never without meaning; but we shall have missed the essence of Daniel's story if we become occupied with things or people rather than with the Lord

Himself. This is the second of Daniel's secrets of a steadfast life: to him the Person of the Lord towered high above
all others. Prophetic truths may interest or enlighten us,
but they will never save us in the hour of testing. Daniel's
chamber was not a study—at least it was not then being
used as such; it was his prayer-room, his audience-chamber
with his God. As we tend to hurry to our best friend when
trouble comes, so Daniel, when he knew the writing was
signed, went straight home to his prayer chamber to
commune with his Lord. He knelt on his knees not as a
matter of routine or ritual, not to list a number of items for
prayer, but to worship and to wait upon his God. As we
have said, he was associated with a very great vision, but
the central and supreme feature of this vision was the
Person of the Lord.

This is as important to us as it was to him. When we
come to the New Testament, we must be careful to give due
weight to every detail of its teaching. It is very wrong for
us to ignore or disobey the injunctions, the admonitions and
the explicit statements of the Word of God. Yet our supreme concern must be with the Lord Jesus Himself. To
follow all the teachings and methods associated with the
House of God and yet lack the overwhelming Presence of
the Son and Owner of the House is to substitute an empty
shell for the living reality.

Daniel's vision of the Lord was so great that it involved
the eclipse of all his enemies. No doubt they were very
imposing, 'the presidents, the deputies, the satraps, the
counsellors and the governors' (v. 7). Whatever Daniel
thought as he considered this long and formidable list, he
gave no indication of being greatly concerned by it. He
went off home to meet with his Lord . . . *"as he did aforetime"*. To have his eyes on the Lord did not mean that he
ignored his enemies or pretended that they did not exist.
It only meant that because of their hatred he drew nearer

to his Lord, realizing that at all costs he must not be drawn away from that committal and that communion which represented the very heart of the Divine purpose. He was determined to keep on positive ground. It can be merely negative to get preoccupied with our enemies, or with the things that menace God's purpose. We shall never reach God's end by chasing negatives.

Daniel refused to be diverted from the main issue. He would not even turn aside to pray about his own perilous position. He had but one answer for his foes, and that was to continue straight on in his devotion to the will of God. We need to follow his example. Satan will always try to divert us from the positive end of God. If we can be drawn out into side issues, he will always provide such for us. They may be things that provoke us, some matter that never fails to arouse our irritation or anger. If we turn aside to pray too much about them, we shall have missed the real call to positive prayer. It is true that Ephesians 6 stresses the call to prayer conflict, but it comes at the end of a letter that is devoted to the main vision of God's purpose in His Son. It is for this, and not for lesser or personal matters, that we are called into the spiritual battle. Or the devil may even keep us busy with some side issues which we like, good things in themselves, perhaps, but diversions from the principle one. The man of the Spirit refuses to be diverted. Like Daniel, he goes determinedly on.

Daniel's vision was so great that it also eclipsed his friends. There is no mention here of Shadrach and his two companions. We do not know where they were. Perhaps they were praying for him in secret. We do know, though, that there are times when we must go through alone with the Lord. This is no contradiction of spiritual fellowship. Such fellowship can only be healthy and vital if in all things the Lord Himself is the One we keep in view. Darius

13

was also Daniel's friend. As a matter of fact he did his sincere best to help him. But it is not recorded that when Daniel knew that the writing was signed he sought out Darius, to talk the matter over with him or to seek his help. No, he went straight away to the Lord. With all his apparent power, Darius proved helpless in this matter. Daniel knew the Lord as 'high over all'. He could not have held quietly on his way as he did if he had not known a constant walk with his Almighty Lord.

The Power of Prayer

In the third place Daniel had learned complete confidence in God's ability to answer prayer. Nothing could deter him from waiting on God, for he knew the power of prayer. Daniel was well acquainted with power; he had lived at the seat of it for many years. As a lad, he had seen in his own land the amazing things that could be done by this world-power. Together with his fellow Jews he had been taken captive by the mighty emperor, the "head of gold" surmounting all the Gentile kingdoms; and now for a very long time he had had his place at the heart of that terrifying world authority. He knew all about the decrees of an absolute despot and about the "law of the Medes and Persians, which altereth not" (vs. 8, 12). And when he had considered it all, he was more than ever convinced that one man on his knees was more than a match for it all, that there is more power in the simple prayer of faith than in the greatest empire that this world can ever produce. He had learned his lesson. To him it was no mere theory, as, alas, it often is to us. He had proved it in the past and he was content to go on proving it. It was a special occasion, but he sought for no special remedy. He just went on praying *"as he did aforetime"*.

When a man is up against something of satanic origin, he is forced back to prayer, for only God can deal with the

14

great enemy. It is significant that the signed decree was based on a lie. Darius put his signature to it because of deliberate untruth. Those who brought it to him insisted that it had been agreed among "*all* the presidents of the kingdom . . ." (v. 7). Daniel was at least equal to his fellow presidents, and he had had no part in it. Had Darius known the truth it is certain that he would never have agreed to pass the law. Wherever there is a lie, Satan is not far away. And when we get involved in his activities we do well to stand back for a moment, to consider the whole thing, and to decide—as apparently Daniel did—that only God can deal with this situation. Of course we may need to state the truth or point out the lie, but how often God's servants have only got themselves into greater difficulties by trying to grapple with something that was too much for them, too strong or too subtle, when the very presence of a lie in the situation could have warned them that this needed not carnal but spiritual weapons. This is not a matter of opinion or judgment—we all make mistakes—but of an untruth in the realm of facts. What do we tend to do when we meet such a lie? Usually we want to fight it, to argue about it, to try to deal with it by our own actions. What did Daniel do? He went straight back to God, got on his knees and found a place of spiritual authority over it. He dealt with it all in the place of prayer.

That is where it was all done. The rest was simply the outworking. A painful outworking if you like, for it did not relieve him from the necessity of going down into the lions' den, to the great distress of his friend, Darius, who spent a wakeful night worrying about him. He need not have worried. His own power had failed to deliver Daniel —human power always does fail in the face of spiritual opposition—but the man on his knees is the man in touch with the Throne. We are not told what sort of a night Daniel had, but it may well have been one of great inward rest. And this not because he had prayed about himself, but because he had devoted himself to the Lord's interests and could therefore afford to leave his own needs in the Lord's hands. He did not pray because he was faced with an emergency; he prayed because he was a praying man. He believed in the supreme power of prayer, and he practiced what he believed. If only we would do the same!

Daniel had had to pray in order to obtain his vision. A man is no prophet unless he is first a man of prayer—". . . he is a prophet, and he shall pray for thee . . ." (Genesis 20:7). But that was only the beginning. We must not think that revelation as to the will of God is an end in itself; it is but the first phase of a prayer ministry. When Daniel had prayed through to an understanding of the ways of the Lord, he then set himself three times a day to persevere in prayer for their fulfilment. His prayer ministry took him into the lions' den, but it also brought him out again, and he was able to see the thing right through to its glorious end. "So this Daniel prospered . . ." (v. 28). *So*—by praying through, unmoved and undismayed by plots and threats— this Daniel prospered. *This* Daniel—not the Daniel of the presidential office, but the Daniel of the lions' den—this Daniel prospered, not only in the reign of Darius but also in the reign of Cyrus the Persian, who was the liberator and restorer of Jerusalem.

This all happened in the last years of his life. That may be because the time of Jerusalem's liberation was at hand, and Satan the more fiercely attacked the man who was standing for it in prayer. If so, there is a special message for us, who surely have our testimony to give in the closing days of the dispensation. The kingdom for which we labour in prayer is not earthly, but heavenly: it concerns "the Jerusalem that is above" (Gal. 4:26). Let us therefore encourage one another not to be moved by the things which threaten to quench or divert our prayer-life.

And let us remember that this very experience was the way by which Daniel was brought to his appointed advancement. He went to the Throne by way of the lions' den. Our Saviour ascended to the Throne by way of the Cross. We can only reign with Him if first we suffer with Him.

Part Two

"Windows Open Toward Jerusalem"

"And when Daniel knew that the writing was signed, he went into his house; (now his windows were open in his chamber toward Jerusalem;) and he kneeled upon his knees three times a day, and prayed, and gave thanks before His God, as he did aforetime."

(Daniel 6:10; A.S.V.).

The key to this verse, and indeed to the whole chapter, is that little parenthesis—"his windows were open in his chamber toward Jerusalem."

These chapters of Daniel are not in chronological order. Chapters 7 and 8 both come before chapter 5, and then after chapter 5 comes chapter 9 which occurred in the first year of Darius. Chapter 6, although it does not say so, clearly occurred after the first year of Darius: there was an order of things already in the realm, there was a relationship between Darius and Daniel, there were enmities which must have taken time to mature: so that chapter 6 follows chapter 9, and chapter 9 explains the open windows.

A Revelation of God's Purpose

Daniel had a revelation from God. Chapter 9 tells us how he humbled himself before God over the state of God's people and of God's city, and how from heaven there came illumination, and Daniel, with the eyes of the spirit, saw the Divine purpose in its immediate effect (for Jerusalem was to be rebuilt) and in its larger, fuller and final outworking—the day when the people of God and the city of God should indeed be a praise to Him, all transgression forever finished, everlasting righteousness brought in, all the prophecies fulfilled, and God's dwelling-place with men. Daniel saw that; he was able to enter into God's purpose concerning His people; and, whether his windows had been open before that or not, from that day onward they were open—the windows that looked toward Jerusalem—and Daniel made it the persistent, continual, purposeful exercise of his heart to get down before those open windows and pray for God's purposes.

Daniel's Committal to God's Purpose

The opening of the windows was a symbolic act. It meant that he was committed to God and to that to which God was committed; he was with God for that which God intended to do; and the open windows were, humanly speaking, his undoing. Other people saw him at the open windows and realized that here was a trap, a way by which they could ensnare him. And that is, as I understand it, the setting for this chapter 6—not a young man, but the old servant of the Lord, being faced with two alternatives, either to close his windows and leave off pursuing this utter attitude of co-operation with God, or else to go into the lions' den.

The Enemy's Antagonism

Of course, as far as the story goes, it was just the hatred of men and a convenient way of getting rid of him. But we know that there are spiritual lessons in it, and that it always happens like this—that heavenly revelation, and the committal of the heart utterly to the Lord for its fulfilment, provoke an assault which is meant either to make us desist or to destroy us.

Earlier on, Daniel's companions had been in a similar

position with regard to the fiery furnace; but for them it was a matter of whether they were on the Lord's side or not. If they were on the Lord's side, well then, the fiery furnace; if they wanted to avoid the fiery furnace, they must break with the Lord. And we know, and Daniel knew, how the Lord delivered. We all know something of that as Christians. So soon as we are truly on the Lord's side we meet, as they met, an antagonism which calls upon us either to desist or to know the fiery furnace.

I think this experience of Daniel's marks a step in advance of that. This was not for him a question of whether he was the Lord's or not. He could have closed his windows, he could have desisted from this which was the cause of his being thrown into the lions' den, without breaking with the Lord; in the quietness of his own heart, in the seclusion of his own room, he could have prayed. It was not now the question of whether he was the Lord's or not, but the question of an utter position in the light of heavenly revelation, or of desisting from that. It is always so. That is the treatment that we may expect if we too have seen something of what God is desiring and intending to do, and have given Him our hearts and our hands that we are with Him for it.

The Delivering Power of the Heavenly Vision

But the message of this verse to my own heart lies here—in such conditions, in the midst of that bitter assault and antagonism, how did Daniel behave? What a lesson for us all! When he knew, he just went on praying toward Jerusalem. It did not make the slightest difference to him. It was not that he suddenly opened the windows—the windows were open; not that he suddenly began to pray— he had been praying and giving thanks three times a day toward Jerusalem. All the threats and fury of the adversary made not the slightest difference to him. Without any sense of strain: without any twisting of himself up and suddenly getting into a tense condition over it all: in quiet, noble dignity, he went on with the Lord. How important for us to be ready for the assault when it comes! I think one of the reasons why Daniel was so steady and calm under it all was that his revelation was something so much bigger than himself that it carried him through. What I mean is that if Daniel had seen Jerusalem being rebuilt and himself a kind of Nehemiah or Zerubbabel taking the lead: if his vision, while being of Divine things, had brought himself into prominence: well, the lions' den would have been a first-class problem. How could the vision be realized if he went into the lions' den? And that is the disturbing feature in our spiritual lives—that so often, when God reveals Divine things to us, we somehow manage to introduce ourselves into the picture. A certain thing is going to happen, and we are going to have a part! and all too subtly we begin to see ourselves having a prominent place in the realization of it. Then, when the assault comes upon the revelation, and upon us because of it, we are disturbed, we are worried. But Daniel was not going back to Jerusalem, though, as we find, he was told that he should have his place in the end (Dan. 12:13); so far as he was concerned, he forgot himself, he was nothing. The people of God and the city of God, and the purpose of God in that people and city—they were what he saw when he opened the windows. Excuse me putting it this way—it was not a mirror he went to pray in front of, it was an open window. He did not see himself as the chief feature; he saw—though no human eye could see it at that distance—the city of God, he saw the Divine purposes. What did the lions' den matter to them? What did it matter what men did to Daniel so long as that end was realized? In the light of what God had shown him, he could not stop praying for Jerusalem, and, what is more important, he could not stop giving thanks for Jerusalem.

We need a little imagination to put ourselves in his place. When he knew that the writing was signed, what did he do? Begin to pray for Daniel? No, that is what Darius did. Daniel gave thanks that Jerusalem was going to be rebuilt. Oh, the delivering power of a vision big enough, heavenly enough, Divine enough to swallow up all our little petty and personal interests! That is the secret—the open windows. Dear brother, dear sister, look out to God's purpose! Of course, if you do, it will involve the lions' den. What did Daniel care for the lions' den? When he had heard all about it, he just went home, went on praying, went on thanking God.

The Futility of Earthly Endeavour

I like to compare Darius with Daniel. Darius was supposed to be the king, but Daniel was the man reigning in spirit. What a bad time Darius had! and that does not express to us the bad time that evil people have, but the bad time that the well-intentioned man has, who is concerned for the interests of the Lord without really knowing the Lord. It was to Darius' credit that he was so moved and terribly anxious. You notice what it says: this shows the difference of attitude: Darius, when he had been tricked into this experience, "was sore displeased, and set his heart on *Daniel* to deliver him." That is a good enough, reasonable enough, sincere enough exercise. "He set his heart on Daniel to deliver him." And what happened? "He labored till the going down of the sun to rescue him," but all his labour did not make the slightest difference to the lions' den; nor did it make the slightest difference to the Divine deliverance when it came. You can imagine those men who were the means of bringing Daniel into the lions' den. How they enjoyed the problem, the dilemma in which Darius was! He laboured, but they outwitted him; he tried in vain to think how he could outwit them and express his power, and they laughed at him. And the devil laughs at us when we are in the position that Darius was in. And, while the Lord did not laugh at him—I am sure the Lord appreciated the good that lay behind it all—He would have said to Darius, Don't trouble, you are wasting your time, I can manage without you.

Then the night came and the matter seemed irrevocable. What a night the king had, the restlessness, the bitterness, the disappointment! Bring him food—he doesn't want food; music?—he cannot listen to music; sleep?—he cannot sleep. What a night! While Daniel, down among the lions, was having a nice, peaceful, quiet night! Which things are a parable. Daniel or Darius? I am afraid I am often Darius. Darius was a man of the earth, Daniel was a man of heaven. When you are a man of the earth and when you face Divine things as here on earth, that is the kind of condition you work yourself into. Darius was frantic, strained to breaking point. He wanted to deliver the Lord's interests and he laboured and he fought and then he broke his heart because he felt all the Lord's interests were in the lions' den. He tried to meet the enemies of the Lord's interests on their own level. They plotted—he tried to counter-plot; they had exercised their power—he sought the means for overruling with *his* power; he was wrestling with flesh and blood, and he was losing and he was suffering. "Our wrestling is not against flesh and blood" (Eph. 6:12). When Daniel knew that the decree was signed, he did not set his heart to deliver Daniel. He did not labour till the going down of the sun to try and find a way out. Daniel went on looking to Jerusalem, and the peace of God which passeth all understanding kept his heart and mind. But Darius, with the best of intentions, was struggling and striving and trying to do something to help the Lord, and he only succeeded in working himself into a state of restlessness and strain that are beyond description.

23

What is the secret? Surely it is as I have said—Darius was concerned for Daniel, for the human side, for the servant of the Lord—a very good concern in his case, because quite unselfish—but it did not help. Daniel was not concerned for the servant of the Lord, he was concerned for the interests of the Lord, for the heavenly revelation, and the result was that he was kept in perfect peace while Darius was worked up into a fever and a fret.

Well now, let the Lord apply the message and the lesson to each of our hearts. How does it work out with us? Are we on earthly ground or on heavenly?

The Devil's Seeming Triumph

The devil seems rather to be limited in his ability to foresee the deliverances of God. He thinks—and indeed it looks as if he is right—that he can engineer situations in which there are only two alternatives; it was so with the three young men, it was so with Daniel, and in His time it was so with our blessed Lord. Two alternatives face the servant of God. Either he must relinquish the vision or he must be destroyed; and having, like some diabolical chess-player, engineered a situation from which there are only two possible moves, Satan stands back. In either case, he is triumphant. If those three young men will avoid the fiery furnace at the expense of denying the Lord, the devil does not mind their going free—they have denied the Lord, the spiritual interest is marred. Daniel can, if he will, save himself from the lions' den, he can close his windows, he can relinquish that utter position of abandonment to the heavenly revelation; he can—and alas many do—avoid the lions' den. It can be done, and Satan has triumphed either way; and that is the diabolical ingenuity of it. It is a cleft-stick. Either we must relinquish that utter position concerning that which the Lord has shown us, or Satan will break us, he will finish our usefulness, he will mar our lives. So we have to sit down with the two alternatives.

God's Counter by Resurrection

But the devil is limited, happily. There are not really only two ways, there is a third way. The young men proved it, Daniel proved it. In the case of our Lord, and in New Testament language, it is Resurrection. The word used in Daniel is "deliverance." There is a third way; the young men may not have known about that, Darius did not know about it. Did Daniel know? I wonder. Neither he nor the three young men stopped to think when the alternatives were placed before them. They did not take any time to decide, they were committed to the Lord; what happened to them was a secondary thing. Yet I think Daniel did know. He knew in the way in which we may all know. He could not foresee the way in which God would deliver him. That is what we want to know—we want the Lord to explain, we want that somebody else should have gone the same way, and nobody has gone that way before: it always is to us as a new experience, we cannot see the way out. Nor could Daniel in that sense; but spiritually he could see that his association with the Lord was the safe way, and though with his mind he could not understand, with his spirit he knew that to be on the Lord's side was the safe way, and that is why there is this air of quiet calm about him. He did not see the way out, but he did know the Lord; so he would open his windows and pray and praise.

"Is thy God, Whom thou servest continually, able to deliver thee from the lions?" Well, let the next morning and the light of day show, and the king shall see there are not just the two alternatives. That is what the devil thinks—maybe even persuades himself. That is what man thinks as he looks at it from a human level. That is what we shall think unless we have the windows open toward Jerusalem. Two alternatives—either we must compromise in this

matter of utter abandonment to what the Lord has shown
to be His will, or we shall be broken—one or the other. If
we say, in any case I cannot abandon what the Lord has
shown, my heart is set upon Him: we shall find that there
is a third way. There is the vision, and there is deliverance.
Thank God, that is true for us, He is the God of resurrection, the God of deliverances. So let us keep the windows
open.

A Great Victory

See what happened as the result of this. There is
always spiritual gain when we are faithful to the Lord.
Daniel heard all their threats, knew what was going to
happen, foresaw it all, and quietly went on with the Lord.
That is all Daniel did, but you see the extraordinary
results. This experience of his was a great victory. Without
feeling revengeful about men, we must feel there is a
certain spiritual satisfaction at the end of the story in the
fact that the ones who had plotted Daniel's overthrow were
cast into the den themselves; and the spiritual lesson is a
true one. Daniel's quiet faithfulness and his deliverance
were not just things in themselves, they were the overthrow
of the enemies of the Lord. It was a great victory. And it is
always like that. Daniel did not wrestle and strive. He did
nothing concerning his enemies; he kept his windows open
to Jerusalem. But so long as he did that, God was quite
capable of dealing with his enemies. Let the rest, the quiet,
the calm dignity of that assurance flood our hearts. Darius
was trying to deal with the enemies and could not; Daniel
was holding fast to the Lord and his steadfastness was the
undoing of all his enemies.

"The God of Daniel"

And the second feature which emerges from this story
is the great testimony to the Lord which was set up because

of Daniel. The Book of Daniel has a number of titles of God which are very striking, and some of them very wonderful. He is the "Living God"; He is the "God of heaven"; He is the "Ancient of days"; and so on. But come to chapter 6:26, and He is "the God of Daniel." In all that list of glorious titles, here is one more—"the God of Daniel." What a testimony! It is not that Daniel stands for anything, but what makes the King and all others to marvel is, 'What a God Daniel has!' *Would that that might be added to the many titles of the Lord, with my name and yours in the place of Daniel's!* We are not important, but nor was Daniel in his own eyes.

Our windows open toward Jerusalem, our going on with the Lord, mean the lions' den; but we go on with the Lord, and after all we come out of the lions' den and there is a great victory, something established in the earth that never was before of a testimony to the greatness of the glory of God. "The God of Daniel." *The Lord grant that this may be true in our case.*

Part Three

Meekness of the Man of God

"And there hath not arisen a prophet since in Israel like unto Moses, whom the Lord knew face to face; in all the signs and the wonders, which the Lord sent him to do in the land of Egypt, to Pharaoh, and to all his servants, and to all his land; and in all the mighty hand, and in all the great terror, which Moses wrought in the sight of all Israel."

(Deut. 34:10–12).

"Now the man Moses was very meek, above all the men which were upon the face of the earth.

(Numbers 12:3).

The prophet Micah described the man who pleases God as the one who loves mercy and walks humbly with his God (Mic. 6:8). Moses was outstanding in his humility, not only in his own days but through all time. In connection with this, it is helpful to realize that he was a man who loved mercy. He had reason to do so, since he himself owed everything to the grace of God. There seems to be no greater man in all the sacred record—certainly not in the Old Testament; and the mark of his greatness is that he was very meek.

A Christ-like Virtue

His meekness was not a superficial guise which he assumed, but a profound characteristic of the man. The actual statement about him was made in connection with a period of great provocation. He was tested—tested

28

severely and often; and from it all emerged the Divine verdict that he had passed the test: he was indeed a truly meek man.

Meekness is, of course, a Christ-like virtue—"I am meek and lowly in heart" (Matt. 11:29). Perhaps it is one of the greatest virtues, for it was the Lord Jesus Himself Who not only pronounced a special blessing on the meek, but promised that they should inherit the earth (Matt. 5:5). He knew very well that meekness is not natural to humanity; indeed it was in order that men might be instructed in this quality of life that He called them to come unto Him and to take His yoke upon them. "Learn of Me . . ." , He commanded, with the clear inference that we sinners would never be meek or lowly unless we did.

This was certainly true of Moses. Nobody would suggest that the man Moses was naturally meek. Nor would the years of training and luxury in the Egyptian court have taught him such a lesson. He learnt much from the Egyptians, but he certainly never learned meekness. His outburst in Egypt, and the one flash of impatience in the wilderness which cost him so dearly (Num. 20:8–12), give clear indications of the kind of man he was by nature. The more wonder, then, that this man, of all men, should be meek, and the supreme wonder that he surpassed all others in this Christ-like virtue.

Not that Moses was a mere dreamer. Meekness is not a characteristic of the contemplative; it is a virile virtue. Moses was a man of action. "In all the mighty hand, and in all the great terror . . ." He was the leader of the greatest venture of all history, the pioneer of the Israelitish nation. God was mightily with Moses. When Joshua took over the leadership of the people there was no greater encouragement which God could give him than to assure him that he should have the same backing: "As I was with Moses, so I will be with thee" (Josh. 1:5). What was the explanation of the wonderful experiences of Divine power which Moses had? Surely this very fact, that he was meek above all other men. His meekness was his strength.

Meekness Because of Mercy

As we have said, the prophet made a close association between mercy and meekness: the man who loves mercy will walk humbly with his God. It may well be that the greatest contributory cause to the supreme meekness of Moses was that his life was transformed by an overwhelming realization of God's mercy to him. It is possible, of course, to take God's blessings in a wrong way; to become conceited, as the Jews did, vainly imagining that God's kind treatment of them was due to some innate superiority of theirs. Such men may use the right phrases, and talk of God's grace, but it is only phraseology; they cannot be said to "love mercy". If, however, we do appreciate the amazing patience of God, and His goodness to the utterly undeserving, then we begin not to boast of mercies, but to love mercy. There is surely nothing so calculated to make us truly lowly in heart as a realization of the greatness of God's grace, even to us.

Mercy at His Beginning

Moses' life began with a very great mercy. At that time every other baby boy had to be drowned. He alone was saved, and saved by the mercy of God. We can give every credit to his mother who thought of the plan and executed it, to the sister who watched by the ark of bulrushes and intervened so successfully, and even to Pharaoh's daughter who showed such true and unexpected compassion. But it was not the mother, the sister, the ark, or the princess, who delivered him, but the great mercy of God. Moses himself contributed least of all. When the casket was opened, he just cried—that was all he could do.

Probably it was the one thing which his mother hoped would not happen, and it may be that Miriam stood by, tense with concern, lest the baby should spoil everything by not smiling at the appropriate moment. All that the babe could do was to wail in complete weakness and so fail to give any help at all. His deliverance was all of God. The name given to him, Moses (Ex. 2:10b), was a lifelong reminder of how he had been pulled out of the waters of destruction by the mercy of God. Such a beginning should keep a man humble.

Yet this, too, was our beginning. We would have been swallowed up by destruction had it not been for Divine intervention. Like the baby Moses, we could contribute nothing but a cry, a despairing wail. It was God Who showed mercy to us and drew us out of the waters of death. We might well ask, as Moses must often have done, why we should have been the favoured ones when others all around us have no such history. Many have had the same opportunities, the same, or even greater privileges; yet we are the Lord's, and they are not. The grace of God is amazing. ' 'Tis mercy all! '

Mercy of Recovery

A time came when the Lord met him at the burning bush, met him with a commission and a promise. "Come now therefore, and I will send thee", He said to him (Ex. 3:10); and later, "Certainly I will be with thee" (v. 12). It would be impossible to imagine the overwhelming sense of the mercy of God that must have filled Moses' heart as he heard those words.

What a lot of history had intervened between Moses' first sense of call to be the Deliverer, and this present commission! He had begun—where we must all begin—by making a great renunciation. At forty years of age he let go of possessions, prospects, everything selfish and earthly, in order to be a servant of the Lord. This was not wrong; it was right, and nobody can serve the Lord without such a complete renunciation. He let everything go—or at least he meant to do so. This, however, did not make him meek. Many of us have passed through a similar experience, and been most sincere in our dedication, but it did not make us meek. Perhaps it made us the very opposite, giving us a false idea of our superiority to other Christians.

For Moses there followed a complete fiasco. He tried to serve the Lord in his own strength, in his own way and at his own time. Meek men don't do that sort of thing. The result was abysmal and utter failure. Away he fled into the land of Midian, and for forty years he had to live with his own sense of complete breakdown. Perhaps it was borne in on his soul that God's work could not be done by the kind of man he was, even when such a man had made great sacrifices. There must have been a collapse of any imagined ability, a sense of deep disappointment, in the conviction that he had spoiled every chance he ever had, that he had disqualified himself from ever being a servant of God.

We, too, must go this way, though happily it need not last for forty years as it did with him. But there is a spiritually symbolic meaning in that number: it is meant to indicate the thoroughness of the weakening process. He had learned his lesson.

At least, he thought he had. But in fact it was only the first half. He had settled down with his own failure, but now the Lord appeared to him, with this surprising call to go back again to the work which he had ruined by trying to do it in his own strength. He went back, unwillingly, hesitatingly, full of doubts as to his own ability or worthiness, but he went with the new and emphatic assurance: "Certainly I will be with thee". How amazing the grace of God must have seemed to him, rescuing him from his failure and despair, offering to one who had broken down in the past such high and privileged service. We know, of course, that it was this very self-despair which made possible such power as he had never known before. It was the proof that the forty years, far from being wasted, had done the necessary work of undoing. To receive back his original commission by such a miracle of mercy was calculated to make Moses feel deeply humbled.

There is a sense in which God's true servant is always a defeated man. The one who drives on with the sense of his own importance, who is unwilling to appreciate the worthlessness of his own best efforts and is always seeking to justify himself—that one will not be meek, and so will lack the essential power by which God's work must be done. Our brokenness must not be feigned; we must not be content with the mere language and appearance of humility. We, too, must be as conscious of Divine mercy in our being recovered for God's service as we are of the original mercy which drew us from the waters of death.

Mercy of the Exodus

God abundantly fulfilled His promise to 'be with' His servant: Moses was used in a unique way to do the work of God. This, too, he realized, was pure mercy: "Thou in Thy mercy hast led the people which Thou hast redeemed" (Ex. 15: 13). Moses did not need the deliverance for himself. He was free; he had never been a slave; he could walk in and out as he pleased. He was sent, however, to his people who were in 'the house of bondage', and was faced with the impossible task of getting them released so that they might worship and serve God. The miracle happened; the great emancipation came; and Moses had been the man whom God used to bring this about. The old Moses, full of his own importance, might have been ready to take some credit to himself for this. Alas! it is all too easy for the servant of the Lord to get puffed up, even if he has been used in only a small way. Even the new Moses, deeply aware of his dependence on the Lord, had severe tests in Egypt which threw him back even more on the absolute grace of God, and he was only able to share in the great Exodus when it had become abundantly clear that God alone was doing the work.

This is the case with every spiritual servant of God. He has to be so dealt with that any tendency to imagine that he is anything in himself, or at all superior to others, must be purged from him. Then, to see God working in power and deliverance, as Moses saw Him, to be the instrument of a work which is so wholly and absolutely of God—this can only bring a man very low in humble worship. Really, the man who is most used should be the meekest of all. When Christ turned the water into wine, we are told that, while the ruler and the guests at the feast did not know the secret, those who did the carrying did. "But the servants which had drawn the water knew" (John 2:10). They knew how gloriously Christ had worked, and that they themselves had been spectators, rather than agents, privileged to be so used, well aware that all the glory belonged to the Lord and none to man.

Mercy of Answered Prayer

Think, also, of the wonderful way in which the Lord answered Moses' prayers. There were miracles of preservation, miracles of provision, miracles of progress. Every time when a new crisis of need came upon them, Moses turned to the secret place of prayer and called on the Name of the Lord. And on each occasion there were fresh blessings which could only have come by way of the trials. The people could not pray for themselves. More often than not they doubted and complained. Moses was the man who prayed, and so Moses had the full spiritual blessing which comes to those who see their prayers answered, especially if these prayers are for others rather than for themselves. After all, when the people lacked food, Moses was as hungry as any of them. He, too, could have died from thirst, just like the rest. When they were attacked by their enemies, Moses was as much in danger as any of them —possibly more. It seems, though, that, as a true intercessor should, Moses forgot himself and his own needs in his shepherd-like concern for the people. He prayed for them, not for himself; and, as he did so, he could hardly ignore the fact that they were as unworthy as he. When the prayers were answered—and what a wonderful record of answered prayer the wilderness journey provided!—then anew he would be impressed with the greatness of God's mercy.

There were, of course, deeper spiritual needs than the physical and material perils of the wilderness way. There were times when the whole nation was likely to be destroyed, because of its disobedience and sin. There were individuals, like Aaron and Miriam, whose only hope of survival could be in the mercy of God. Moses was the man who prayed for that mercy, and God graciously responded to his selfless intercession. There are two ways of receiving answers to prayer. The wrong way is that of conceit, as though we or our prayers had some kind of merit in them. A prayer ministry will not continue for long, nor remain effective, if any such spirit is allowed a place in the heart of the intercessor. But there is the other way, when those concerned are humbled to the dust by the sheer goodness and grace of God. Even more than suffering, even more than chastening, the very abundance of God's mercy can melt our hearts in lowly gratitude. Such people do not have to try to be meek. They do not even have to pray to be made meek. It is the goodness of God, so amazing and so undeserved, which produces such meekness.

The Influence of a Meek Man

It was after the people's greatest sin, and God's gracious pardon, that the new promise was given: "My presence shall go with thee, and I will give thee rest" (Ex. 33:14). The 'rest' here spoken of was something more than comfort or easement: it implied that the expedition would reach its successful end, and that the people would be led into the land of promise, which was God's 'rest'. Moses had earlier lost all confidence in himself. He knew that he had failed God. Now, in a very thorough way, he had reason to lose confidence in the whole people who had sinned away all their prospects. Only one hope was left to him, and this was the hope now inspired by God's new promise. It was hope in the mercy of God.

We know that the nation did get through. Although Moses himself was not allowed to lead them in, Joshua, his assistant and successor, led them into their inheritance. On the Divine side, this success was due solely to God's great mercy; on the human side, to the shepherding ministry of the man Moses. What was his secret? We are told: it was that he excelled in meekness. So we are left with this definite implication, that in any people who are in danger of breakdown and failure, the one contribution which has most value among them is meekness. If there be but one truly meek man or woman in that situation there is still hope. "The meek will He guide in judgment: and the meek He will teach His way" (Psalm 25:9). There are various qualifications for the man who would serve the Lord, but this is probably the most important. The one who excels in meekness will be the one who knows face-to-face communion with God, and proofs of the mighty hand of God which are denied to all others. *May we, too, learn something of the meekness of the man of God.*

Part Four

The Tragedy of the Unfinished Task

This evening we move in thought into the Book of Judges—and how very different it is from the Book of Joshua! I think the Book of Judges is the most terrible book in the Bible! And why is it such a terrible book? Because it is the book of the unfinished task.

In the Book of Joshua the people of Israel went into the land, and had a wonderful history of victory after victory, moving more and more into God's full purpose. Then, before they had finished the work, they settled down. In the last chapters of the Book of Joshua we see the people just settling down before the work is perfect. They had heard the great call of God. God's purpose had been presented to them and they had made a response to it. They had moved so far, and then, before it was all finished, they settled down. The Book of Judges follows, and that is the book of the tragedy of the unfinished work.

None of us will say that there is nothing like that in Christianity today! There are many Christians who make a wonderful beginning. They see the vision of God's great purpose, and certain words in the New Testament make a great appeal to them, such as: "Called according to His purpose" (Romans 8:28). That is a wonderful vision! "According to the eternal purpose which He purposed in Christ Jesus our Lord" (Ephesians 3:11). Such a thought makes a great appeal to these people and they make a heart response. They go on so far, and then many stop too soon. They lose the vision; they lose the inspiration; they lose the sense of purpose; they lose the energy to go on, and of some we have to say: 'Something has gone out of their faces. What was there with them once is not there now. They were so positive once, so occupied with the heavenly calling, but something has happened.' These people may not be altogether conscious of it, and they would not tell you that something has happened, but it is quite evident that something *has* happened. They have just lost something, and you do not get the response now from them that you once got. They are not so interested now as they were. The heavenly vision has gone out of their lives. That is true of many Christians, and it could be true of all of us.

And the Book of Judges is our instructor in this matter. What I say now is not in judgment—although it is from the Book of *Judges!* I have a very great deal of sympathy with these people. Oh yes, I know how wrong it was, and how this book spelt the failure of these people. I know how sorry the Lord was about it, but from my own experience I cannot help being sympathetic, for I think I understand.

Weariness In The Battle

Why did these people stop short of finishing the job? I think that very likely it was because they became weary in well doing. The battle was long drawn out. It was spread over years and was very exhausting. No sooner had they gained one victory than they had to start fighting again. They did not have much rest between one battle and the next one. It was a long drawn-out warfare; they got weary in battle, and in their weariness they lost the vision, they lost heart, and they lost the initiative.

I am so glad that with all the strong things that the New Testament says, it says some very kind and understanding things about this: "Let us not be weary in well-doing; for in due season we shall reap, if we faint not" (Galatians 6:9); "Wherefore, my beloved brethren, . . . your labour is not vain in the Lord" (I Corinthians 15:58); "God is not unrighteous to forget your work and labour of love" (Hebrews 6:10). What a lot of things there are like that! And Jesus said to His disciples, who were being brought into the battle: "Let not your heart be troubled!" (John 14:1), while we can hear the Lord's words to Joshua: "Be strong and of a good courage; be not affrighted, neither be thou dismayed" (Joshua 1:9). Again, the Lord Jesus said to His disciples: "He that endureth *to the end*, the same shall be saved" (Matthew 24:13).

These people in the Book of Judges were discouraged by weariness—and we are all capable of that! Sometimes it is not easy for us to give up—or perhaps I ought to say that it is not *difficult* for us give up!—because we do not want to get out of the battle, and yet, at the same time, we do want to get out of it. The battle is inside, and even so great a man as the Apostle Paul had that battle. He said: 'I really do not know what to do! I have a strong desire to depart and be with the Lord in order to get out of the battle, and yet I know that duty to the Lord would keep me in the battle. I do not know whether to give up or to go on!' I say that that is a possible temptation to every Christian, and the Lord knows all about that! The New Testament is full of understanding things about it.

The first reason why these people settled down too soon, then, was discouragement. It was not because they had had no victories—they had had many—but because they said: 'There is no end to his battle! It looks as though we shall *never* finish!' So in weariness and discouragement they settled down too soon.

I feel sure that this Book of Judges recognizes that. Every time these people stirred themselves again they found that the Lord was very ready to go on with them. This book is a picture of an up-and-down Christian life. One day these people are down in despair, and another day they are up in victory. It was that kind of Christian life which was always up and down, but when they turned their faces to the Lord they found that He was waiting for them. The Lord had not given up. He was always ready to go on. I think that is the first great lesson in this Book of the Judges.

The Loss Of Heavenly Vision

But what was the effect of this loss, of this stopping too soon? It was the loss of vision. They only saw the things that were near and lost sight of God's eternal purpose. They lost sight of what Paul calls the "prize of the on-high calling" (Philippians 3:14). Now this sounds like a contradiction, but they lost sight of the things that are not seen! You say: 'What do you mean by that? That is nonsense! How can you see the things that are not seen?' Paul says: "The things which are seen are temporal; but the things which are not seen are eternal" (II Corinthians 4:18). They lost sight of the things which are eternal because they were looking too much at the things which are seen. They lost the heavenly vision for they became satisfied too soon. It was all good so far, but the good became the enemy of the best.

The first thing that happened, then, was the loss of the heavenly vision. It works both ways. If we lose the heavenly vision we settle down too soon. If we settle down too soon we lose the heavenly vision. And what do we mean by settling down too soon? We mean: losing the warring spirit. In this Book of Judges the Philistines resorted to a very subtle strategy: they took all the weapons of war away from Israel, and all that they had left was one file to sharpen their agricultural instruments, so that every farmer in Israel had to take a journey to the blacksmith to sharpen his farm instruments. All the sharp instruments had been taken away, and the spirit of *war* was undermined.

The Philistines had made it impossible for Israel to

fight and you know that there is a very big Philistine about! The strategy of this great enemy of the inheritance is to take the fighting spirit out of us. Oh, what a lot of mischief the Philistines have done to Christians! What about our prayer life? There was a time when we were mighty warriors in prayer. We fought the Lord's battles in prayer. What about our prayer meetings? Where can you find the prayer meetings now that are out in spiritual warfare? Yes, we ask the Lord for a hundred and one things, but we do not battle through to victory on some situation. There is some life in terrible bondage, there is some servant of the Lord having a hard time, and there are many other calls for battle, but where are the prayer groups who take up these issues and will not give up until they are settled? The warring spirit has gone out from so much of the Church. That is a clever strategy of the devil! Lose the spirit of spiritual battle and you will stop short of finishing the work.

The Spirit of the World

The next thing that caused these people to settle down too soon was the spirit of the world getting in amongst them. What is the spirit of the world? It is the spirit of: Have a good time! Let us have a good time! Let us eat and drink, for tomorrow we die! And these people of Israel looked at the world around them and, if I understand it rightly, they said: 'These people do not have all the hard time that we do. Our life is a life of continual battle. They do not know so much about that, but they believe in having a good time.' I think that is how it was at this particular time.

Of course, up to this time Israel had given the people round about a bad time! But Israel had lost the fighting spirit now, and the world was having a good time because the Church was no longer fighting it. Instead of fighting the world they made friends with the world. They made the world their friends, and so they did not finish the work. Compromise is a dangerous thing to the inheritance! Trying to be on good terms with the world and having an easy time will result in our losing a large part of the inheritance.

Recovering the Fighting Spirit

But let us finish on a better note. As I said before, God did not give up, and whenever the people took up the battle again and turned again on the Lord's side to fight the enemy, they found the Lord waiting for them. So we have the story of Deborah, the story of Gideon—and dare I mention Samson? However, although Samson was a poor sort of man, if only the Lord gets a poor chance, He will take it. You may not think much of Samson—but do you think better of yourself? We are all poor creatures! We have all been discouraged, we have all been tempted to give up, we have all stopped too soon, we have all been weary in well-doing, but take the sword of the Spirit again! Take up the battle again, and you will find the Lord is ready and waiting for you.

Gideon—Deborah—Samson—and all the others. But I think there is one who is better than them all—do you remember that beautiful little Book of Ruth? Everybody is charmed with that book! What a lovely book of spiritual recovery it is! What a picture of the Lord's patience, the Lord's readiness to take advantage of every opportunity! How does that book begin? "And it came to pass in the days when the judges judged. . . ." The Book of Ruth was in the times of the Judges, which until then was the most terrible time in history of Israel, but God was ready to change the whole picture. There are the two different pictures: the Judges and Ruth, but both were in the same period. Do you see what I am trying to say?

Dear friends, we are in a great battle, and it is long drawn out. We can get very weary in the fight. We can become discouraged and give up too soon. We may have to stop before the work is finished. That is always our temptation, the tragic possibility in the Christian life, but the Lord does not give up. He does not faint, nor is He discouraged, and if we will turn again to Him, rise up again, recover our fighting spirit and continue to fight the good fight, we shall find the Lord is ready every time, and He is always wanting to help us to fight to the end. He will help till the day is done!

Part Five

"Gather My Saints Together"

"Gather My saints together unto Me, those that have made a covenant with Me by sacrifice."

(Psalm 50:5; A.S.V).

"Now we beseech you, brethren, touching the coming of our Lord Jesus Christ, and our gathering together unto Him."

(II Thess. 2:1).

"Not forsaking our own assembling together, as the custom of some is, but exhorting one another; and so much the more, as ye see the day drawing nigh."

(Hebrews 10:25).

In all of the above passages there is this one common factor, that an end-time movement and feature is dominant. It must be remembered that the Psalms themselves represent what remains when a history of outward things as to the general instrumentality has ended in failure. The history of Israel in its first great phase closed with the Book of "Kings" in a calamitous and shameful way. Weakness, paralysis, declension, reproach, characterized the instrument in general. But out of that history now so concluded the Psalms are carried forward, and they represent what has *spiritually* been gained and is permanent. This is pre-eminently a personal, inward, spiritual knowledge of the Lord gained through experience. That is why they always reach the heart and never fail to touch experience at every point. To them the saints have turned in times of deep experience. They are the ministry of experience to experience, the only ministry which is permanent. The end-time instrument will always be that which inwardly knows the Lord in a deep and living way through history fraught with much experience of the heights and depths. What David gave to the Chief Musician for the wind instruments and the stringed instruments touches the highest and deepest note of a mortal's knowledge of God. Worship, Salvation, Sorrow, Appeal, Victory, Battle, Faith, Hope, Glory, Instruction, are all great themes interwoven with the mass of matters touched, but the point is that all came in *real life*; He passed through it all. It is this, and this alone, which can serve the Lord when what He first raised up has failed Him as a public instrument. So the Lord would take pains to secure this, and this may explain much of the suffering and sorrow through which He takes His chosen vessels.

It does not need pointing out that, in the other two passages with which we commenced, the end-time is in view; they definitely state it.

There is a further common feature, however, which is more particularly the subject before us. They all definitely refer to gathering together as something related to the end-time. The Day is drawing nigh, therefore there is to be a "so much the more" assembling together. The Lord is coming, and there is a gathering to Him.

A history of a religious system which sprang out of something which the Lord raised up in the first place has ended in weakness, chaos and shame. Therefore, there is to be a re-gathering *to the Lord* of His saints.

Before we deal with the nature of this end-time gathering, we must get clearly in view those that are concerned in it. The passage in the Psalm would embrace and include those referred to in the other two passages.

"My Saints . . . Those That Have Made A Covenant with Me by Sacrifice"

It need hardly be remarked that when all has been said and done through type, symbol and figure, the covenant means an entering into what the Lord Jesus has done by His shed Blood. It is an appreciation and apprehension of Him in His great work by the Cross. The Lord, by His Blood, has made a "New Covenant" by sacrifice, and we, His spiritual people, have entered into that covenant and set our hand to it. Christ as "the mediator of a new covenant" stands for both parties, for a covenant requires two parties. On one side He is God, "The Son of God"; on the other side He is Man, "Son of Man". In Christ we are made the humanity side of the covenant, and by taking our place by faith in Him we enter into the covenant. Just as, in Christ, God has come out to us in a great committal, so also—as in the case of Christ—we in Him go out to God in a like utter committal. The Blood seals the covenant, that is, makes us wholly the Lord's, and the Lord wholly ours.

If we see the meaning of "a covenant by sacrifice" then we shall see who it is that will be in this gathering together. It will certainty be only those to whom the Lord is everything, to whom He is all and in all; and those who are all for the Lord without a reservation, a personal interest, or anything that is less or other than Himself. Spiritual oneness is only possible on this basis.

The Lord's word to Abraham in the day of covenant was, "Now I know that thou fearest God". Malachi's end-time word was "Then they that feared the Lord. . . ." The fear of the Lord is an utter abandonment to Him at any cost; His will being supreme, claiming and obtaining the measure of a whole burnt-offering.

The Nature of the Gathering Together

Having then in view the kind who are concerned, which forms a test as well as a testimony, we are able to look at the nature of the gathering together. We are well aware that there is a widespread doubt as to whether we are to expect anything in the way of a corporate movement or testimony at the end. Indeed, it is strongly held by some that everything at the end is individual, and this conviction rests, for the most part, upon the phrase "If any man", in the message to Laodicea.

Let us hasten then to say that we here have nothing in mind in the nature of an organized movement, a sect, a society, a fraternity, or even a "fellowship" if, by that, any of the foregoing is meant.

Having said this, however, there are some things on the other side which need saying quite definitely.

The Church of the New Testament never was an organized movement. Neither was there any organized affiliation of the companies of believers in various places with one another. It was a purely spiritual thing, spontaneous in life and united only by the Holy Spirit and mutual love and spiritual solicitude. There were other factors which acted as spiritual links which we will mention presently. Further, and still more important, was the abiding fact that a "Body" had been brought into being. This is called "the body of Christ". You can divide a society and still it remains, but you cannot divide a body without destroying the entity.

Are we to understand from the exponents of the individualistic interpretation that all the teaching of the Lord, in nearly all the Scriptures concerning the House of God, and in nearly all the Letters of Paul concerning the Body of Christ, is now set aside or is only an idea without any expression on the earth? Are we to blot out the mass of the New Testament and live our own individual Christian lives with no emphasis upon working fellowship with other believers? Surely not. This would be contrary to all the ways of God in history, and would certainly spell defeat, for if there is one thing against which the Adversary has set himself it is the fellowship of God's people.

Ultra-individualism is impossible if the truth of the "one body" still stands, and what is more, the Lord's people are becoming more and more conscious of their absolute need of fellowship, especially in prayer. The difficulty of 'getting through' alone is becoming greater as we approach the end.

What then is the nature of this gathering together? It It is a gathering to the Lord Himself. *"Gather My saints together unto Me"; "our gathering unto Him"*.

In times past there have been gatherings to men, great preachers, great teachers, great leaders; or to great institutions and movements, centres and teachings. At the end the Lord will be very much more than His vessels or instrumentalities.

God's end is Christ, and as we get nearer the end He must become almost immediately the object of appreciation.

Our oneness and fellowship is not in a teaching, a 'testimony', a community, a place, but in a Person, and in Him not merely doctrinally, but livingly and experimentally.

Any movement truly of God must have this as its supreme and all-inclusive feature, that it is the Lord Jesus Who is the object of heart adoration and worship.

The two great purposes of the 'gathering' are prayer and 'building up': "supplication for all saints", and spiritual food. These two things have ever characterized Divine gatherings or convocations—representation before God, and feeding in His presence.

This, then, is the meaning of "call a solemn assembly" (Joel 1:14; 2:15). The need more than ever imperative as "the day" approaches is the gathering together *unto Him*.

May we see more of this as His Divinely inspired movement to meet the so great need!

Part Six

"Whither the Tribes Go up"

"Whither the tribes go up, the tribes of the Lord, unto the testimony of Israel, to give thanks unto the Name of the Lord." (Psalm 122:4).

"Gather My saints together."

(Psalm 50:5).

It was a beautiful thought in the mind of God when, in His divine economy, He prescribed for the periodic convocations of His people. Away back in the time of Moses, He commanded that all the males in Israel should journey three times in every year to some place of His appointment (Deuteronomy 16:16), the details of which are worth noting. It is clear that David laid great store by such convocations. Psalm 122 is by its heading attributed to David, as were other "Songs of Ascent," or pilgrimage. It was due to division resulting from spiritual decline that such gatherings ceased for so long, until Josiah had a great recovery celebration (II Chronicles 35: 17–19). It was therefore a sign of spiritual recovery and strength when the Lord's people so gathered from near and far.

We can briefly summarize the values in the Lord's thought for such convocations:

1. They were times when the universality of God's church, or "Holy nation," as on the basis of the Passover (the Cross) was preserved in the hearts of His people. "They left their cities"; that is, they left exclusively parochial ground. By the gathering from all areas they were preserved from all exclusivism, sectarianism, and the peril

49

of isolation. They were made to realize that they were not the all and everything, but parts of a great whole. Thus the ever-present tendency to make God in Christ smaller than He really is was countered.

2. Thus, they were times of wonderful fellowship. People who belonged to the same Lord, but had either never before met, or had been apart for so long, discovered or rediscovered one another, were able to share both "their mutual woes, and mutual burdens bear," or tell of the Lord's goodness and mercy. Loneliness, with all its temptations and false imaginations, was carried away by the fresh air of mutuality. New hope, incentive, and life sent the pilgrims back to their accustomed spheres with the consciousness of relatedness.

3. They were times of consolidation. The Psalm says: "For a testimony unto Israel." The testimony of the great thing that the Passover (the Cross) means in the heart of His people. A testimony to the unifying power of the blood and body of Christ. The gatherings held a spiritual virtue in the livingness of the presence of the Lord. If they had been assailed by doubts, fears, and perplexities, they went away confirmed, reassured, and established in their common faith.

4. They were times of instruction. The Word of God was brought out, read and expounded. They were taught, and they "spake one to another." In a word, they were fed. There was spiritual food. The initiation of these convocations was connected with three "Feasts" (Deuteronomy 16). Eating and drinking in the presence of the Lord. They returned fortified, built up, enlightened, and with vision renewed.

5. They were times of intercession. Possibly not every individual was able to "go up." For various reasons—infirmity, age, responsibility, or some other form of detention—kept some from the blessings of joining with the pilgrims.

But God's idea of the gatherings was—as put into later words—"My house shall be a house of prayer for all peoples." The New Testament is clear and strong on this point, that the representation of the "Body of Christ" in any place *can*, and *should* have real spiritual value for all its members because "the Body is one."

So, let the lonely, detained and isolated ones realize that when the Lord's people are together, they are being supported. And let those who are not so deprived of the "gathering together" realize how vital it is, and what a necessity there is in expressing this Divine thought.

Would to God that all our gatherings were after this sort!

Part Seven

Gathered of God

"Also the foreigners that join themselves to the Lord, to minister unto Him, and to love the name of the Lord, to be His servants, every one that keepeth the sabbath from profaning it, and holdeth fast My covenant; even them will I bring to My holy mountain, and make them joyful in My house of prayer: their burnt-offerings and their sacrifices shall be accepted upon Mine altar; for My house shall be called a house of prayer for all peoples. The Lord God, Who gathereth the outcasts of Israel, saith, 'Yet will I gather others to him, besides his own that are gathered.'"

(Isaiah 56:6–8; A. S. V.).

In the latter part of his prophecies Isaiah concentrates on the return from captivity and the restoration of the Lord's testimony in Zion. It is impossible to exaggerate the importance of this recovery, for at its heart, the goal and explanation of it all, we find the house of God. It is God Himself Who is most concerned about re-gathering His people, for this is essential to His own will and glory.

Scattered Ones Gathered into
Fellowship in God's House

The Lord's declaration that His house *"shall be called a house of prayer for all peoples"* does not primarily mean that it shall be a place from which prayer shall go out on behalf of men everywhere. It is true that the house does become a centre from which there radiates a ministry of life and blessing in answer to believing prayer, but the context shows clearly that the first thought is of that house as a centre of gathering, a rallying point to which all who will may come. The Spirit's work is to unite in practical fellowship those who have been delivered from the kingdom of darkness, and to unite them under His own authority in His own house. It is, of course, a blessed privilege for those concerned. They have trusted and proved the Lord in their scattered state, but they have known that they were not experiencing the fulness. There is always something lacking when believers know the Lord in isolation only or in sectional groups.

The Word of God had set before the "outcasts of Israel" prospects which were far beyond their present experience— promises of the glory of God in the midst and of feasts of fat things in the mountain of the Lord. All this was to be accomplished by a great Divine gathering of those who had hitherto been scattered and in limitation. God would make them joyful in His house of prayer. The greatest values, however, were not to be personal and local, but universal and Divine.

It is God's great desire to manifest Himself in and through His people: *"that now . . . might be made known through the church the manifold wisdom of God"* (Eph. 3:10). When God's scattered people are freed from every bondage and brought together in true oneness, the impact of His presence and kingdom will be tremendous in its range. This gathering is of supreme importance to the Lord, for it provides Him with His house and ministers to His satisfaction. Who can calculate the effect of the unrestricted and ungrieved presence of God in a people? The house of God is no hollow pretence; it is not a relic of what used to be, nor a vain ideal of what ought to be; it is meant to be a present, spiritual reality. *"For where two or three are gathered together in My name, there am I in the midst of them"* (Matt. 18:20).

They are not gathered together for their own name, nor

for any other earthly name; not for any personal interests, nor even for the furtherance of a cause. They have been drawn by the Spirit into the house of God where all things are of Him and all things are for Him. In that house God is given His rightful place in everything.

During the captivity there was no place on earth where the Lord could truly reign among His people. There were individuals like Ezekiel, or those of whom we read in Daniel, who faithfully represented Him and maintained the testimony to His universal sovereignty. These, however, did not cease to long and pray for the day of recovery, when the house of God would once again come into being. They knew that the Lord's purposes required a re-gathering of His scattered people, with their establishing in a united fellowship in Him. This is the spiritual meaning of the house of God. For us it is not a building or a locality, nor must we be content to regard it merely as something doctrinal into which we enter when we become the Lord's. It is a practical life together in the fellowship of the Spirit.

Gathered on the Basis of Grace Alone

Isaiah's ministry was one of comfort, or perhaps better, of encouragement. The purposes of God are so often hindered by timidity or lack of inspiration among His people. There are so many objections, so many arguments and questions, that we tend to accept the low level of things as they are, instead of responding to the heavenly vision and call. The house of God seems to be a dream or a vision; we gaze upon it but take no active steps to enter it in a practical sense and to enjoy the blessings that are to be found therein. From the words of Isaiah we gather there were two groups particularly susceptible to a spirit of discouragement, the eunuchs and the foreigners. The prophet's message is to assure them that they are to share in God's gathering. He speaks to those who are ineligible on natural grounds, assuring them of the abundant grace of God. His house is not concerned with what we are in ourselves; admittance cannot be governed by human considerations; grace has made it a house of prayer for *all* peoples.

But there must be some qualification, for God's house is holy. Why are these outcasts received, and given so warm a welcome? How is it that God says, *"Even them will I bring . . . and make them joyful in My house of prayer?"* There are three statements which seem to give the answer to this question. They love the name of the Lord, they keep the Sabbath and they hold fast His covenant.

Gathered in Virtue of Christ's Finished Work

The second and central feature really includes the other two. They are true keepers of the Sabbath. This stress upon Sabbath observance is the more remarkable since the prophet is particularly strong in expressing God's indifference to mere ritual. Nobody could be more emphatic than Isaiah in assuring the people of God that the whole realm of religious observance, even though prescribed by the Scriptures, is in itself of no value to the Lord and rejected by Him. His message to the people was often in such terms as, *"Your new moons and your appointed feasts My soul hateth; they are a trouble unto Me; I am weary of bearing them"* (Isa. 1:14; A.S.V.). In spite of this, Isaiah lays great stress on the need for keeping the Sabbath. This is surely because of the spiritual meaning attached to that day.

What is this spiritual meaning? It is simplicity and utterness of faith as to the finished work of Christ. This is a term which we make much of in relation to the salvation of sinful men; we rejoice that redemption is secured by the finished work of Christ upon the Cross. But what is true as to the justification of the ungodly is equally true in regard to every phase of spiritual life and experience. The whole work is completed in Christ. Human effort can provide nothing at all, for God's rest is based upon the fact that in Christ and by His Cross all the work is finished. We are called on to find all our life and energy on this basis—that we keep God's Sabbath. Some people, of course, talk a lot about the finished work of Christ and yet live lives which are not glorifying to Him. This is as though they were approving of the idea of the Sabbath—marking it, as it were, upon their calendars—and yet failing to be governed by it in a practical way. God is calling for those who are true keepers of His Sabbath, those who by faith are proving in ever new ways and ever greater fulness the glorious perfection of the new creation in Christ.

We can profane the Sabbath in two ways. The first is by trying to do something, or thinking that we can do something, to add to God's work in Christ. It is the intrusion of self-wisdom or self-effort into the spiritual life. The second is by failing to count on the Lord's sufficiency. If we are governed by some lack or weakness of ours, or succumb to our own sense of unworthiness, the purposes of God in our life are hindered and we are in effect denying the finished work of Christ, profaning the Sabbath.

Gathered into Fellowship with God Himself

There is an indication in verse 3 of the doubts and fears of the stranger who has joined himself to the Lord. To him the house of God seems so high and holy that he is inclined to despair of having a place in it. Seeing that he has no nature standing, no virtues or abilities of his own, he is worried as to whether he can claim admittance. He begins timidly to enter in, conscious all the time of his strangeness, and half expecting that before long someone will come up to him and tell him that he is an outsider who has no right to be there. It is as though while he is thus troubled, fearing that any moment he will surely be separated from God's people and turned away from His house, the High Priest himself comes forward and gives him a cordial welcome. He is taken by the hand and led, stranger though he is, not just into the outer court nor only into the holy place of priestly ministry—which he never expected to see—but taken right through into the very presence of the Lord. Far from being rejected, he finds that God Himself gives him a warm welcome, giving him full right of access to His holy mountain. No wonder that his heart overflows with joy! *"I will ... make them joyful in My house of prayer"*.

God comes out to the man who approaches Him on the grounds of grace. He had been forced to reject many who claimed a place of prominence, because they sought to be something in themselves, and to deal with Him on purely natural grounds. They felt that their name, their education, their orthodoxy or their experience gave them the right to demand God's approval. It was these men and this spirit which really caused the destruction of God's house. The greatest enemy to God's house has never been the enemy from without, but religious pride within. Uncrucified flesh spells the destruction of true spiritual fellowship. There is a spiritual significance in the fact that the foreigner, timid and diffident, and the eunuch, weak and despised, are particularly singled out as being welcomed to fellowship; in the restoration God bases His acceptance on pure grace.

This entrance into the house of prayer is described as being taken up into God's holy mountain. A mountain is a place of vision. The Lord's mountain is where everything is seen in its right proportions in relation to Him. When we are in the valley even small things seem to tower over us, and we are easily governed by petty and personal considerations. True fellowship in the Spirit will raise us into heavenly realms, not away from practical realities but into the clarity and breadth of things as God sees them—to spiritual ascendency, and to fellowship with God in His great universal purposes of grace and glory.

Gathered to Enjoy God's Full Approval in Christ

The second reason for rejoicing is that *"their burnt-offerings and their sacrifices shall be accepted upon Mine altar"*. What an amazing experience this stranger is having! He feared that he would not be permitted to enter at all, but now he finds not only that he is welcome, but that all his offerings are brought to the altar and receive the seal of God's approval. No wonder that he is glad! Somehow nothing else seems to matter if we know that the Lord is pleased with us. This is the meaning of the burnt offering—that God is well pleased with the offerer. It is a blessing indeed to know that our sin offering is accepted, for that means that God has nothing against us. Those who have known deep conviction and concern about their own guilt will know the value of the sin offering and the blessed relief of being sure that God has nothing against them. But when heaven's verdict was given upon the Lord Jesus the voice did not say, 'This is My Son and I have nothing against Him'. God affirmed, *"This is My beloved Son, in Whom I am well pleased"* (Matt. 3:17). The burnt offering identifies us with this good pleasure, in Christ.

Many Christians who are rejoicing in the sacrifice of Christ as taking away all their sin, know very little of the deeper joy of being assured that in Christ God is satisfied with them. Does this sound presumptuous? What about Enoch? The whole secret of Enoch's walk of holy and happy fellowship with God was that he had the witness that he was bringing pleasure to the heart of the Lord. In ourselves we can never do this, but on the basis of Christ we can and we ought.

God does not merely tolerate the foreigner, but finds

great pleasure in his company; and this, not because of anything inherently good in the man, but only on the basis of the altar. Christ is our burnt offering, to be daily appropriated as our sufficiency to bring pleasure to God. Even while we are seeking to walk nearer to the Lord, to be disciplined by His Cross and transformed by His Spirit, the very secret of our holy living is to rejoice in fullest acceptance in Christ. Thus the burnt offering will exercise a mighty sanctifying power in our lives.

And we are to do this in the house of God. Nothing must discourage or divert us from finding our place there. In active association with God's people we are to be rejoiced at the privilege of setting forth something of the perfection and glory of His Son. If we come by way of the altar God will welcome us and God will accept us—even the weaklings and the outcasts.

Gathered into the Fellowship of Christ's Sufferings

This sacrifice has cost the stranger something. When Scripture speaks of God's acceptance of our offerings it refers primarily to the acceptance of Christ's offering on our behalf, but it also includes our sharing in the sufferings of Christ and the sacrifice of the altar. Those who are pledged to walk in faithfulness with the Lord will find that this is a costly way. That cost may be ignored or despised by others, be treated as the stranger's sacrifice would probably be treated by those who resented his intrusion. How few know the real nature of what we are bearing for the Lord! Men do not appreciate; perhaps some even misunderstand and despise; but God takes full note of the value of the offering. The house of God is not for human glory. Our offerings are not made for men, to be approved or praised by them. When in some solemn hour we joined ourselves to the Lord to minister to His pleasure, we were given a place in His house, not that men might praise us but that our sacrifices, through Christ might bring joy to the heart of God. He is dealing with us on this basis. So often we are tempted to discouragement; it is as we come nigh to God in His house that we know our sacrifice is precious to Him, and we hear His promise anew *"I will . . . make them joyful in My house of prayer".*

Blessing for Others Because of the Gathered Ones

This will be bound to bring life and blessing to the scattered multitudes. True fellowship with God always provides a centre from which blessing is ministered. If God truly has the first place, if people live a life together in which Christ is supremely honoured, then this provides an expression of the house of God which is a house of prayer for all peoples. *"The Lord God, Who gathereth the outcasts of Israel, saith, 'Yet will I gather others to him, besides his own that are gathered' ".* When God's own people are scattered, wandering in unbelief and profaning His Sabbath, instead of being strong and united in loving communion in and with Him, there is little prospect of blessing for the outsiders. The gathering work must begin with the Lord's people. The house of God must be the place of joyful worship and communion before it can become a centre of life and light. When the outcasts of Israel are gathered, then the Lord can gather in more, for there is a family and a home into which they can be welcomed. What the world needs is not merely a proclamation going out into all the nations, but a setting in the midst of them, however small and weak in itself, of a true representation of God's house of prayer, whose doors are wide open with a welcome for the lonely and outcast. What a need there is for a gathering into true oneness of the scattered people of God, and so of a further adding to Christ of others besides!

Brethren,

As we were reading in the 1968 magazine of "A Witness and A Testimony," we came across an announcement by Brother Sparks. He wrote of two fellow-prayer warriors who were a true representation for God's House of prayer for all peoples. These testimonies were such a blessing to us that we would like to share them with you.

Gathering Home

"From time to time in the course of the years we have had, with regret, to tell of the home-call of friends and fellow-workers who have been our partners in this ministry. A third such one in recent times is our beloved sister, Madame Ducommun. We first met her when we used to go to Paris to minister in conferences of the 'White Russian' refugees. A link of fellowship was then formed which has borne much fruit. Our sister had made it her main ministry to translate the printed ministry into French, and these translations have gone from her little room in Paris, not only all over France, but to many other French-speaking areas. *A number of friends have met regularly in her room every week for prayer.* She has truly been a 'Mother in Israel' to them and to others. We shall miss her at our conferences in Switzerland.

This is one of whom it can be truly said: 'Her works do follow her.' Will you pray for those who will miss her most in Paris, and that guidance may be given as to the carrying on of that ministry.

Madame Ducommun passed into the presence of the Lord quite peacefully on Sunday, May 26th."

"We have now to report the home-call of another of those who have been so valuable a help in the work. Many of our friends in many parts of the world have known our sister Lady Ogle. For over forty years she has been very closely bound up with this ministry and has been a "helper of many". *Her prayer ministry* has been such a great strength, and she will be one for whom we shall give thanks on all remembrance. She was called Home on Monday, 27th November, in the late evening. After a short illness and no suffering she opened her eyes, smiled, and was gone. *May the Lord fill the gap made by this loss with others who will take up her ministry of prayer in—at least— as strong a way."*

Beloved, when two or three are gathered together in any place, and they pray in the Holy Spirit, they represent the whole Church, and become the House of prayer, functioning for all peoples—a universal ministry.

Part Eight

"A House of Prayer for All People"

Reading: II Chronicles 6; Isaiah 56:6–7; Mark 11:17; Eph. 6:18.

"My house shall be called an house of prayer for all people."

The sixth chapter of the second book of Chronicles is a magnificent example and illustration of these words of the Prophet. In the dedication of the House by Solomon, prayer of a universal kind inaugurated the ministry of the House, introducing its function. The characteristic words of that chapter are: "This house" and "Thy name". "When they shall pray toward *this house*, because of *Thy name* which is upon it. . . ."

You will remember the words of the Apostle concerning certain people, that they 'blasphemed that holy name which was called upon you'. The House is the link between the two passages historically and spiritually, and the Name called upon the House.

What was true of the temple of Solomon, as the House with the Name called upon it, is true of the Church, the Church of Christ, with the Lord's Name upon it. We have no difficulty in identifying the anti-type of Solomon's temple as being the Church. You are no doubt sufficiently acquainted with the Word to make it unnecessary to quote Scripture in this connection. Many passages will come to your mind which bear out that statement. The Church is God's House; "whose house are we", says the writer of the letter to the Hebrews; "a spiritual house to offer up spiritual sacrifices", says Peter. The identification is not at all difficult. And that the Name is upon the House is also quite clear. It was because of the Name which they bore at the beginning that the Church was so mighty in its going forth. The power of the Name was ever manifesting itself in their ministry. That is all very simple and needs no labouring. Then there are these other factors.

Sonship Marking the House of the Lord

The temple of Solomon was really the temple of David. It came in in revelation through David, and in realization in sonship, David's son. We know that in the Word both David and Solomon are types of the Lord Jesus, that He is great David's greater Son, and that He combines all that is spiritually represented by David and Solomon of sovereignty, kingship, exaltation, universal triumph and glory. You will remember how the Lord sent Nathan to David, to tell him that though he himself should not build the House, he was nevertheless to be the one to gather all that was necessary for it, and so be the instrument of making it possible. This so satisfied David that in the inspiration of it, and the tremendous stimulus of it, he went out and subdued all those nations which had been historic thorns in the side of Israel. And when he had subdued all the nations round about, and a universal triumph had been established, then the House came into being through Solomon.

We carry that forward into the triumph of the Lord Jesus by His Cross. He possesses the universal victory. He is exalted, enthroned, in virtue of all His enemies being overthrown by His Cross, and on resurrection ground the declaration is made: "Thou art My Son, this day have I begotten Thee." A fresh declaration of sonship is made, by reason of resurrection, and in resurrection, and in that sonship He builds the House, and the Spirit of sonship enters into every member of that House, and it becomes a 'sonship House' (Acts 13:33; Galatians 4:6).

The Ministry and Vocation of the House

That all leads the way to this particular thing, namely, the ministry and vocation of the House, of the Church. The House itself has to provide the Lord with a place, a sphere, a realm, a vessel, through which He can reach all people. That is the working outwards; that is God securing to Himself a means of universal blessing. God moves universally through His House, and therefore He must have a House constituted on a prayer basis. Do you notice the two movements in this chapter of II Chronicles 6? There is a movement outwards, and a movement inwards. The outward is through the House, with Solomon, so to speak, ministering the Lord. He is, as it were, bringing out from heaven the gracious goodness of God, the interventions, the undertakings and resources of God, world-wide. He is making the House the vehicle of what God is, and what God has, unto all peoples. When you reach a certain point in the chapter the movement changes, and you see people coming to the House because of the Name. That is the movement inwards. They shall "pray toward this house, because of Thy Great Name", said Solomon. That means that the circumference is going to find, not a direct access to God, but its blessing through the House of the Lord.

I suggest to you that those two things very greatly govern the New Testament revelation of the Church, and the Church's vocation. The one thing which embraces all is that God in Christ has bound Himself up with His Church, the Body of Christ, for this world's good, and that the fullness of the Lord will never be known nor entered into in an individual or individualistic way; that anything like mere individualism, separatism, will mean limitation. Any kind of detachment and isolation leads to being deprived of the larger fullnesses of the Lord, or, to put it the other way, to come into the fullness of the Lord we have to come into the fellowship of His people as the House of God. That is one law, and that is established.

That is the line which is more severe. There is a frown, perhaps, about that. It sounds hard. But it is the warning note which is very necessary, and especially in the light of the fact that there is a continuous, unceasing, incessant drive of the adversary in the direction of separation, isolation and detachment. It seems that at times the devil releases his forces and concentrates them upon people, to get them to run away, to get out of it, to break away, to quit because the strain seems so intense. Their whole inclination is to get away alone. They think that they are going to get an advantage by that. They are sometimes deceived into thinking that it will be for their good if only they get right away alone. They sometimes put it in this way: that they 'want to get away and think it all out'. Beware of the peril of thinking it all out! You can never think out spiritual problems. The only way of solving them is to live through them. If you have tried to square down to your spiritual problems, and bring your mind to bear upon them, and to solve them by 'thinking it all out', you know that you never get anywhere, and that the Lord does not meet you in that way. Spiritual things have to be lived through to clearness. We can only get through to clearness in spiritual things by living through them. If you do not understand that now, you probably will understand when you come up against another experience of this kind. Thus one aspect of the enemy's drive is to get you to run away. Why does the enemy want us to get away? Why is it that this whole force, this whole pressure, is to make us quit? He has a very good reason. He knows that it means loss and limitation. The Lord, to put it in a word, has bound up all His greater fullnesses with *spiritual* relatedness, and there can be nothing but grievous loss in failing to recognize the

66

House-law of God, the fellowship-law, the family-law. There can only be loss if we *take ourselves* out of God's appointed relatedness. Be very much aware of any kind of movement or tendency which is in the direction of either detachment or putting you into a place where you are apart. The enemy has many ways of getting his end. If he cannot drive us out from the midst of the Lord's people, he very often tries to give us a too prominent place in the midst of them. He can isolate us just as much by our being too much in the limelight, and we at once become uncovered, exposed. There is no more dangerous place than to be made too much fuss of, to be *someone*. There is such a thing as finding a hiding within the House of God.

But our particular consideration at the present time is this vocation and its outward direction, the House of prayer for all peoples. The Church, the Lord's people, form for Him a ministering instrument by which He has ordained to reach out to all the ends of the earth, a universal instrument wherever gathered together, even when represented only by two or three. The test of any company of the Lord's people, and of our position, is this vocation.

The Fact of Representation

You begin with the representative fact, the fact of representation. Representation begins with two or three, and that immediately swings us completely clear of all earthly grounds of judging and estimating. It indicates the essential heavenly nature of the Church. In the Lord Jesus every member of the Church is included. If Christ comes, the whole Church comes. The Holy Spirit is the Spirit of the whole Body, uniting all the members in one. You cannot be in the spirit and in Christ anywhere but what you are there in *the spiritual realm*, in *the heavenly realm*, with the whole Body, and the whole Body is there spiritually. Two or three? "There am I!" The whole Body, then, is bound up with the two or three. The fact evidences the heavenliness of the Church, the Body of Christ. This is not a possibility on the earth. You cannot bring the whole Church together in any one place on this earth literally. It is not the Lord's way, and it cannot be done. The Church is scattered worldwide, so far as the earthly aspect is concerned. And yet the Church is a heavenly thing gathered up in Christ, its Head, by one Spirit baptized into one Body, and when we come into the Spirit, into the heavenly realm, we are in the presence of the whole Body; not with earthly intelligence, that is, the whole Body is not conscious of the fact from the earthly standpoint, but spiritually it is true. That is the whole Church represented in the two or three if truly "in the Name". What the two or three may do in the Holy Spirit becomes a universal thing.

The Prayer Meeting

What we are seeking to press home is that this is so different from having a local prayer meeting, in the usually accepted meaning of that term. Suppose that where such an outlook obtains the announcement is made: 'We will have a prayer meeting on Monday night.' Who will come to that prayer meeting? People will say among themselves: 'Shall we go to the prayer meeting?' or, perhaps: 'Well, it is only a prayer meeting!' That is one way to look at it, as a local thing in a certain place at a certain time. But if I were to say: 'Will you come and minister to the whole Church of Christ universally in such-and-such a place at a certain time, and your business is to go and minister in that range to the whole Church!' that puts another point of view. It gives an altogether new conception of what we are called to. Let your imagination take flight, if you like, and see the whole Church from the ends of the earth literally gathered together, needing to be ministered to, and the Lord saying to you: 'Now you come and minister to the whole Church! Thousands of thousands, and tens of thousands gathered together, and I want you to minister to them. I have placed the resource at your disposal and will enable you to do it.' Perhaps you might shrink, and be fearful, but you would see the tremendous significance. You would not stay away because you were unimpressed with the importance of it.

This is not exaggeration. We are not straining the point. We are seeking to get to the heart of this ministry which is ours. When two or three are gathered together in any place, and they pray in the Holy Spirit, that is what is possible and it happens. They represent the whole Church, and become the House of prayer, functioning for all peoples, a universal ministry. We need to lift the prayer business on to a higher level. When we see the range, the significance, the value of a time of prayer together in the Name of the Lord, we shall stop our trivialities and take things seriously. We shall come together saying: 'Now, here are nations to be entered into tonight, and things which are world-wide and of tremendous significance to the Lord Jesus, and we are called to deal with them in this place!' There is no greater ministry. It is a tremendous thing to have a ministry like that.

It all comes back to asking whether this is true of the Church. What does this mean? Is it merely a passage of Scripture? Is it a nice idea, but falling short of any real meaning? What is the meaning of: "My house shall be called a house of prayer for all people?" It certainly does not mean that the whole Church can literally be gathered together in one place to pray, and it certainly cannot literally mean that the whole Church can pray together at the same time, though scattered. The situation is different in all countries. Day and night govern different parts of the world, and other factors come in. It is necessary to get away from the earth to explain this. And if you get off the earth and see that where two or three are gathered together into the Name all the rest are represented, and because the one Spirit is there the whole is therefore touched through that one Spirit, as well as involved, then the possibilities are tremendous. "A house of prayer for all peoples" is God's ordained way of ministry.

The Need for Prayer Ministry

Leaving the great spiritual truth, and coming to what is immediate, so far as one's own heart is concerned, in this word, I do feel that there has to be a fresh registration in our hearts of a call to this ministry and the need for it. We may pray a lot, but I feel that we have to take this matter of the prayer ministry even more seriously, to regard it as our supreme ministry. The order is *everything by prayer*; not everything and then prayer, but everything by prayer. Prayer comes first. Everything comes by prayer. Prayer is the basis of everything, and nothing else must be attempted or touched except on the ground of prayer. We have to gather into our prayer the universal interests of the Name of the Lord. "Because of Thy Name!" The Name is in view, and is involved. It is the interests of the Name which govern the functioning of the House, and all the interests of the Name of the Lord have to become the definite and solid prayer business of the Lord's people. Oh, the Lord cut clean across that thing which makes us so casual, and which makes corporate prayer times so optional, and bring into our hearts, with a strong, deep, set conviction, the witness that prayer is universal business, and that we are called to it!

It may be that before long there will be very little else that we can do. It may be that before long the Lord's people world-wide will find that their other activities are brought to a standstill, and they are shut up. What is going to happen then to the Lord's interests? Is that the end of ministry? Is that the end of functioning, of value, of effectiveness? It may be that before long the Lord's people in all the earth will need, as they have never needed before, the prayer co-operation of other members. It may be that the Lord's Name has suffered because we have not regarded this ministry as we ought to have done. We are not blaming anyone, but simply saying that there is room for far more serious entering into this tremendous thing which the Lord has appointed for us. Only to dwell upon the words quietly and thoughtfully will surely mean that their implication will come upon our hearts? The Lord has not said that He is going to move directly out to the universe. He has said: "My *house* shall be called a house of prayer for all peoples." To put that in other words we might state it thus: 'I have ordained to meet universal need through an instrument, through a vessel, and My people, My Church, form that vessel. That is My appointed way. If My Church fails Me, if My instrument does not take this matter seriously, is occupied with itself rather than with the great world-wide needs of My Name, then I am failed indeed!'

Now this means that we must recognize that where but two or three gather into the Name, where it cannot be more, there is nothing merely local about such coming together in prayer, but that the farthest ranges of the Lord's interests can be advanced, helped, ministered to, by the twos and threes. If it is possible for more to gather, then the Lord desires that, but it is ministry to the Lord by prayer for which He looks to us. We must see to it that it is our first, our primary business to pray. It is strange that so many more will come to conference meetings than to prayer meetings! Is the mentality behind that, that it is far more important to hear teaching than it is to pray? Would it not be a great day and represent some tremendous advance spiritually, something unique, if the prayer gatherings were bigger than the biggest conference gatherings, or at least as big as the biggest?

Let us lay this to heart! Remember that the enemy is always seeking to destroy the essential purpose of the House of God. "Ye have made it a den of robbers." That was one attempt of his to put out the real purpose by changing the whole character of things. God forbid that anything like that should be true in our case, but it is just possible to allow the primary thing to take a secondary place. The primary thing is prayer for all peoples. That, the Lord says, is what His House is for, and that is our real ministry. We cannot all be in the ministry of the Word, but we can all be in this ministry. We can all be in spirit out to the Lord for the interests of His Name.

There seems to be weakness and failure along this line: that we are not functioning in prayer to the point of seeing things through. We pray about many things, and we preach many things, but we do not see them through in prayer, and the Lord's Name is involved in that. You will know whether the Lord is speaking to your own heart. I believe this is a fresh call to the primary ministry which is so very, very much needed. All those who go out into the nations need very strong prayer support. If we fail them we do not know what may happen. They may be in all kinds of difficulties which they need not get into if we were wholly faithful in this prayer ministry. *The Lord lay it upon our hearts as a burden!*

Part Nine

The Church's Prayer and Spiritual Increase

"And in these days came prophets from Jerusalem unto Antioch. And there stood up one of them named Agabus, and signified by the Spirit that there should be great dearth throughout all the world: which came to pass in the days of Claudius Cæsar. Then the disciples, every man according to his ability, determined to send relief unto the brethren which dwelt in Judæa: which also they did, and sent it to the elders by the hands of Barnabas and Saul."

(Acts 11:27–30).

"Now about that time Herod the king stretched forth his hands to vex certain of the church. . . . Peter therefore was kept in prison: but prayer was made without ceasing of the church unto God for him."

(Acts 12:1, 5).

"But the Word of God grew and multiplied. And Barnabas and Saul returned from Jerusalem, when they had fulfilled their ministry, and took with them John, whose surname was Mark."

(Acts 12:24–25).

We may get great help from the incident recorded in Acts 12 if we realize the vast implications of it. When verse 24 speaks of the Word of God growing and multiplying it is dealing not merely with what happened at Jerusalem after the release of Peter, but with the spread of the Gospel into all the earth. Here was a notable turning-point in the

73

affairs of the people of God—*"But the word of God grew and multiplied."* The explanation of it, however, is surely in the earlier statement which discloses the secret crisis which brought about this turning of the tide—*"But prayer . . ."* (Acts 12: 5).

Everybody knows, of course, that chapter 13 marks a new division of the Book of the Acts, and that it introduces a very important development in the life of the Church. From that point there was an amazing and altogether new sending forth into all the earth of the testimony of Jesus Christ; the Word of God was indeed multiplied. But the narrative runs straight on from chapter 12, and is closely connected with it. We must not imagine that this new development was unrelated to what had gone before, but rather take note of how closely related were the events at Jerusalem with what was initiated from Antioch.

Significance of the Time

(1) Spiritual Triumph at Antioch

"Now about that time . . ." What time? The time of great spiritual victory and blessing at Antioch. The Spirit of God was mightily at work in the city, and for a year Saul and Barnabas had been ministering there among the new converts who were notable for the great grace of God which could be seen in them. Then, in the midst of this happy time of fellowship and instruction, a practical matter arose. By means of a prophet who came down from Jerusalem, the Holy Spirit presented them all with a practical challenge. He always does this. And very much depends on how we react at such a time of challenge. The saints at Antioch were told of an impending famine in Judæa, and thus, in a very practical way, they were tested as to how much they had really profited from what they had learned. It was a critical moment. By means of the Prophet Agabus they

were being proved as to whether the grace of God was
really working effectively in them. They stood the test.
Their response was immediate and whole-hearted. They set
aside any feelings which they might have had as to their
remoteness from Jerusalem or their independence of it.
Their brethren were in need. That was enough. Love
triumphed, as they determined to send help, every man
according to his ability.

"Now about THAT *time, Herod the king put forth his
hands."* Is not that just like the devil? Just when there is
a new movement of the Lord among His people and a fuller
expression of the triumph of His grace in their hearts,
Satan reacts with increased hatred and opposition. This is
all so true in our own experience.

(2) The Beginning of an Apostolic Partnership

Another significant feature in the timing of this evil
attack was that it also marked the beginning of a very
important association of two men—Barnabas and Saul.
They had known each other before, indeed it was Barnabas
who first brought Saul to Antioch. Now, however, there
was coming into being a most vital and significant movement of God, which demanded the joint ministry of the two
men. In the providence of God they were found together at
Jerusalem at this very time; it may be that they were
present at the special time of prayer for Peter. We must
not surmise too much about those movements of the
apostles which are not recorded in the Word, but surely the
Holy Spirit has a purpose in recording their presence in
Jerusalem immediately before and after the story of Peter's
deliverance from Herod. Chapter 11 ends with the arrival
of Barnabas and Saul in Jerusalem. They had come with
their gifts for the needy saints of that city. It is true that
no further mention of them is made up to chapter 12:24,
but when the narrative is resumed at verse 25 we are told

of the fulfilment of their ministration and their return from Jerusalem. This seems to show clearly that the chronicler wishes us to understand that Barnabas and Saul were still in Jerusalem during the intervening period. A further confirmation seems to be found in that the prayer took place in the house of the mother of John Mark (Acts 12:12), who was the very same young man who accompanied Saul and Barnabas back to Antioch. This Jerusalem prayer meeting seems to be taking on an altogether new significance. It is related to issues much larger even than the ministry of Peter and of the local church. It first checks and then reverses the rising tide of spiritual opposition, opening the way for a mighty release of the Spirit's energy through the whole Church.

(3) The Time of the Passover

There is one more point which should be noted with regard to the time element, and this is that it was the time of the Passover. *"Those were the days of unleavened bread."* It seems that in some general way the saints still kept the Jewish feasts; indeed in Jerusalem it was impossible for them not to do so. Even if they did not strictly observe the Jewish festivals, at least they would keep the Passover. We cannot fail to take some note of them. There is no doubt that as the Passover was being celebrated they would be vividly reminded of that other Passover, not so many years before, when the Lamb of God was offered up for their redemption. But there is always a danger that our commemoration of spiritual things should become formal and lifeless, instead of expressing up-to-date and living values. The Lord has to take precautions to deliver us from this peril. He may have seen that at Jerusalem they were inclined to celebrate the victory of Calvary as a matter of past history, a deliverance that belonged to a former day, and so permitted Herod to stretch forth his hands in a new attack, in order that the people of God, being forced into fresh conflict, might prove anew in a personal way the present power of Christ's glorious victory. So this was not so much Satan's timing as the timing of God. There was no question as to the ferocity of the assault upon them. *"But prayer. . . ."* And we may truly add, *"But God. . . ."*

Do not let us be discouraged when the enemy renews his attacks, nor fall into the mistake of imagining that the Lord is against us, just because life is difficult and full of problems. There is a timeliness about what is happening. Great things are afoot. It was precisely when the church at Antioch was responding whole-heartedly to the Lord, when a new day was dawning for the world-wide testimony of Christ, and when God was about to give His people fresh proof of the completeness of Calvary's triumph. *"Now about* THAT *time Herod the king put forth his hands to vex certain of the church."*

This will help us to appreciate an important fact, namely that our personal difficulties and trials, our local, corporate experiences of spiritual conflict, have a vital relationship with far bigger activities of God than we can imagine. *"But prayer was made earnestly of the church . . .";* *"But the word of God grew and was multiplied."* These two things are very closely connected.

God's Use of the Famine

It was the famine which occasioned the presence of Barnabas and Saul in Jerusalem. We know that there was such a famine, and that it was very extensive. Not only are there other authentic accounts of the great dearth in Jerusalem itself, but there are also records of famine conditions in Greece and Rome. It was one of those times when the whole world was in straitness and suffering. While it may be exaggeration to suggest that the world-situation happened in order that God's purposes might be realized among His people in Jerusalem and Antioch, there is no question but that world-conditions are used both by the devil and by the Lord for specific activities and interests among God's people.

Now, suppose that the saints at Antioch, who apparently were not themselves affected by the famine, had been unconcerned and unmoved concerning the needs of their Jewish brethren. Barnabas and Saul would not then have gone to Jerusalem at this time; they might have missed some Divine purpose, and there might have been no missionary developments at Antioch, as described in chapter 13. A great deal may have come out of the sending of relief to Jerusalem. None of us knows how closely inter-related are spiritual issues.

An ordinary Christian, one of those who met for prayer at the house of John Mark's mother, might have thought that he had nothing to do with the great apostolic mission, and the triumphs of the Gospel through Barnabas and Saul. He himself might have thought that he had nothing to do with it. God alone knows what spiritual energy is released to the ends of the earth when even a simple group of saints meet for prayer, and not only meet for prayer, but win through in prayer. The conflict may seem to relate to some purely local situation or personal need, but if those who are so beset rise up in the Name of the Lord, claiming the fulness of His victory, the local and personal victory will become the occasion for the release of spiritual forces in a widespread way.

The Test of Persecution

We find that the famine was followed by persecution, by Peter's imprisonment, and by severe testing for all the believers. What was the devil's purpose in this persecution? Was it not to scatter the saints, to divide them, to make them lose heart, and perhaps to compromise, or even to give up altogether? We, too, are affected by world-conditions, as they were by the famine. It may be that some of us are not involved in actual persecution, but we also suffer from Satan's attempts to discourage and divide us. Peter, it is true, was the one actually in prison, but the whole church was on trial; they were all being tested as to whether they would stand firm in the evil day and win through to victory. It is so easy to enjoy meetings, to appreciate Bible teaching and to be loud in our praise to the Lord, and then, when the conflict comes, to go all to pieces. It would not have been difficult for them to lose heart. James had been taken violently from them; Peter was in prison and apparently finished; everything seemed to deny the reality of their faith. What would be the use of going to a prayer meeting?

And, of course, the human element usually comes in. We may be quite sure that Peter was not a perfect man, and that under such a stress it would be very easy to remember his faults. It might possibly have been argued that if he had behaved differently he might have avoided arrest. Satan's effort was to break into the midst of that flock, to destroy their close fellowship, to get them doubting, questioning and arguing—anything but standing firmly together in faith. They might have felt that this imprisonment was Peter's business and not theirs. They might have let him find his own way out, perhaps putting up a little perfunctory prayer for him, but feeling in general that it was his own personal concern. And we, too, are exposed to these same perils and temptations. We do not have to wait for active persecution, for Satan is always seeking to make us divided in spirit, suspicious and critical of one another, or at best rather coldly independent. The devil focuses his attention on making the church lose faith, lose hope and weaken in love. We are not now treating of whether one should go to a prayer meeting—some of the most important elders could not be present at this one—but remarking on the spiritual principle of resisting every attempt at scattering.

The church in Jerusalem did not succumb to this temptation, but rallied together in earnest prayer and love, not for Peter only but for the will and glory of their Lord.

The Victory in Jerusalem

"But prayer. . . ." Here is the spiritual answer to a spiritual challenge, and very much depended on the outcome. If the victory had not been won at Jerusalem, if the saints had been scattered, disheartened and defeated, what would have happened to the Word of God? The real battle was concerning the release of that Word. The supreme concern was not what should happen to the church in Jerusalem, nor even what should happen to Peter; what really mattered was what should happen to the Word of God. When the saints gathered for prayer at Mary's home, though they probably did not realize it, they were fighting out the battle of world-evangelization, of the growth and multiplication of the Word of Christ. There are two 'buts' in this chapter. The first of them was the responsibility of the church: they refused to be moved. Satan was attempting to overthrow, to scatter, to destroy love and to turn faith into despair, when he was suddenly checked by a mighty spiritual resistance—*"But prayer. . . ."* It was a turning point. The whole course of events was arrested, and there followed a blessed sequence of Divine acts of deliverance. It was straightforward after this, for God had taken matters in hand, and was sweeping aside all opposition, that His people might be led out and onward to new triumphs. In verse 24 we have the great Divine 'but,' "BUT *the word of God grew and multiplied.*" This was the answer to their praying; the first responsibility lay with them, then God took things up in a mighty way, and said 'but' by

releasing His Word far and wide.

Like the church at Jerusalem, we too, shall be confronted with attacks upon our faith, our patience and our love. If we do not resolutely face up to these personal and local conflicts, pressing through to victory in the Lord's Name, what hope is there of increase and multiplication? On the other hand, if we do take up the challenge as they did, by stemming the onrush of spiritual disaster with our *"But prayer . . ."* God will surely respond with His 'but,' and clear the way for increase and new fulness.

The Far-reaching Effects

So it appears that there was a very large background or setting to the prayer battle in Mary's house. The Christians at Jerusalem thought that they were being assaulted on a purely local and personal issue. They felt, and rightly so, that by prayer they could win an immediate and local victory. Thank God they did. But what they did not know, what they could hardly have imagined, was that this was a turning point in Divine strategy, a victory which would produce a great release of the Lord's servants and of His Word. An ordinary rank and file believer in Jerusalem might have questioned whether it really mattered so much whether he was triumphant or defeated, whether after all very much depended on his loyalty and faith. It mattered far more than he could realize. It always does. It matters tremendously. There are far-reaching issues involved in the spiritual victories or reverses of the people of God.

And so when Peter was released, something else was released, the whole situation was released. For a time it seemed as though everything was shut up. The one man, Peter, seemed to be an embodiment of the whole state of affairs. He was shut up, he was in chains, and it seemed as if an end were coming to all the activities of the Spirit through the church. Everything then depended on whether the Lord's people would accept what appeared inevitable, whether they would give way to the opposition and be defeated by it. Had they done so, there is no guarantee as to what might have happened. But instead of giving way, they rose up in faith to assert that the Passover was no mere commemoration of a past victory, but the celebration of the ever-present power of Calvary's universal triumph. God responded by releasing Peter, but more than that, He gave new and mighty increase to the whole testimony of the church.

We now move on into Acts 13, to find that Barnabas and Saul are on the eve of being thrust out by the Holy Spirit into the uttermost parts of the earth. We must remember that they had just come down from Jerusalem in the spiritual good of a great victory, they had come down on a tide of glorious life and power, released in answer to believing prayer. From many points of view, Jerusalem and Antioch may have been different, but there can be no question as to their spiritual relatedness. The organic nature of the church means that we depend very much on one another. It is never the Lord's way to confine His working to limited and localized matters. He takes hold of our trials and conflicts, making them the occasion for the registration of important spiritual victories which will bring great and widespread increase. In actual experience the people of God are bound up together in vital association for the interests and glory of the Lord.

A Word of Warning

There remains just a word of warning concerning the young man who came down with Barnabas and Saul. Mark, of course, had every encouragement to be a missionary. He had been through all these thrilling events. With others he had been plunged into the darkness of battle, he had felt the sorrow of seeming defeat, he had heard the prayer and he had witnessed the wonderful answer. When Barnabas and Saul returned to Antioch, full of the story of God's marvellous deliverance, Mark went down with them, thrilled with a sense of the overwhelming power of God. So enthused and inspired was he that he had no difficulty in offering himself to go to the ends of the earth for Christ. We are therefore informed that when Barnabas and Saul set out *"they had also John as their attendant"* (Acts 13:5). But it did not last long. *"John departed from them and returned to Jerusalem"* (Acts 13:13). It seems that he was not prepared to travel quietly on into dark and forbidding territory, steadfastly believing that the God Who answered prayer at Jerusalem was still with them. Just the outward experience of things does not carry us very far. Saul and Barnabas had something more than that; they had a deep inward knowledge of the triumph of Calvary, and of the ever-present reality of the conquering Lord.

This is a note of warning, lest we should be among those who take up the matter of prayer warfare in a superficial way. We cannot live on thrills and wonders. We shall not always get quick results. The increasing spiritual conflict will call for an ever deeper and inward knowledge of the Lord. Mark's enthusiasm did not carry him very far. Perhaps he did the best thing in returning to Jerusalem. It may be that for the time being it would have been far better for him never to have left it. After all it was there that he had learned something of the power of God. We do not know. But we do know that in a simple home in that city, a gathering of ordinary and unnamed Christians fought a mighty spiritual battle, and won through to a victory which had repercussions in the lands and nations far beyond. *And this may be true of us all.*

Part Ten

The Church His Body

"The Church, Which is His Body" is the vessel, the 'embodiment', of the Lord the Spirit, in which and by which He is to express Himself. If the Church, as we met it and moved amongst its members, accorded with the Divine idea, we should know what the Lord was like. Let us take this to heart: that our very existence as the Church is in order that people may know what Christ is like. Alas, we fail Him so much in this. It is often so difficult to detect the real character of the Lord Jesus in His people. But that is the very first meaning of the Body of Christ.

But further—and here we are on familiar ground—a physical body is an organic whole. It is not something put together from the outside. It is something that is marked by a oneness, by reason of a life within; it is related and inter-related in every part, dependent and inter-dependent; every remotest part is affected by what happens in any other part. That could be much enlarged upon. But we have much more yet to learn as to the actual spiritual application of this reality about the Church as the Body of Christ. We need to be brought right into that great 'sympathetic system' of the Body. And that demands a real work of grace in us. There are many ways in which that is expressed in the Word. We are to "remember them that are in bonds, as bound with them; them that are evil entreated, as being yourselves also in the body" (Heb. 13:3); that is, we are to get into their situations by the Spirit. It is an organic whole. 'If one member suffer, all the members suffer with it' (I Cor. 12:26). It is probable that we suffer a good deal for things that we know nothing about. There is suffering going on, and we are involved in it: the Lord is seeking to involve us in the needs of others, to bring us into their conflict.

But, whether or not we apprehend this truth, whether or not we are alive to it and understand it, it is God's fact that it is so. Believers in one place are dependent upon believers in another place; they are affected. This is such a whole; there is one sympathetic nerve-system running through the whole body. If only you and I really became spiritually more alive, the expression of the Body would be much more perfect. Our deadness, our insensitiveness, our lack of real spiritual aliveness, results in there being more suffering, more loss, than there need be.

If only we could—not mechanically, and not by information, but on the principle of the Body—be moved into a universal sympathy and co-operation with the people of God! Our moving is so often mechanical; we have to read or hear letters, somehow receive information, in order to be stimulated to some measure of prayer. But I believe that, altogether apart from those means, if we were really in the Spirit, the Spirit would lay burdens for people on our hearts. Do you not think that it is a matter that we ought continually to bring before the Lord? *'Lord, there is someone praying to-day for something: is it possible that I might be the answer to their prayer? If so, show me, lead me, lay it on me.'* That is spiritual relatedness, aliveness. The oneness of the Body is a great vocation.

Part Eleven

Corporate Prayer

While it is true that a very large place is given in the Bible to individual and personal prayer, it is also true that a very great value is put upon corporate prayer. Indeed, a value is given to corporate prayer which cannot be known in individual prayer. In the New Testament the prayer-meeting has a very vital place in relation to the people and the work of God. It can be rightly said that the prayer-gathering is the index and register of the church's life. Show us your prayer-gathering and let us hear how the believers pray, and we will tell you what kind of church that is.

But what is church-prayer? In other words,

What Should
The Prayer-Meeting Be?

It may seem a truism to say that it should be

(1.) The Church AT PRAYER.

That is, the church as an entity, a corporate entity. Such a gathering together should be the solid expression of the organic oneness and spiritual unity of the local company of believers. The mere congregating of a number of individuals without an organic integration, and with so many personal interests to express or have expressed, may have values and would be better than nothing at all, but it would not be the solid and effectual prayer of the church as an entity.

There is a history behind the prayer of the church, as

such. It is the history of a work of the Cross in which each member has been brought on to the ground of identification with Christ in death, burial, and resurrection, and by that common history has identical life and fellowship. Such a church has *gone through* something in experience and that something has become subjective.

If two people have gone through a similar experience which has deeply affected their inward life, they have a mutuality of understanding, and they can speak with one voice. So it was in the prayer-life of the New Testament churches. They shared and expressed locally what was fundamentally true of the Church universal. It was a crucified and resurrected Church, having been baptized into the sufferings and victory of its Head. That victory should be inherited by the local church, and be manifested in the effective working and issues of its corporate prayer.

There, in the gatherings—or coming together—for prayer, the very nature and vocation of the Church universal should be in expression. Its nature is that of a spiritual organism because it has been born "not of man, nor of the will of the flesh, but of God," "born of the Spirit." Its vocation is to express the greatness, the rights, and the authority of Christ. Prayer is essentially vocational, and this is pre-eminently so in corporate prayer.

Vital relatedness, both of the persons and of the prayer, is indispensable to effectual prayer. How easy it is for someone to come in with something quite discordant or irrelevant, and so swing the prayer away from its strength of purpose and positiveness.

While many particular matters may occupy the foreground of required prayer, there should always be a looking beyond the thing itself to how it really relates to and touches those three factors just mentioned—the greatness, the rights, and the authority of Christ. We must have an adequate case in our prayer, and that is the Lord's glory.

(2.) Corporate Prayer Must
BE AUTHORITATIVE

The church at prayer must be on the ground of absolute authority. It must not be in doubt, uncertainty, or weakness, but in assurance and confidence. There must be the ground of authoritative appeal to God. There must be the ground of authority over the evil forces at work in any given situation. The church must have the assured right in its position and in its intercession.

That right and authority is respectively the infinite virtue and efficacy of the Blood of Christ and its testimony, and the Name of Christ as above every other name.

The church—at all times, but—especially when at prayer must be consistent with all that the Blood of Christ means as a testimony against sin, condemnation, and death. These things mean a closed door to Heaven and God. The Blood of Christ has for ever been the ground, and the only ground, of "the new and living way" to the Throne of Grace. The Name of Christ is the very synonym for supreme authority. But even so, it is not just a title, but the embodiment of a nature wholly satisfying to God; of a work perfectly accomplished; and of a position fully accorded Him. These are the elements of authority, and the ground of authoritative prayer. On this ground the church has a right to pray and expect. It can do more than ask upward; it can challenge outward—"in the Name."

(3.) Corporate Prayer Should
BE EXECUTIVE

When we use the word 'executive' we mean decisive. If you were a member of an executive body in any business concern, you would be a person marked by certain features, that is, if the concern with which you were connected was of a really vital character.

(a) You would be recognized as a person with a real business mind. That concern would give a seriousness to your demeanour and attitude. It would rule out diffusiveness and irrelevance, and knit you together with your colleagues as one with an integrating objective.

(b) You would be a person who would be marked by a will for decisions. Wasting of time; indecision; tentativeness; carelessness; and all such things would greatly disturb and trouble you. Your soul would be saying, 'Don't let us be always and only talking about things; waiting for something to happen, and hoping that it will, some day. Let us *be* executive, and have issues settled, and conclusions reached. Let there be an element of decisiveness and conclusiveness about our transactions. Let us reach for and be set upon a verdict.' Surely, such features are traceable in the prayers in the Bible, with Abraham, Moses, Daniel Nehemiah, etc., and in the New Testament Church and churches!

Our praying in meetings is all too tentative and indecisive. We do not really go out for a verdict. We stop before we have the assurance that we are *through* on that issue. There is such a thing as taking as well as asking. We ought to go away, not wondering, to say nothing of forgetting, but rather expecting and looking for Heaven's answer. That answer ought to be already in our hearts. If what we have said is true of any Executive worthy of the name, who has a serious Concern to serve, should it be less or otherwise with the church which has the greatest of all interests to serve, responsibilities to carry, and Name to honour? We should not go to the place and time of prayer just because it is 'prayer-meeting night'; or to do our duty to our 'church,' or for conscience sake; certainly not to give certain others the occasion to pray while we listen and—more or less—agree. We *are* the church. We *are* in the greatest of all business! We should go thus-minded and with 'purpose of heart' determined to co-operate and—so help us God—to have outstanding, urgent issues settled for 'the sake of the Name.' On arriving our instant action should be to take the right ground and ask fervently that all should be taken into the hands of the Holy Spirit. One word remains for this present.

(4.) Corporate Prayer Must
BE COMBATIVE

It is impressive that in that part of the greatest *Church* letter in the New Testament where its militant character is emphasized and its armour portrayed, the Apostle gives such a definite place to prayer (Eph. 6).

There is nothing which draws out the "wiles" of the evil powers so much as corporate prayer. Everything is done to smother, blanket, confuse, divert, pre-occupy, disturb, distract, annoy, hinder, weary, waste time, and many other things, all with the object to see that there is no real impact of Christ's authority upon their kingdom.

If we realize this we shall 'gird up the loins of our minds,' we shall 'stand and withstand.' Being alive to what is involved and what is happening, we can be no more passive than a soldier could be if he saw his country's interests and his comrades' lives involved in his attitude and action.

There is a real combativeness in corporate prayer, and we shall not get anywhere if our fighting spirit—not in the flesh, but in the Holy Spirit—has been let go or taken from us.

Part Twelve

The Divine Ministry of Delay

One of the great dangers of life is that of losing sight of God's great design in the details by which that design is worked out; and it has been well said that we entirely lose the value of any experience if we isolate it. That is, if you take your sorrow and regard it apart from the great designing love of God, if you take your losses, your temporary setbacks, your momentary depressions, and dwell upon these things as if they were the only experiences of God's providence, and as if they were not related to the great central control of His love—you will entirely miss their value. It is that we may be saved from such peril that we are meditating together thus on some of God's unlikely but never unkindly ministries.

With this brief recapitulation let me ask you to turn to the word which is the occasion of our thought this morning in regard to the Divine ministry of delay by which God oftentimes tests His people. I will ask you to turn to the words of Jeremiah the Prophet, in the Book of Lamentations, in the third chapter, at the twenty-fourth verse:

"The Lord is my portion, saith my soul; therefore will I hope in Him. The Lord is good unto them that wait for Him, to the soul that seeketh Him. It is good that a man should both hope and quietly wait for the salvation of the Lord" (verses 24–26).

It is especially on those last words that I want our meditation to be based: *"It is good that a man should both hope and quietly wait for the salvation of the Lord."*

Let us frankly admit at the outset that one of the great difficulties of life with many of us is concerned with the fact that God sometimes seems to delay His answers to our prayers. The most perplexing problem of many a Christian life is just this: that God apparently does not answer, and apparently does not even heed much of our crying. By His grace our faith in Him has not been finally disturbed. By His grace this conflict has been carried on courageously in secret.

Outside our own heart no one even suspects that there is such a conflict. But you know that there is, and I know that there is, and sometimes the only word that rises from our hearts when we come into God's presence is almost the last word which came from the Saviour's lips: "My God, why?" This is not the first question of the Christian life. Faith's first question is usually "How?" There is a stage in Christian experience when we are constantly saying "How?"—"How can a man be born when he is old?" "How can these things be?" "How can this Man give us His flesh to eat?" "How are the dead raised up, and with what body do they come?" These are some of the first questions of the Christian life. But as we go on with God, as life deepens, as its necessities become heavier, its sorrows more acute, and our perceptions more alert also, the question which rises from the heart of many a disturbed and distressed believer is: "My God," not "how?" but "WHY?"

I have already suggested that what many of us are seeking at this time is not comfort, nor sympathy, nor even the lightening of our loads. We are seeking some explanation, some interpretation from God Himself as to what He is doing in these our lives. Some of us are distressed almost to the point of desertion—desertion of our own allegiance, and desertion of His colors, because He seems to delay, indeed almost to deny the things we ask Him.

Yet, I would remind you that there is nothing which the Word of God so amply encourages men to do as to pray. There are promises attached to prayer which do not attach to any other condition. There are riches which are covenanted to men as the result of prayer and waiting upon God, which they can obtain in no other way. And it is just because the promises with regard to prayer are so great, so high, so wide, that these delays of God perplex us, and we cry out this morning, "My God, why?" There are times in life when nothing but sheer belief in God's goodness saves us from despair; when nothing but simple reliance upon God's love, without any present evidence of it, can save us from hopelessness; when nothing but almost reckless faith in His omnipotent wisdom, will prevent us from sinking into positive moral apathy and spiritual lethargy.

Therefore, it is my present endeavor to help some here to a recreation of that sheer belief, that simple reliance, and that reckless faith in God which trusts Him when His face is veiled, and they do not even feel the grip of His hand. Faber well sang:

> "Thrice blest is he to whom is given
> The instinct that can tell
> That God is on the field, when He
> Is most invisible."

That is the instinct which may God grant every one of us to have in these days.

Now these words were spoken by the Prophet Jeremiah in a day when the nation's desire, its best desire, was perhaps never so evident. The people had begun to see the fulfilment of God's promises and the working of His providence. Their foes were being pushed from their land, the beginnings of recultivation were taking place, and the broken-down altars of God were being rebuilt. But all was being done so slowly that they could not reconcile the slowness of God with the implicit assurances upon which their faith in Him rested. They were impatient and restive under His apparent inactivity. Faith saw God's beginnings and, like the disciples of later days, "thought the kingdom must immediately appear!"

There is a great deal to be said for the faith of a little child which cannot understand the reason of delay. But you will not misunderstand me when I say that there is a great deal more to be said for the faith of a grown man who has come to know that God has an entirely different scale for the measurement of time from those we commonly use. There is still more to be said for the faith of the man who is perfectly content to rest in the fact that a thousand years are as one day with Him, and one day as a thousand years. This was the faith of Jeremiah. He had looked into the depths of the Infinite God, and had seen that He was unhurried, and that His ways were the more certain because they were not the more obvious. So he waited calmly, and sought to renew courage and patience and hope in the people, just because these things were the expression of his own soul. Hence he says: "It is good for men that they are kept waiting, that they have to quietly hope for the salvation of God."

You will readily understand that these words of his are of infinitely wider application than to the Israel of that day. I believe they are apposite to the case of every one of us here today who is perplexed because, for instance, the expected deliverance from sin in his own life does not come as he thought it would. Or the petition he offers for some good of which he conceives himself to be in great need is not granted. Or the loved one for whom he prays is not immediately converted; and though he goes on praying he has almost lost heart about it. Or the revival in his work, for which he has conscientiously wrought to the very last ounce of his strength, does not seem to be even on the horizon. We want to know why this delay, and what the spiritual good of having quietly to wait and hope so long.

I am very sure that when the last word of human experience about prayer has been said, we are still in the presence of the greatest of all mysteries. The man who thinks he knows so much about prayer, that he can frame a philosophy of prayer, really confesses that he knows little indeed. How prayer liberates spiritual forces, who knows? Why God has ordained that men should wait upon Him, uniting their wills with His in order to exert the saving power of His grace both in their life and through them in the lives of others—who can say? With regard to this greatest of all subjects, there is really nothing further to be said than that which Paul said about all knowledge of God—"We know in part, and we prophesy in part." But, thank God, we do know! What we know we know with a certainty which nothing can shake. But we only know in part. Therefore they are mere suggestions that I venture to offer you today, suggestions which have come with some degree of light and encouragement to my own heart in regard to this assertion—that it is good for a man to wait and hope for the salvation of God.

It is almost unnecessary to say that there is no thought in this word of any man having to wait until God is willing to bestow upon him the primary gifts of pardon and peace and forgiveness, the salvation which is His free gift in Jesus Christ. The sinner who cries for pardon, the weary and heavy-laden who ask for rest of heart, the lonely who seek the fellowship of love, are never kept waiting for the fulfilment of their desires. The prodigal is welcomed before he utters his prepared confession. The sinking man who cries "Lord, save me", is at once conscious of being grasped by the Hand of power. The Evangel of Christ bears the age-less superscription that "now is the day of salvation". In this respect, indeed, it is never God who keeps men waiting, but men who keep Him waiting. But, in regard to that aspect of His mercy which is concerned with the strain of our present discipline, with the anxiety of future uncertainty, with the relief of immediate discomfort, with the weariness of unremoved burdens—it is in that realm of life that we want to know why God delays. Nor is it unnatural that we should be impatient.

For instance, here is a good man who reads that "All things work together for good to them that love God", but who sees nothing in his life today but chaos. His affairs have been completely ruined. His home has been invaded by sorrow and disappointment, until the nerves of all are on edge, and no one knows with certainty what an hour is going to bring forth of fresh calamity. That man has rested upon that Divine Word with implicit confidence in its truth, but the delay in realizing its fulfilment has almost staggered his faith. Is it to be wondered at that he should be asking today what it all means?

There is a young man yonder, and there has been illumined to his soul's vision this word: "In all things we are more than conquerors through Him that loved us." And yet he has been defeated ever since he came to Keswick, and this morning his face is toward the ground, and not toward the Lord. He says, "What does it mean? I have rested my whole weight, as I believe, upon this promise of God, and my Lord delays His coming in power to me. What does it mean?"

There is the busy worker—I have met him since I came to Keswick—who has come from some far-off missionary field, in which for the last ten years he has been pouring out his life, seeking to live the life of a citizen of the Kingdom of God, resting upon that word—"My word shall not return unto Me void, but it shall accomplish that which I please" (Isa. 55:11). And he confesses today that he has seen it accomplish hardly anything. What does it mean?

There is the great promise upon which every member of Christ's Church just now is building more solidly than ever a temple of hope: "Behold, I come quickly" (Rev. 3:11; 22:7). It seems as though Christ was never so much needed as He is today. It seems as though international relationship can never again be restored as we have known it. It seems as though the scattered units of Christ's Church can never be gathered together again in one, save by His coming. And the Church cries out: "Amen. Come quickly, Lord Jesus" (Rev. 22:20). But there is not a sign of His coming. What do these delays of God mean?

I am going to suggest three things, and they are mere suggestions; but may they bring light to you, as they have brought to me in past days. The first thing I want to say about God's delays is this: It is only by *enforced* waiting upon Him that we come to know God with that knowledge which is the foundation of all character. I use the word enforced waiting upon God, because it is only by being forced to wait upon God that some of us ever do wait on Him. We are naturally impatient, we are naturally impulsive, we naturally chafe at anything like slowness; and God, by withholding the answer for which we have looked, keeps us at His feet in order that we may come to know Him. He is infinitely more concerned in the making and remaking of our lives than in the gratifying of our minds. He is infinitely more concerned in making us men and women of His own pattern, and to deepen His life in our souls, than to gratify some of the desires which we often express in unconsidered prayer. For we cannot come to know God, and inferentially we cannot come to know ourselves, in an hour. God's delays do not indicate any caprice on His part, but rather His concern and compassion for us. They are directed toward saving us from hurrying away from His presence before the lessons of His grace have been more than mentally received. God is preparing us, by keeping us waiting upon Him, worthily to receive, to interpret, and then to use the gifts He will yet give in answer to prayer and in fulfilment of His word.

I constantly see tourist visitors to London rushing about from Park to Palace, doing what they call the "sights". And after a fevered week they go back home thinking they know London. But do they? One of Ruskin's students once said to him, on returning from a first Italian visit: "Sir, immediately I entered the Gallery at Florence, I knew in a moment what you had always impressed upon us as the supremacy of Botticelli." Ruskin's reply was somewhat cutting. He said: "Oh, you found that out in a moment? Well, it took me twenty-two years to discover it!" And there are a great many people who think they know God in the light of a single experience! We are kept waiting upon Him that we may become of the number of those who really do know their God, and who consequently are empowered to do exploits.

God is making us; do not let us be impatient under the process. God is making us; do not let impatience and impetuosity take us, therefore, from under the hand of the Master Workman. He is eliminating the flaws, and remaking the marred vessels. The two qualities which we need most—endurance and radiance—are not imparted to any man in a single hour. God keeps us waiting that in His presence, beholding His glory, we may be changed into the same image from glory unto glory.

The second thing I want to say is this. Many of our prayers must be passed through the refining medium of God's wisdom, that is, of God's love; many of them must be edited by God before they are answered. For well-intentioned prayer is not always well-informed. Like those who made requests of the Saviour, God often has to say to His children, "Ye know not what ye ask". If some of our prayers were immediately answered, the consequence would be almost certain moral and Spiritual disaster. Our prayers have to be passed, I say, through the refining medium of God's wisdom, sometimes with regard to their motive. "Ye have not because ye ask amiss."

There are men and women, for instance, who pray for power, while their real objective is pre-eminence. What they really mean by power is that which will make them prominent in His service. When our motives are altogether unworthy of the words we express, we have to be kept waiting until God turns upon us the searchlight of His love, and learning the untrustworthiness of our own impulses, we yield us to that gracious Spirit Who makes intercession in us according to the will of God.

Not only in regard to the *motive*, but in regard also to the content of our prayers, Christ has to say again and again, "Can ye drink of the cup that I drink of; are ye able to be baptized with the baptism wherewith I am baptized?" For often we know not what we ask, and hence God's delay in response. I have seen children—we have all seen them—who have been utterly spoiled by the weak good-nature of parents who gave them at once everything they wanted. For human love may be entirely lacking in wisdom. But the love and wisdom of God are one. When He keeps us waiting for secondary mercies, it is in order to make us know the value of the primary and spiritual. We have to learn that God's "No" is just as much an answer as God's "Yes". We have to learn that God's "Not yet" is just as truly an expression of Divine love as God's "Immediately". The day will come to every one of us when we shall know that God's silence was in reality His most loving speech to us. For we shall see that while seemingly inactive God has all the time been working in us, bringing us into moral correspondence with His will, which alone capacitates men to receive His gifts.

Well do I recollect, some years ago, in the city of

Dublin, a man coming into the vestry-room of a church and saying: "Sir, I want to thank you for that message about God's love. I believe every word of it now, but I did not six months ago." His eyes filled with tears; and as I said: "What does it mean, my brother?" He went on: "Six months ago my home was bright and happy, and the shadow fell. I prayed earnestly that God would save my wife and our infant. But He took them; and I have come to know that He took them only in order to bring me back to Himself, from Whom I had wandered." God's silence in that man's life was His richest and kindest speech. And others of us have found this to be true also; and more of us will find it so ere these dark days in which we live have passed away.

The things we try to get rid of by prayer are often the very things we can least afford to lose. Some of those things we call burdens, of which we try to get rid in the Sanctuary, are the things that God has placed upon us for the steadying of life and the guiding of our energies into channels which otherwise we should overlook and miss. Paul learnt that there was something infinitely better than the removal of the thorn-pain—infinitely better! Thrice he besought the Lord to remove it—with what interval between those prayers we know not. But surely Paul, like the rest of us, was perplexed at God's delay. And he ultimately found that God was preparing something far better than the extraction of the thing which caused a throbbing wound—"My grace is sufficient for thee." If he had not had the thorn-pain, like the nightingale which is said to sing sweetest when its breast is pierced, he had never learned the song: "Most gladly will I glory in my infirmities, that the power of Christ may rest upon me!" We learn, as we are kept waiting at His feet, that the cord which we would have had God cut, He disentangles, and so saves for purposes of His service. God's ways are always justified of His children, if they will patiently tarry His leisure.

Ere I pass on to the third and last suggestion I have to make, may I say that surely we get an illustration of all this in the burden of prayer which is increasingly descending upon us for our nation. There are not a few of us who are perplexed that God has not already intervened to stay this terrible conflict. We look out from this place of quiet rest, and see across the Channel the sons of God being butchered upon the fields of France and Belgium; and we cry to God to give victory to the cause which is inherently right, and about which we have no shame. Yet He does not do so. After a whole year, and despite the sacrifice of thousands of precious lives, the battle-line is drawn substantially as it was at first. Why does God not put forth His power through our Forces, and by scattering the nations that delight in war bring this unspeakable strife to an end? Why have we no answer back from Heaven that our cry is heard? Why does He delay His coming when by one word He could end the whole conflict?

Ah! it is not that God cannot, nor that He will not; but that an immediate victory for our land might only mean a revival, in the basest form, of our national sins. As a nation we are far from being morally ready for victory, for there are few signs in our common life that we have learned and taken to heart the lessons of this chastisement. That is why God is keeping our nation waiting. We have to be brought infinitely lower yet. We have to learn yet what the law of God stands for. We have to learn yet what the hideousness of sin in a man or nation means. We have to learn that sin brings pain and bloodshedding to man, as it brought pain and bloodshedding to God. Then when the nation is morally prepared and renewed I believe that victory will not be delayed by an hour. But it will not come one hour sooner. Hence the necessity of our quietly waiting for the salvation of God. Though remember, in the last analysis, it is not He Who delays the answer to our prayer for victory. It is we who delay Him.

The third thing I want to say is this. Faith can only be trained by being tested. As a man's muscles are only hardened by exercise, so his faith only becomes strong and ultimately invincible by being subjected to the discipline of strain. For until it accepts the will of God, not under compulsion, nor because there is no alternative, but by free choice and glad surrender, faith is lacking in essential quality. But when we are unmoved by the fact that we are kept waiting, calmly conscious that God's glory is intimately bound up with our lives and prayers, and content that if He can afford to wait, so too can we, one of life's greatest lessons has been learnt. For faith reaches its triumph only when its exercise ceases to be a deliberate activity and becomes an instinctive attitude.

Sometimes we learn this by our own impetuous efforts to hurry God. There are two conspicuous examples of this. Do you remember Moses and his undisciplined effort at the deliverance of his people? How disastrously it ended for him! God had to take him into the schoolhouse of the desert and keep him there for many a weary year. By his impetuosity he had embarrassed God; and so, too, do many of us. Do you remember Abraham with a wonderful promise to support him, with a vision so great that it staggered him, attempting to expedite God's purpose? You know the dark story of Hagar and Ishmael, and all that it afterward led to. Sometimes God likewise delays the promises of His faithfulness in order that we too may learn the utter futility of our every effort, and all the sweat of our souls, apart from Him. For remember that the faith of God must be vindicated in us before it can be verified through us, and before we can be His effective messengers to the world.

One last word. There is nothing in common between quiet waiting upon God and lethargic indolence. We have known those who excuse their non-participation in the enterprises of Christ's Church because of this necessity of quiet waiting on God. Let me say that there is no greater mistake than to wait for subjective manifestations and to neglect objective opportunities. True waiting upon God expresses itself in the expenditure of every energy of the soul at the clear directions for whose interpretation we do not need to wait an hour.

Oh, the supine folly of the man who in these days of tremendous opportunity is content to "wait upon God" to open doors, to "wait upon God" to enlarge opportunities, to "wait upon God" to organize success and influence for him, while he himself does nothing in the way of sacrifice—of giving himself, of losing his life, for the Kingdom's sake! God does not co-operate with dreamers. We cannot live in fellowship with God and let evil stalk unchallenged, by neglecting the wide-open doors of the world which call to our faith and our loyalty.

I cannot forget that God did once say to His people: "Stand still, and see the salvation of God." But I also remember that that word was given to men and women, a great host, who were walking in implicit obedience to His leadership, and who in that pathway had come up against the impassable. There are times in life when God says these words to us, but only when, like Israel, we are walking in the light of His will.

> "We are not here to play, to dream, to drift;
> We have hard work to do, and loads to lift;
> Shun not the struggle! face it! 'Tis God's gift.
>
> Say not, 'The days are evil! Who's to blame?'
> And fold the hands, and acquiesce—oh, shame!
> Stand up, speak out, act bravely in God's Name.
>
> It matters not how deep entrenched the wrong,
> How hard the battle goes, the day how long;

Fight on! fight on! tomorrow comes the song!"

As we wait upon God in this energy of implicit obedience to Him, He will vindicate all His delays. He will do it as we stand, like men who wait for their Lord, doing His will to the very utmost of our power; knowing that when He comes He will perfect that which concerns us; pushing the battle to the gate, in the confidence that at the strategic moment He will bring up reinforcements which shall mean the final factor in victory; quietly hoping for that we see not; saying to our souls again, and yet again, "We see not yet all things put under Him, we see not yet the fulfilment of our every desire; but we see Jesus crowned. Blessed be His Name for ever!"

Part Thirteen

The Eternal Reward of Labour and Suffering

Reading: Numbers 27:1–7; Joshua 15:13–19; Romans 8:17.

I have just one thought that I want to pass to you here. It relates to inheritance. In the New Testament that word is found to compass quite a lot. In the first place, inheritance is there shown to be a matter of birthright; then it is extended to a bequest, a gift; and then still further it applies to reward for labour, for service. It is in this last connection that my word lies.

While it is fully recognized—not for a moment would we detract one iota from the grand fact—that everything is of grace; even enablement to work for reward is of grace—while that is true, this other aspect of inheritance, or heirship, as a matter of reward for service and suffering, is very fully revealed. Inheriting by labouring, entering into the fruits of labour; inheriting by warfare, entering into the spoil of battle; entering into suffering and being recompensed for suffering. It is surely inherent in labour, in suffering, that there should be some gratification, and the gratification is the wages. While we know that it has been grace that has enabled to suffer and to labour, nevertheless we *have* suffered and we *have* laboured and we *have* battled, and there is something for that, by the faithfulness of God—there are wages, there is that sense of achievement. There is no greater gratification than to know that, through labour and suffering, something has been achieved.

Inward Relationship to the Object in View

It is just there that I put my finger. The very heart of suffering, the very heart of co-heirship with Christ, is this wonderful sense of inward relationship to the object in view, inward relationship to the inheritance, inward relationship to the result, the reward. And that is the explanation of suffering, of labour, of conflict. The Lord does not just give to us without cost. He always brings us into the cost of that which He is going to give. It will be grace all the way through, but He brings us into the cost of the reward. In the end, let us repeat, we shall acknowledge that any part we have had in it of suffering, labour, warfare, has been infinitely outweighed by what He has given, and that is where grace will always be our theme; but I do believe that mingled with our gratitude will be this sense that the Lord enabled us to achieve, that He did not act without us and apart from us. He brought us into it, and there will be this deep, inward, heart-relatedness to the result, that we share with Him the gratification. That is the very heart of suffering, I believe.

Now why am I saying this? Where was this born? How was this born? Well, in a very practical way. I have just returned from a time in the United States, and it has not by any means been an easy time—very much otherwise. But we have been profoundly grateful all the time that you dear friends were so many hours ahead of us. In the Eastern part of the States you were five hours ahead. When we got further West you were six hours ahead, and we constantly reminded ourselves that your prayer gatherings were ahead of us. They had gone before and we were just following on, in our own prayer and in the conflict and the pressure; following on, and, as we believe, being carried through. And there came to me this: Those dear friends are right in the battle, and if there is anything here that really is for the Lord, if anything results for the Lord, it belongs to them, quite as much as it belongs to us. It is theirs; in a certain sense they will own this; it will be, so to speak, their property. They have battled for it, suffered for it, endured for it, toiled for it. They have gone on ploughing the way, pioneering the way, and it is theirs.

That is the thought right at the heart of this word, that there is something that becomes ours through suffering. Yes, it is the Lord's, and it is all of His grace, but it is ours.

Suffering Is a Purifying Thing

And that means surely that what we have laboured for, suffered for, travailed for, becomes something over which we are very jealous. Suffering for anything is a very purifying thing. Take the matter of the child for which there has been suffering, travail. Well, other people who have not so suffered and travailed and gone through for the child can see all the defects and pass all the criticisms and arrive at their judgments, good or bad, about that child, and just stand apart and say their say about the child. But the mother may see very little of that. There is something for the mother which transcends all that. 'Oh yes, you may say that, but that child is very precious to me. I have suffered for that child, that child is my child, the child of my heart and the child of my travail, and, while l may see its faults, there is something which covers them all, there is the jealousy of a love born of suffering'.

Now you see what I am getting at. There is nothing that is precious to the Lord, and which He would make the property of His people, but there will be suffering for it. It will only become their property—in that sense—as they suffer for it, and then woe betide who criticizes that! If you are detached from a thing, if you are detached from a testimony, from a work of God, you can do all the criticizing you like. You have no inward heart-relationship to it, and so you pass your judgments upon it. But if you are in it and you have suffered, if it has been a costly thing where you are concerned, then you are seeing more than all the failings, more than all those faults. The people who can criticize like that and judge and point out faults are the people who have not suffered.

On the other side, we may know all the terms, all the phraseology, all the doctrine, all the truth, and it may be just objective, something we have heard; we have lived in the midst of it, it is familiar to us. But what the Lord will do if that is to become ours is to take us into travail over the matter. He will relate that thing to our hearts in a deep, inward way, so that none of us will be able to say, 'I know all about that, I have heard all about that, I could tell you all that you could tell me about that'. The Lord would so work in a costly, deep and painful way in relation to that, to make it ours through travail, that we are brought into a new position. We are not spectators, looking on, criticizing; we are on the inside, looking out, defending. We are jealous over it. Suffering is a great purifying thing. It destroys selfishness. It destroys that self-interest that is the cause of so much of the trouble. It makes us in a disinterested way jealous for what is of God. Yes, suffering purifies, and suffering makes this deep, inward link.

It gives an extra feature to things. That extra feature where we cannot just be occupied with faults and be people of a criticizing attitude, the extra feature with a love which covers a multitude of sins. We have suffered together. When we suffer together, what a lot we get over! We have gone through it together, perhaps through the years. We have been in the fire together, and there is a love, there is a jealousy which, let people say what they will about the other persons, simply rises up in us because we have suffered.

Joint-heirs with Christ Through Suffering

"Heirs of God, and joint-heirs with Christ; if so be that we suffer with Him, that we may be also glorified with Him" (Rom. 8:17; A.S.V.). This is not just an official thing, something that is a gratuitous gift in a mechanical way, as much as to say, 'Well, you have done a bit of work; here are your wages'. That thing has been wrought in us through the suffering and the cost and the warfare and the labour, and there is this sense of an inward co-heirship with Christ, if we suffer. It will be a very blessed thing, to us who know how much we are dependent upon the grace of God, how little we can even bear without the support of His grace; it will be a wonderful thing when at last He says, 'This is the reward of your suffering'. We shall say, 'Well, after all, it was our *light* affliction—in the light of the far more exceeding and eternal weight of glory. How have we earned this?' But there will be some gratification in recognizing that the Lord has taken account of what we have gone through, and has brought us into a sense of His own gratification, and given us to feel—'Well, it was not in vain, it was not for nought'.

Why did I read those passages in the Old Testament from Numbers and Joshua? They both have to do with inheritance. I read them for this reason, that here were people who, in the first place, were concerned, were jealous, for the inheritance. And then they were people who were prepared to enter into the cost of the inheritance, after which, when they had got it, it was theirs. Yes, it was the Lord's, but it was theirs. Do you see what I mean? It is theirs. And many of us have gone through the years in toil, in suffering, in labour and warfare in the Lord's interests, and if there is anything that comes out of that at all, it is ours, in this sense—that we are jealous over it with a right kind of jealousy. It belongs to us in the Lord. Yes, it is the Lord's, but it belongs to us in the Lord, the fruit of suffering and of travail and of cost. Your faithfulness in prayer, and in prayer-gatherings—it is not without cost that you continue like that. Your faithfulness in the upholding of those who go out—it costs. Taking the years over, it is not without price if there is anything. The Lord has given it to you as your inheritance; that is yours. All that eternal spiritual value is yours in Christ. Now look after it, cherish it, watch jealously over it, and from all attacks defend it. If only we had this inward sense of relatedness to everything that costs, what a difference it would make, how less ready we should be to see the defects and the faults!

The Lord bring us to understand that the meaning of the conflict and of the suffering, from His standpoint, is not only—and I say this quite reverently—not only in order to get something for Him. It is because He wants us in an inward relatedness to it, as a very part of ourselves. I believe that is the very essence of this joint-heirship with Jesus Christ. What does it mean to inherit if we suffer? Surely it means—'This is what you have earned through the grace of God. Here it is: you have paid for this in fellowship with Christ'. I do not understand all this in the New Testament about 'suffering together with Him', 'filling up that which is lacking of the afflictions of Christ for His Body's sake, which is the Church'—I do not understand unless it is this, that the Lord wants us not just as bits of a machine to work out some piece of work for Him. He wants a real heart-relatedness; so that, as we suffer with Him—and we are suffering with Him, there is no doubt about that—as we suffer with Him, we shall be gratified with Him. Glorified—yes, but gratified; the deep sense of gratification that we had a share in this. *The Lord give us a right attitude toward all the cost.*

Part Fourteen

Recovery of the Glory

"And she named the child Ichabod, saying, The glory is departed from Israel: because the ark of God was taken, and because of her father in law and her husband. And she said, The glory is departed from Israel; for the ark of God is taken."   (I Samuel 4:21–22).

"And it came to pass, when the priests were come out of the holy place, that the cloud filled the house of the Lord, so that the priests could not stand to minister by reason of the cloud: for the glory of the Lord filled the house of the Lord."
(I Kings 8:10–11).

Ichabod! This dying widow spoke a good deal of truth when she lamented the glory that had gone, but she did not speak all the truth, for she could not foresee what would follow. The Ark of the Covenant was more than a material emblem: the Lord's Name and honour were associated with it. Israel had suffered a great loss, but the Lord was still well able to look after His own interests and act in jealousy for His own Name. The subsequent chapter relates His immediate reaction with regard to that Testimony and that Name.

Jealousy and Mercy

If the Ark was taken into the house of Dagon, then so much the worse for Dagon. When God's people tried to make selfish use of the Ark, bringing it out to back them up in their conflict though their hearts were estranged from the God whose covenant it represented, they found that the Ark seemed powerless. It was as if God had no interest in it—did not care what happened to it. But when the Philistines presumed to take liberties with that same Ark, they found, to their cost, that it mattered very much to the Lord. Dagon, their god, was first humbled, then smashed to pieces, as the Ark was placed in his temple. And the Philistines concerned had no doubt about the supernatural power involved, for it left a lasting impression of awe upon them all. Jehovah is a jealous God, and He showed His ability to crush this would-be rival, Dagon.

If the men of Ashdod thought that they could trifle with Divine things, they, too, had to learn a painful lesson. "But the hand of the Lord was heavy upon them of Ashdod ..." (I Sam. 5:6), so that they soon took steps to get rid of this troublesome Ark. To Israel it seemed powerless, but to those in Ashdod who trifled with God's glory the power of Divine judgments was overwhelming. It may be, then, that some godly Israelites who heard of these events would take heart, in the realization that God was still God, jealous in holiness for His great Name; so that, mingled with their regret at their own sin and failure, there would come the assurance that He would still take care of His own interests. His power was the same, even if His people had failed Him. 'He cannot fail, for He is God!'

The Lord is also great in mercy. Perhaps Ichabod's mother was so overcome by her own sorrow that she forgot that most precious part of the Ark, the Mercy Seat. The longsuffering and grace of God were represented in an integral part of that Ark of the Covenant. Even when His people had so badly failed Him, seeming to throw away all right to a further place in His purposes, recovery was still possible, because the holiness of God had also the accompaniment of the blood-stained Mercy Seat. 'God does not cast off His people whom He foreknew' (Rom. 11:2). He is not only able to take care of His own interests, but able also to bring back the glory to an undeserving people. Thank God for the

Mercy Seat. The Ark came back, and more quickly than might have been thought possible. It needed no army, no rescuing party, no help at all from the Israelites. God made His presence felt in such a mighty way that those who held the Ark were glad to be rid of it, and themselves arranged for its return to Israel. 'Ichabod' was not the last word.

Priestly Intercession

When Phinehas' widow expired with the pronouncement of "Ichabod", she was overlooking the fact that God had already laid His hand on a man who would be the instrument for bringing back the glory. Samuel had lived in her house. He must have been always around, and she would know him and see him often. But he was so small and insignificant that she would never expect him to influence events. He was not even a priest. If the High Priest and his two sons had gone, then it must have seemed that there was no one left to take responsibility for the interests of the Lord. So we see Samuel set over against Ichabod. The Lord had already provided Himself with this instrument of recovery—so humble and small that men took no account of him, but so wholly given over to the will of God that he could provide that priestly intercession which Eli and his sons had failed to give. Here, then, is a further cause for wonder. Not only can the Lord look after His own interests, not only will He in mercy bring back the glory to His erring people, but even before the disaster He has provided Himself with the human instrument needed for the purpose. Eli's daughter-in-law knew nothing of this. The natural eye could see only tragedy—the tragedy of the departed glory. Ichabod.

What was the cause of Israel's tragic failure? In part, at least, it was due to the failure of the priesthood. We read in the story of the sad conditions in Eli's household, and we are told little about Eli himself to suggest that he exerted any spiritual influence for good in the whole situation. So it is plain that the priesthood of that day was gravely at fault. In reality, however, that breakdown was only the end of a long process, just the last stage in what had been wrong with the people of God for many years. When Joshua's days were finished, Israel passed into a period when there was no God- given leadership. Occasionally judges were raised up by the Lord, and for a time there was some semblance of order among the people, but it seldom lasted for very long.

Even more notable was the lack of priesthood. Only in the last chapters do we find mention of Levites, and then in the most depraved and lamentable connections. It would be a true comment on those times to say that there was no priest in Israel, just as much as there was no king. Even in the brighter days, when for a season leaders did arise, bringing relief and victory to a defeated people, even then there is no mention of this basic, essential, though often hidden, serving of the Lord's interests by a ministry of intercession. The reader passes from the unwholesome records of Judges into I Samuel (though with the inset of Ruth), only to find this ominous opening: "And the two sons of Eli, Hophni and Phinehas, priests unto the Lord, were there" (1:3), which is soon followed by the further comment: "Now the sons of Eli were sons of Belial; they knew not the Lord" (2:12). 'Ichabod' indeed! It is always true that, when there is no vital ministry of intercession, then there is no glory.

This is the negative side. But it was not the end. Later the glory came back, and it came back in very great fulness—"the glory of the Lord filled the house of the Lord". As we have already said, this was due to the sovereignty of God, and also to the greatness of His grace. But it was also due to the fact that first a prayer ministry had been provided. Behind it all we find the figure of Samuel, God's priestly instrument.

It may be objected that the glory was a long time in coming back. It was. Samuel's was a long life, and he never lived to see that day. But patience is an important feature of priestly ministry—persistence in faith and perseverance in waiting upon God. These were the secrets of a life which had such a tremendous influence on the whole course of the history of God's people; for surely it is no exaggeration to say that the man who contributed most to the recovery of the glory was Samuel. Samuel, the intercessor.

Samuel's Simplicity

If this is true, then it must be a profitable study to consider the essential traits which characterized Samuel. For many of us live under the shadow of Ichabod. We, too, feel that the glory has departed. Although we could easily despair, there is with us also an inner conviction that the Lord's desire is to bring the glory back, once more to fill His spiritual House with His glory. There are many projects and suggestions that men may offer for the recovery of this departed glory. They may be right or they may be wrong, but they do not deal with the root cause or effect the radical cure. With us, as with Israel, the greatest need is for a mighty ministry of intercession—if necessary prolonged like Samuel's, if necessary to extend beyond our own lifetime as it did beyond his—but a ministry which will turn all the 'Ichabods' into 'Hallelujahs'.

The first thing to be noted with regard to Samuel is his simplicity. Samuel was not a priest. He had no official place in the priestly order. So far as we know he was never anointed by men nor ordained by them. It is true that his father was a Levite, but even so he does not seem to have been engaged in any Levitical work. People would have regarded him as a very ordinary boy in a very ordinary family.

Of course he was not this. One cannot class as ordinary a child who has such a miraculous entrance into the world as Samuel had. He himself was an answer to prayer. It would, indeed, perhaps be correct to say that this mighty ministry of intercession had its commencement with his mother, Hannah. This, then, was his beginning—God brought him in. And this is the way in which every true intercessory ministry begins: it is initiated by God Himself. This, surely, was what enabled Samuel to continue through all the long and testing years: this knowledge that it was no natural contrivance and no effort of his own, but an act of God which had brought him into being.

Even so, there was something very simple about this vessel of God's service. "The child was young" (1:24). "But Samuel ministered before the Lord, being a child" (2:18). "Moreover his mother made him a little robe" (2:19). All this seems to point to a homely insignificance, which meant that he was completely overlooked by Ichabod's mother. What could this feeble lad contribute to the recovery of the glory? This, however, is just the one who can serve God in the place of prayer, weak and despised in himself, but mighty in intercession. He turned the tide for God. "The sin of the young men was very great . . . men abhorred the offering of the Lord. *But Samuel* ministered before the Lord, being a child, girded with a linen ephod" (2:17–18). Once again there is a Divine "But. . . ." And it was a child in all his natural inadequacy who faced and stemmed the flood of evil and hopelessness. He stood his ground with the Lord, and in the end the glory came back. No one need be ashamed of their simplicity or insufficiency! It seems as though this was what the Lord was needing, someone small enough and humble enough to be usable. In Samuel He found just what He wanted.

Samuel's Teachability

Furthermore Samuel was willing to be taught. His first uttered prayer, the introduction to a long and fruitful life of intercession in the secret place, was just the childlike request: "Speak; for Thy servant heareth" (3:10). The secret of a true ministry of intercession is to have an open ear to the Lord. The first utterance must come from Him, not from us; our speaking to Him can only have value when it is preceded by His first speaking to us. Great stress is laid on Samuel's growing up, itself an important spiritual matter; and as he grew it is stated that "the Lord appeared again in Shiloh: for the Lord revealed Himself to Samuel . . ." (3:21). It is not said that prayer became mighty in Shiloh, or that Samuel broke through to God in prayer. No, the emphasis is on God's side; He revealed Himself again, because He had found a young man who, in spite of his youth, was ready to be shown the will of the Lord, and to maintain his first attitude of the bended knee and the listening ear.

And as he grew old he still retained that sensitiveness to the Lord. He mistook Jesse's eldest son for the man to be appointed king; he went so far as to conclude, "Surely the Lord's anointed is before Him" (16:6); but he did not act rashly. God was able to check him, to correct him, and to show him how not to exercise natural judgment—"as man seeth"—but to receive Divine guidance. What a contrast to the blind and set old man, Eli! It is a great mercy, and an indispensable condition for a fruitful prayer life, that a man should always have his heart attuned to the voice of the Spirit.

Samuel's Heart Purity

The third great secret of Samuel's power in the secret place was the unblemished purity of his life. Did his mother know the corrupt influences to which he would be subject among Eli's sons? If she did, she must have been a woman of remarkable faith, to commit her young lad to live in Shiloh, in those evil days. Her faith was vindicated. It is quite evident that Samuel was never tainted by the evil all around him. It was a miracle, to keep pure in that atmosphere, and God did the miracle. There can be no power without purity.

Later on in his life, when Samuel was dealing with the matter of Saul's appointment as king, he was able to issue an open challenge concerning his procedure from his youth until this advanced time when he was old and gray-headed, and with one accord the people testified to his integrity (12:1–5). If it was a miracle that the boy Samuel should be kept pure, how much greater was the miracle of maintained purity of spirit, during years when he could very easily have made some personal profit out of his position. It was this which gave him his unique standing before men as well as before God—he could claim to be free from impurity in his daily walk.

Saul's reign brought him nothing but sorrow. Yet, just as he had meekly accepted being set aside at Saul's appointment, so he remained with an unoffended spirit through all the heartbreak of that unhappy reign. He reproved Saul, but he still mourned and prayed for him. He allowed no bitterness of spirit, nor did he of his own choice seek an alternative. He returned to his place of quiet at Ramah, to continue his ministry of intercession, until, by the urging of the Lord, he went to Bethlehem to anoint David.

These, then, were the features of God's man of prayer—Simplicity, Teachability and Purity. And this was the man who brought back the glory and reversed the verdict of 'Ichabod'.

Samuel Spanned the Gap

There may be some who doubt whether Samuel did, in

fact, play such a vital part in spanning this gap between the departure of the glory and the full recovery in Solomon's Temple. Apart from the actual narrative, there is an indication of what both God and men thought of the part he played, in the titles given to the two historical books which tell the story. Up to I Samuel 25:1, it can be argued that Samuel was only one of the principal characters. Then he dies, and is no longer on the scene. Yet, in spite of that, both books are called by his name—First Samuel and Second Samuel—though originally, we are told, they were treated as one single book. Who gave the title of "Samuel"? We do not know. But it is singularly appropriate, as many have pointed out. It was Samuel's influence and Samuel's ministry, largely in the unseen realm, that reversed the tragic experience of 'Ichabod' and brought in the fulness of the glory. Where are the Samuels to-day? Surely they are as greatly needed in our day as he was in his.

When Saul turned against Samuel, we are told that the prophet returned to his home at Ramah (15:34). And Ramah, so they say, means *'heights'*. Earlier on he had built an altar at Ramah (7:17). How much Israel owed, and how much David and Solomon owed, to this man whose home was in the *heights* by the altar!

Part Fifteen

Discipline unto Prayer

"And the Lord turned the captivity of Job, when he prayed for his friends: and the Lord gave Job twice as much as he had before"

(Job 42:10).

There is a very striking sequence about the arrangement of many of the Books in the Bible; though chronologically it is all wrong to take the order: Nehemiah, Esther, Job; spiritually it is all right. Each of these books centres around, or emphasizes at least, this matter of intercession. Nehemiah is the work of prayer. Prayer is everywhere in Nehemiah; prayer at all times, long prayers, short prayers, but it is all prayer with the work, and work with the prayer. "In everything by prayer and supplication" (Philippians 4:6)—I think that is Nehemiah. In Esther we strike a deeper note: it is the prayer of love, sacrificial love, in the one great moment of intercession of Esther's life. And in the case of Job I think we go deeper still, including, of course, those other two. Here we have not somebody who is marked by what they do so much as somebody whose doing comes out of what they are, the *life* of prayer.

What Job went through! This verse seems to me a kind of peak and climax of his experience, as well as a turning point for him personally. He prayed for his friends. What a prayer! What a need! And what a man to pray it! We must not regard prayer as one of those lesser activities of life. It seems with Job that this is the culmination of all his life. Now he can pray! You may say: 'Now he is rich.' That is true. 'Now he is prosperous.' That is true. But I would say, when we have got through to chapter 42: *Now* he can pray. Not that he had not prayed before, but something had been done in the man himself which gave a quality to his prayer. We remember that in the case of our Lord Jesus the fruit of His conflict with Satan, the culmination of all His experience, is this very thing—that now He lives to intercede. This is not just the fact that we can pray, and the wonder that God answers prayer, or that "more things are wrought by prayer than this world dreams of", or that sort of thing; but something far deeper. "He ever liveth to make intercession" (Hebrews 7:25). How much we owe to His praying! But how much His prayers owe to what He is! The quality of the prayer comes from Him, of course, as the Son of God, the perfect One; but also, as Hebrews tells us, it comes out of a deep experience of discipline and suffering which have made Him an able intercessor.

"The Lord turned the captivity of Job, when he prayed for his friends." You must put the 'friends' in inverted commas. It is very easy to pray for your friends when they are friends, but I think it is not straining this story to say that when Job prayed, he was praying for his enemies. I fail to see anything more that they could have done to make life impossible for him than what they did. The only thing they could have done was to leave him alone, and he begged them to, but they would not. It was not out of affection—that sort of feeling we have for our friends that makes us want to pray for them. It was the men who had caused him so much pain and grief, but who so needed prayer. I wonder if we can see that! Here are men: they know all about God. Some of the precious things that are said about God in the Book of Job are said, not by Job, but by his friends. Job's friends said some of the passages you love. They were right, they knew all about Him, and yet they were utterly different from Him—hard, censorious,

121

ungracious. That is a challenge to us. You may know all about God, but be very unlike Him.

It is very interesting that Job's experiences were taken by the Lord to bring to the surface and disclose, not only his own state and need, but the state and need of his friends. How much may circle round your experience, and mine, for other people as well as for us! It was all coming to the surface; not only what Job was, but what they were, and it was how harsh and critical and unkind they were to him personally. I may be wrong, but I always feel that when Job began to curse his day, that was really caused by his friends. When all the sufferings came, he blessed the Lord and was patient. But these men came to commiserate with him, and for seven days they sat there and did not say anything; but seven days of a critical atmosphere, seven days of eyes upon you, and you know what they are thinking. It was too much for Job, and it is often too much for us. And then they began to open their mouths, and the second phase of their so-called friendliness came in. What a painful experience it was for Job to have the barbed arrows of their unjust interpretation of his experience, their wrong judgments, all thrust into his quivering, suffering flesh. *They* were the people that needed prayer.

You do not think of them like that. You think they need something else, but they need prayer. When God revealed Himself, not only was Job abashed, but these men were stricken. It is a new light upon the harsh, hard, critical people that make life more painful than it is. It is true that when Job saw everything in the light of God's presence, he saw himself, but he also saw the need of those poor men. *They* needed prayer. Well, they were new men in that sense; but what a new man Job was when he prayed for them.

New Power in Prayer

As we have said, he already, before these experiences, served in a priestly capacity. You read about it in the first chapter. He interceded for his family. Job could pray, and he did pray, but this is a new Job, and there is new power in his prayer. What is there that is new about it?

(a) A New Sense of Sin

First of all, strangely enough, there is a new sense of sin. You would not think that that would make you pray better, but that is just what is needed. According to God, Job had said the things that were right; but Job, according to Elihu (and he seems to have spoken for God) was the man who justified himself instead of God. Job was the man who said: "My righteousness I hold fast" (Job 27:6). He was self-righteous, and it was to disclose that fact that the devil was allowed to do what he did to him. Self-righteousness is a great hindrance to prayer. So the Lord brought Job to the place where every shred of self-opinion was utterly forsaken and repudiated. He had a new sense of sin.

You know how the Letter to the Romans makes the discrimination between sins and sin, and it was something like that that was borne home upon Job's heart. His friends were all the time saying: 'You must have committed sins'; and Job said: 'I have not!' But they said: 'You must have done', and he maintained: 'I have not'. When he saw God he did not remember, after all, certain sins that he had committed. Something much deeper came upon him—a conviction that, though he could face his fellow men and hold fast his integrity, when he came into the presence of the Lord it was not so much that he had committed sins, but he was a sinner; his very being was unclean before God.

If Job's friends had prayed for him instead of talking to him, they might have helped a little bit, but I expect they would have prayed very much as they talked: 'Now, Job must have done this. Show him he has done it.' If Job had been on that level—and he might have been!—when the Lord said, 'Pray for your friends', he would have fallen into exactly the same trap. 'Lord, so-and-so said this, and Bildad said that, and someone else something else.' But he came into a realm where he was not looking at particular faults of people, but was overwhelmed with the sense of the holiness of God, and the deep, deep unholiness of man. "I abhor myself."

'Well,' you say, 'the man that is down in the dust abhorring himself will not be much good for prayer.' He *is* the man! We are not much good for prayer because we are not down. This sense of personal unworthiness and sin that humbles us before God, if it does its work in us, brings us to a place where we are able to pray as we never could when we were strong and self-confident. You notice that Job did not offer himself to pray for them. God said to Job: 'Now, you are the man to pray.' 'What me, Lord? But I am horrible! I lay my hand on my mouth, I am unclean, I am a sinner, I abhor myself.' The Lord said: 'You are the one to pray, for you are the only one that can pray the kind of prayer that I mean.'

(b) A New Understanding of Suffering

A new understanding of suffering. Job now knows, and we need to know, what God means by suffering. "My servant, Job." How these men must have opened their mouths and been surprised! The Lord says—and you notice how often He says it—"My servant, Job". If He had said: 'The man who used to be My servant', they could have understood, but He says: 'He *is* My servant.' But what has he been doing? He has been suffering. Is that all? Yes, suffering. He suffered under the hand of God, suffered in the will of God, and in that way he has been serving God. He was God's servant before. God said to Satan: "Hast thou considered My servant Job?" But there is a sense, it seems to me, in which the end of this book just concentrates on the fact that God says: 'This is the man that is serving. Not these preachers who are going around telling people what is right and what is wrong, what they ought to do, and all the theories of God's dealings with men, but the man who has been through the fire. He has been serving Me.' Everybody despised him. 'He used to be a servant of God, but look at him now, stripped of everything! He has nothing at all.' The children mock him, and everybody despises him. God says: "My servant", and the very people that mocked him and despised him had cause to thank God from the bottom of their hearts that Job was God's servant, for it would have been a bad day for them if he had not been.

Then Job found much more about suffering: how suffering brings you close to the Lord if it is taken in the right spirit. How much nearer to God Job was, and how much nearer to Job God was at the end of the book! And all he had done was to suffer. Suffering under God's hand brought that nearness, and it made Job a different man. That was one of the things Elihu said: "Who is a teacher like unto Him?" (36:22). God had been teaching Job, and it is out of such a background that he could pray.

(c) A New Conception of God

But I think that most of all it was out of a new conception of God that Job prayed like this. That was the value of his experience. He had known God before, and he had prayed before, but now he had a new conception of God altogether. He had been apt to treat God on equal terms. That comes out more than once, and he is charged with it—with considering God as though He were a man instead of realizing the utter transcendence of the Lord: "Behold, I will answer thee, in this thou art not just; for God is greater

than man" (33:12). You would not think that a man like Job
needed to be told that, but he did. The Lord took him and
said: 'Now, Job, you have got on wrong terms with Me. I
want intimacy, yes, but not familiarity.' And that is the
danger with us all. We mistake familiarity for intimacy.
So the Lord suddenly turns on Job and says: "Where wast
thou when I laid the foundations of the earth?" (38:4). That
is a question. But Job had been treating God as if he had
been there. That is one of the dangers. I know prayer has
its realms—realms of executive prayer, realms of fellowship
with God, but they are dangerous realms unless we realize,
and have brought home to us in ever fresh power, how
transcendent God is. This is the man who prayed: the man
who sees how great God is.

When he used to pray he treated God as though he
were more or less equal, telling Him what He had done and
what He ought to do. Now he can only bow in utter worship
and wonder. That is the kind of man who can pray. He
knows how omnipotent God is. "I know," he says at the
end, "that Thou canst do all things" (42:2). In a sense, he is
answering all his own questions. It seems to me as though
God deliberately baffled Job. You see, if you know everything that God is doing, somehow it has a bad effect on you.
So God took hold of His choicest servant and took him
through experiences that so baffled and perplexed him that
in the end he did not know anything. "Oh that I knew. . ."
(23:3). His friends, of course, knew it all—or thought they
did. Poor Job says: 'I do not know; oh, that I did know!'
And God has done that on purpose because Job, by all this,
comes to realize the supreme power and wisdom of God.

If we knew all about Him, He would not be any greater
than ourselves. But we see just the hem of His garment,
the fringes of His ways, and the vast realms of His Divine
counsels and His sovereign power we only glimpse here and
there, and we say: 'How wonderful the Lord is! I do not

know what He is doing, but I know He can do everything; I do not know why He is doing it this way, but I am sure He knows.' That is the man who can pray, the man with a new sense of God in all His greatness, His transcendence, His power, and, above all, His grace.

(d) A New Understanding of the Grace of God

I suppose we are apt to think of Job as reinstated, for he has everything back and more than he ever had, and feeling rather good and magnanimous, so he says to his friends: 'Do not say anything more about it.' Nothing of the sort! Job had nothing at this stage. This was the turning point. He was still as stripped, as poor, as low as ever he had been. What had he got, then, that made him pray, and able to pray like this? He had a new understanding of the grace of God, and that is the richest thing you can have. He knew how gracious God is. He could not have prayed for his friends properly if he had not known. He knew how gracious God is in terms of personal experience. God was gracious to him, and God had been merciful to him. Oh, the things that he had said and thought about God, and all the time love was planning and grace was being poured out upon him, so out of a new heart-overflowing sense of the wonderful grace of God, he could pray.

All this is surely for us, too, for if, as a people, we feel we have one thing more than another which is our essential ministry, surely it is prayer. The Lord calls us to prayer again and again. Perhaps the Lord is dealing with us so that we can pray. That is what He did with Job—and see what happened when Job prayed! His friends were delivered from their danger and their need, and the prayer was answered. But the whole point of the verse is, not that the prayer was answered, but that Job came into new fullness because he prayed. "The Lord turned the captivity of Job, when he prayed for his friends." So often we feel that if we

127

could come out and be strong and prosperous, we could pray. But the Lord says: 'If you will pray, I will bring you out.' It is not, of course, a sort of catch arrangement that we make with the Lord—'I will not pray for myself. I will pray for others and then You will help me.' It was not that. Job, I am sure, was not thinking of himself, but, out of this new sense of God, and of sin, and of the command to pray for these poor needy men who had been so hard to him, but who, he now realized, were in such a parlous state themselves, he prayed for them. We must be content to pray for the Lord's will far beyond our own interests and our own borders. We must make our supreme prayer for the needy among the Lord's people and among mankind everywhere. Let Him fit us in where He will to the meeting of that need, but our first thing is to pray for the need.

That is just what Job did. He did not say: 'Make me a great man again so that I can serve You.' He said: 'Lord, have mercy upon these men, who ought to be Thy servants, but who are in need and have been revealed in all the nakedness of their spurious profession of spirituality. Have mercy upon them!' When Job began to pray for them like that the Lord gave him double.

Some of us may be seeking fullness and not finding it because we are critical of the Lord's people, because we are watching, because we have summed them up, because, like Job's friends, we can tell them where they are wrong. Perhaps we do not dare to, but we could if we had the chance. We are finding our emptiness, our leanness along that line, and we shall! Job found his fullness when, out of a deep sense of the grace of God, he prayed for his friends.

May the Lord make us those who have such an experience with Him that we are constituted able intercessors! Then we shall find our fullness; the Lord will give us double.

IN TOUCH WITH THE THRONE

Some considerations on prayer

—BY—
T. AUSTIN-SPARKS

Contents

Chapter One

The Divine Basis of All Acceptable Prayer

As we contemplate the great ministry of prayer, I think it would be most helpful if at the outset we were reminded of the Divine basis of all acceptable prayer. Before we come to what may be more technical we must recognise the spiritual foundation of prayer, and that has to do with the ingredients and the sacredness of the incense which was to be burnt upon the golden altar referred to in Exodus xxx, verse 34 onwards.

It is not my intention to take up these ingredients for exposition, but simply to note that the Lord stipulated certain things for the sweet spices, and then made a very strong statement in relation to them: ". . . ye shall not make to yourselves according to the composition thereof; it shall be unto thee holy for the Lord. Whosoever shall make like unto that, to smell thereto, shall even be cut off from his people." That is the basis of all acceptable prayer. As we know, the sweet spices, the ingredients of the incense, typify the moral excellencies of the Lord Jesus: His graces, virtues, merits and worthiness. The incense is not the prayers of the saints, but the merit and worthiness of the Lord Jesus put into the prayers, mingled with the prayers, and becoming that which brings the prayers in effectiveness and acceptance to the presence of God. There is completeness here, inasmuch as the ingredients are fourfold: the completeness of the graces and virtues and moral excellencies of Christ. And then, as you notice, salt (which always speaks of preserving things in life) is to be mingled with these other ingredients, and that seems to me to suggest that even the presentation of the moral excellencies of the Lord Jesus is always to be free from merely cold formality, which means death, and must remain a living and vital thing. It is so possible for a contemplation of the Lord Jesus to become a mechanical and formal thing, something which we accept in our minds as necessary and true, so that we come mechanically upon the merits of the

Lord Jesus, when the Lord wants the thing to be continuously alive. With every fresh coming to the Lord there should be a fresh appreciation in life of the Lord Jesus. The salt is to keep things from death, to keep them in life, to keep them fresh and to keep them keen, and we are required to have an abiding keenness and aliveness of appreciation of these excellencies of the Lord Jesus. If it is so, then prayer is acceptable and effectual. The salt is not one of the ingredients, but something added in, and that something is that which is incorruptible.

Then we have the very definite stipulation that nothing like this was to be made by man himself or for himself. There was to be no imitation of this, and there was to be no private and personal appropriation of it by man. It was to be held always unto the Lord and to be holy to the Lord, and an infringement of that rule meant death. As we know, on one occasion the offering of false fire resulted in judgment and death. So here we are told that if this thing were made by man, an imitation of it made for himself and for his own personal ends, he would be cut off from among his people. The moral excellencies of the Lord Jesus cannot be imitated. Man cannot have them in himself, and anything feigned is unacceptable to God. There are no excellencies, and there are no glories like those of the Lord Jesus.

Here we have God most definitely and positively saying in effect that there is a uniqueness, an exclusiveness about the character of the Lord Jesus which is unapproachable by man and altogether apart from the very best that man can make of himself. God sees in the Lord Jesus that which is not anywhere else, and for any man to come imitating the merits of the Lord Jesus means death for that man. There is no ground of approach to God in our moral glories, and it is an awful blasphemy to talk about the sacrifice and the laying down of life on the part of men for their fellow-creatures being on a par with the laying down of His life by the Lord Jesus. That is utter blasphemy, and it must come under the most utter judgment of God. No! God sees nothing equal to the moral excellencies of His Son and forbids us to try to bring anything which is an imitation of those, a man-made thing, which does not recognise the uniqueness of the Lord Jesus.

So the ground of all acceptable prayer upon which we approach the Father is that of the moral excellencies and glories, and graces, and virtues, and merits, and worthiness of the Lord Jesus. That is very simple, but it is basic, and we do have to recognise that before we can get anywhere in the matter of prayer.

THE FIVE ASPECTS OF PRAYER

Now we are able to go on with the subject of prayer itself. In the first place I want to say a little about the nature of prayer, or that which makes prayer, from its different standpoints. And while there may be many other aspects, I think we may say that prayer has five main aspects: communion, submission, petition, co-operation and conflict. Prayer is each one of these, and prayer in its fullness requires or involves all of them.

PRAYER AS COMMUNION

Firstly, prayer is communion, prayer is fellowship, prayer is love opening the heart to God, and that is the foundation of all true forms of prayer. We may liken it to the two main activities of our human bodies. When we speak of the activities of these physical bodies we speak of what is organic, and then of what is functional. Organic trouble is a very serious thing, but a functional trouble may not be so serious, and prayer as communion takes the place of the organic in our bodies. One part of our organic make-up is our breathing, which we call respiration. Now, you never stop to think about that! You never reason that out and say: "Shall I take another breath?" "Shall I breathe?" or "How many more breaths shall I take today?" You may do that over a meal, for that is functional, but you never do it over your respiration, for that is organic. You may discuss whether you will walk, or talk, or think, and you may tell yourself that you will stop thinking, or walking, or talking. That is functional. It is controlled and deliberate, but you do not do that over your breathing. That goes on. But if your respiration should give out, your walking, talking and thinking would give out, so that respiration is basic to everything else.

And prayer as communion is in the spiritual life what respiration is in the physical. Communion with God is a sustained thing, a thing like breathing which goes on, or should go on. It differs altogether from those periodical functional activities such as feeding. Respiration is quite involuntary and not just deliberate. We may call it a habit, and a habit is something which easily eludes the full consciousness of the one who is addicted to it. We do things habitually without being aware at the time that we are doing them. When a habit is fully formed it is just an unconscious part of our procedure, and communion with God is that—something that goes on. Prayer as communion is just that: we are in touch with the Lord and we spontaneously and involuntarily open our heart to Him. That is the first foundational thing in all prayer, and that is something to which we shall have to give attention. While we never discuss the question as to whether we will breathe or not, there is such a thing as developing right breathing, and in this sense we shall have to give attention to our breathing.

I think that of all the people I ever met who exemplified this organic life in fellowship with God, Dr. F. B. Meyer was outstanding. It did not matter where he was or what the circumstances were, he would suddenly stop, perhaps in dictating a letter, or in a conversation, or in a business meeting, and just say: "Stop a minute!" and he prayed. And that was his habit in life. He seemed at any moment to be in touch with the Lord. It was like breathing to him, and I believe it represented one of the secrets of the fruitfulness of his life and the value of his judgment in the things of the Lord. Only those who had close touch with him, especially in difficult executive meetings, knew the value of that spiritual judgment which he brought to bear upon situations, and it seemed to come to him just like that, as out from the Lord.

Well, that is prayer in its foundation. It is communion, it is fellowship and the spontaneous opening of the heart to the Lord. It is not the whole range of prayer, but it is life lived at the back of all deliberate activities, life in touch with the Lord, and it is a very, very valuable thing. All other prayer is so much more effective if we have that. It is so different from life being just a matter of prayer in emergencies, and emergencies are very often much more critical than they need be because we have to find our way back to God instead of being there. I think that very often the Lord allows emergencies to come to us in order to restore fellowship with Himself which has been lost, and in the Lord's mind the abiding fruit of such an emergency is that we should not lose that fellowship again. We should keep hold of it.

PRAYER AS SUBMISSION

Then, secondly, prayer is submission, and here we must be aware of the possibility of a contradiction in terms. Prayer is submission. Passive inaction in what is called trust is not prayer. We have heard people speak of trust, which for them means just passivity and inaction, but it is not prayer. Submission is always active, not passive. Submission always involves the will; it does not dismiss the will. Now carefully keep hold of that. Many people think that just trustfully leaning on the Lord is submission, and their address to the Lord takes its character from such a state, but that is not prayer. Unquestioning acquiescence in things as we find them is not submission, and it is not prayer. Submission means getting into line with the Divine mind. That may mean conflict, it will almost invariably mean action, and it will bring in the volition. Prayer, from whatever standpoint you regard it, is always positive. It is never passive. Trust is another thing and does not come into the realm of prayer. Faith comes into the realm of prayer, but faith is always an active thing and never a passive thing. Faith may require a battle, and it very often does, to get to a place of rest, but the "rest of faith" is not what we have called unquestioning acquiescence. The "rest of faith" means that the last stage of adjustment to the Divine mind has been reached. Submission is not merely the suppression of desire, but the bringing of desire into line with the Divine will, and, if needs be, changing desire. Desire may be a very strong thing, a mighty propelling force, but a propelling force ought to be so much under control that it can be switched into the direction of an arresting force. To propel a train, a tremendous amount of power and force is required, but a modern train is so arranged that the mighty propelling force which carries it forward can in a moment be switched to its brakes to pull it to a halt. In prayer, where submission is in view, that is very often what has to be done. That strength of desire has to be arrested in one direction and brought into another direction, perhaps from propelling us forward to bringing us to a standstill in the will of God. That is submission. You see, submission is an active thing, a positive thing.

I anticipate that there will be many questions in this connection, but it is very important to recognise that prayer in its second aspect is submission, which is a positive thing. It is not just collapsing before God and saying: "Well, I trust that everything will turn out all right. I just acquiesce in things as they are and leave it with the Lord." Submission is coming positively into line with God's will, God's desire and God's mind. That very often means the deepest conflict, and sometimes heartbreak, but it is necessary. We will touch that again later.

Prayer As Petition

Thirdly, prayer is petition, request, or asking. That is all the same, whichever word you prefer. Here we touch what is perhaps the major aspect in the activity of prayer. Undoubtedly it has the largest place in Scripture, and it really defines the meaning of the word "prayer."

From a scriptural standpoint prayer is rightly taken to mean petition, and if you go through the Word of God you will find that prayer represents petition in an overwhelming measure. Perhaps we do not need very much argument along that line to prove or persuade that it is so, but I am quite sure that before we are through we shall see that a note of emphasis is necessary, for, after all, our main problems arise in the direction of asking, in the realm of petition. We shall go on praying, of course, and we shall go on asking, in spite of them all. I trust that we shall, but it is as well for us to have the ground well laid for petition, for request, for asking, and for us to recognise clearly, and be fully assured, that there is an objective efficacy in prayer. I do not doubt but that all of us at some time or other have a little catch in our prayers of request and asking because of a little mental something that comes in and undermines certainty. What I am talking about is the objective efficacy of prayer, that is, prayer which has power to change things objectively and not merely have an influence upon us inwardly, prayer which brings answers outside of ourselves. Petition, request, asking, as set over against all false arguments, such as: Divine omniscience makes prayer *unnecessary*; God knows everything; He knows what He will do, how He will do it, and He knows the end of all things from the beginning, so why pray? Or again: Divine goodness makes prayer superfluous. God is good, compassionate, merciful and longsuffering. He will only do the best, for He is love, so prayer is *superfluous*. Why petition the Lord to do good, to be gracious, to show kindness and to do the best for us? Why not trust the goodness of God? Prayer is superfluous. Or once more: Divine foreordination makes prayer *useless*. If God has settled things eternally, predestination holds good, so it is *useless* to pray. Or, running alongside of that, Divine sovereignty—the fact that God rules and overrules, He is in the throne of government and has all things in His hands and in His power—makes prayer *lack of faith*. Why ask, why pray, why petition, why request, when all things are in God's hands and He is ruling and overruling, governing and directing in His sovereignty? Once more: the Divine vastness of law and purpose makes prayer *presumptuous*. It is presumption to ask God to change things when He has fixed everything according to His eternal laws and things are moving in correspondence with a set order. It is presumption to expect the Lord to go out of His order, or to ask Him to do so.*

Now, you may not have put things like that, and those questions may never have arisen in your minds in that way, but I venture to suggest that, whether those words have been in your mind or not, whether you have put things like that or not, what is contained in them has from time to time crept subtly into your prayer-life, has affected it and taken some of the grip out of it. When you have been praying an indefinable something has crept in: "Well, the Lord knows what He will do so why should I beseech Him? The Lord is good and gracious, so why should I ask Him? The Lord knows the end from the beginning, so why should I not just trust Him? The Lord's purposes are fixed, so why should I begin to wrestle with Him to change things? He will work out His purpose and He is of set mind, so who can change Him?" Prayer is affected, if not by the actual framing of the language mentally, by that sense of contradiction which comes in. All these

---

*See chapter iv.

things creep into the mind or heart and have a tendency to deter or weaken in the matter of prayer, and we have to deal with these more fully as we go on. We must recognise that the modernism of our time does set aside the objective efficacy of prayer and only gives to it the place of a subjective value, that is, its salutary influence upon the one who prays in making a change of, perhaps, demeanour, or mind, or reason, by certain qualities of reverence and such like.

Before we take up some of these things more fully, let me say that there are two things to bear in mind always in petitional prayer. The first is the basic need of the other two aspects, communion and submission. For petitional prayer, in which, after all that I have said, we believe, and with which, after all, we shall go on, nevertheless the basic need is communion with the Lord so that prayer does not resolve itself into merely asking God for things, but comes out of a heart-fellowship with Him. And it needs submission, so that our petitions are not for our own ends or personal desires, but, having been brought by submission into line with the Divine will, are based upon oneness with the mind and will of God. You will find that I am only putting in another way what is made perfectly clear in the Word of God, namely: "If you shall ask anything according to His will." That is submission.

Then the other thing to bear in mind in petitional prayer is that, in view of all the mental difficulties which I have mentioned, it becomes preeminently an act of faith. It is these mental difficulties which very largely make petitional prayer an act of faith. Yes, argue if you will along all these lines, about the sovereignty of God, and predestination, and so on; nevertheless, we believe that God will change things. In spite of all the arguments which would undercut and weaken prayer, we are going on asking. That makes petitional prayer preeminently an act of faith. You may say that is a very cheap way of getting out of it. Well, we have not finished yet, but that is the conclusion at which we have to arrive. We do not want to get out of this cheaply.

Prayer As Co-operation

There are yet two other aspects of prayer, one of which we will deal with in this chapter, and the other we will leave for later.

The fourth aspect is co-operation, and this is the governing object of prayer. It gets behind everything else and will set us right as to praying and to prayer in all its aspects. Communion, submission, petition and conflict are all adjusted and set right when we recognise that prayer is co-operation, for all these other aspects and phases of prayer are for co-operation. Co-operation is the motive, the truth, the life, the liberty, the power and the glory of prayer. The motive of prayer is co-operation with God. What prayer is in truth is cooperation with God. To have life in prayer we have to recognise that it is co-operation with God, and we get life when prayer is entered into as co-operation with God. If we are not in co-operation with God we may be sure that we shall have no life in prayer. If we are really cooperating with God we shall know we have life in prayer.

Liberty in prayer comes along the line of co-operation with God, and it is not until we get that adjustment, that coming into line with God's purpose, that we "get through," as we say. Immediately we get into line with the purpose of God and actively cooperate, then we get movement and there is liberty.

In the same way the power of prayer is related to co-operation with God. Co-operation with God is power in prayer. Think of Elijah, and others, coming into co-operation with God and the resulting effectiveness of their prayer. What is accomplished!

And then the glory of prayer. Prayer becomes a glorious thing when it is really intelligently and spiritually a matter of co-operation with God. Co-operation eliminates selfishness and everything that is merely personal. That is one of its chief values, for it means that prayer should bring us into the Divine plan, the Divine method, the Divine time and the Divine spirit, or disposition. All these things are important—not only to know the plan, but God's method of fulfilling His plan; not only to know the plan and the method, but to come into God's time; and then, not only to be on that executive side, but to be in a right spirit for the thing when the time has come, to do it in the Spirit, in the demeanour of the Lord. All that is co-operation. We may be in a right thing, in a right way, at a right time, and yet not be helping the Lord because we are in a wrong spirit that is not the spirit of the Lord.

Prayer in co-operation with God is to make adjustment in all these matters.

There are three factors which are essential to prayer. Firstly, desire; secondly, faith; and thirdly, volition, or will. I just make that statement and leave it as it is.

Then when we put together communion, submission and petition we have co-operation. When they go together and are adjusted to each other, in line with each other and with the Divine will, then you have co-operation.

Perhaps, in closing that phase of things, we might remind ourselves that very often the Lord calls for an initial exercise on our part before He comes in on His side. He very often requires an initiative from us in the matter of desire, of faith and of volition. It is like the drop of water that has to be put into the old-fashioned pump to produce the stream, and you do not get the flow until you have given the pump something. And the Lord just calls for that on our part which may be, in comparison, a very little, but which makes it possible for Him to come out in His fullness. Very often prayer at its commencement represents exercise of will, faith and desire on our part, and then the Lord responds to that. It may be that the Lord does not respond until He sees the desire put into faith's deliberate action of the will to get through to Him. There is very often a good deal of discouragement met with at the commencement of prayer, and the danger is that we should give up too soon because we do not seem to be getting anywhere. The Lord is just asking for that drop of water to start the flow!

So far we have only mentioned four aspects of prayer, and have referred to some of the difficulties which arise in connection with them, but we have not cleared up those difficulties. We shall give two whole chapters to the fifth aspect of prayer, and then proceed to deal at greater length with the difficulties by way of seeking to answer them. These difficulties, however, are really only in the realm of the mind, and while they may sometimes get in the way of faith, faith will triumph over them, and leave behind a history of mighty things in spite of them.

Prayer As Warfare

Reading: Nehemiah iv. 9, 17, 20.
Ephesians vi. 18.

The Christian life has very often been likened to a warfare, and the appeal has been made to "come and join the ranks and enter into the battle of the Lord." But there is an irregularity about such an appeal, because, while it is true that there is such a warfare and such a militant company, the real consciousness of the fight, the battle, the warfare, does not exist until we are saved and are "on the Lord's side." The unconverted do not know anything about this battle. For them it is something merely reported and spoken about, something objective—outside of themselves and something about which they have altogether confused and wrong ideas. It is not until we are really in Christ that we either know the reality of the battle or understand its true nature.

But it is not just the warfare of the Christian life in the general and ordinary sense with which we are concerned here at this time. It is that warfare which is especially connected with, and related to, the full testimony of the Lord Jesus. The general conception of Christian warfare is that which has to do with evils, wrongs, vices, the things in this world, and human conditions which ought to be otherwise, and it is there that the mistaken apprehension of unconverted men and women is found. They think that to enter into the Christian army means to go out to battle with the evils, the wrongs, and the vices which abound in this world. But when you really come into touch with the full testimony of the Lord Jesus you very soon develop another consciousness: that it is not merely evils, wrongs and sins that you are having to deal with, but spiritual forces—intelligent, cunning, artful, venomous, malicious forces—which are at the back of everything else. It is that warfare with which we are concerned just now, that which is related to the full testimony of the Lord Jesus, to

His absolute and perfect sovereignty and lordship in this universe, and that warfare is not with things but with spiritual persons, headed by a great spiritual personage, the evil one.

Spiritual Conflict Implies a Spiritual Position

This warfare is related to a position. It is a consciousness which only comes to us in a certain realm. You may be a Christian, and as a Christian you may realise that you are up against adversities, difficulties, oppositions, and things which make the Christian life strenuous and full of conflict, calling out all the militant features of life, and yet you may not have entered into the ultimate things of the testimony of the Lord Jesus and the ultimate realm of the battle of the saints. But if you come as a believer to a revelation of the fullness of Christ in His personal sovereignty and lordship, in the greatness of the work of His cross in every realm, and then into the light of the Church which is His Body, you enter immediately into a new realm of conflict, the battle changes its character, and you begin to develop a consciousness, or a consciousness begins to grow in you, that you are up against something far more sinister, far more intelligently evil than those wrongs that abound in the world. You become increasingly conscious that it is with the devil, directly and nakedly, and with his forces that you are having to do.

But that consciousness is bound up with a specific position, and the experience of believers is that as they go on with the Lord (which means going upward, away from the earthlies to the heavenlies, more and more away from the old creation to the new creation life, and more and more away from the flesh to the spirit) the more closely do they come into contact with the ultimate spiritual forces of the universe, and the conflict assumes new forms and the warfare takes a new character. It is a warfare linked up with a specific position to which the believer comes, and with the consciousness which comes in only in a certain realm. It is in a fuller measure a spiritual warfare, and being that, it presupposes a spiritual state on the part of the believer.

To put that in another way: the more spiritual we become, the more spiritual does the warfare become; and the more spiritual the warfare is in our consciousness and in our knowledge, so we may realise that we have become more spiritual.

When we are carnal our warfare is carnal, and I refer to believers and not to unbelievers. The unbeliever is not spoken of as carnal. He is natural. When we are carnal as believers, our warfare and our weapons are carnal. That is, we meet men on their own level and answer back their challenge with that with which they challenge us. If they come out in argument we counter with argument; if they come out with reason we meet them with reason; if they come out with fierce temper we meet them in the heat of the flesh; and if they come out to us with criticism, well, we give them what they give us and try to go one better, meeting them always on their own level.

That is carnal warfare, using carnal weapons. When we cease to be carnal and leave all carnal ground, becoming wholly spiritual, we find ourselves in a new realm at the back of men, dealing with spiritual forces directly and not with merely carnal forces. We have come into touch with something at the back of carnal man, and the carnal man is utterly helpless in the presence of a spiritual man for the simple reason that he cannot get the spiritual man to come down to his level. Therefore he is disarmed, and sooner or later he will have to recognise that that spiritual man is his superior. But the superiority is not just in that the spiritual man is on a new level. It is that he is meeting not the man naturally, but the forces behind the man. It is spiritual warfare now. We cease to fight after the flesh; we cease to fight man; we cease to battle with flesh; our warfare is in another realm altogether. That represents spiritual advance, spiritual growth, and it represents spirituality. And when we come into real spiritual warfare a spiritual state is presupposed. In that realm the natural man's resources are utterly useless. They are ruled out, because for that warfare only spiritual equipment is either permissible or effective. The warfare then is with spiritual weapons, spiritual resources and spiritual equipment. So Ephesians vi. finds us in the heavenlies, battling, not with flesh and blood, but with principalities and powers, but we are equipped with a spiritual armour, the armour of God.

THE PRAYER-LIFE—THE OBJECTIVE OF THE ENEMY

That is all preliminary. What we are coming to immediately as the thing of basic importance for us, having seen

the nature of our warfare, is that the battlefield of this warfare is prayer. When the Apostle Paul has shown us the whole
panoply of God, the armour in all its parts, and exhorted us
to take it up and to stand, and withstand, he, as it were,
spreads the ground under our feet and says: "With all prayer
and supplication in the Spirit, and watching thereunto with
all perseverance and supplication for all saints." The batt-
leground of this warfare is prayer. What I mean is this: that
this battle is won on the ground of prayer, these forces are
dealt with and defeated on the ground of prayer, and, that
being so, the chief objective of the enemy is the prayer-life
of the believer. That is the focal point of all the enemy's attention and strategy.

Now if we said no more than that, that is the supreme
thing for our grasping and for our recognition. We have said
the most important thing that can be said in this connection. The focal point of all the enemy's attention and strategy
is the prayer-life of the believer. If he can destroy that by any
means he has gained the day, defeated the saints and frustrated the ends of God. The enemy fights prayer persistently,
energetically, violently and cunningly, and he fights the
prayer-life of the believer. He fights it in various ways. First
of all, he fights it along preventive lines, in the direction of
prevention, and there has to be a tremendous battle and conflict to *get* prayer—not only to pray, but to have prayer, get
prayer—and there is nothing in all the range of his wit, his
cunning, his craftiness, his ingenuity and his resourcefulness
that the enemy will not employ to prevent real spiritual
prayer. I think it will probably be enough for us if we con-
centrate upon that just now.

THE BATTLE FOR PRAYER

I am quite sure that I have the agreement of most of the
Lord's people when I say that one of the most difficult things,
if not the most difficult thing, is to be able to get to prayer
and give ourselves to prayer. When we contemplate prayer
we meet a host of unsuspected and unforeseen difficulties
which suddenly rise up as ambush forces breaking out upon
us. Anything to prevent prayer! I am not saying something
that you do not know, but I am saying it in order that you
may recognise it clearly, definitely and deliberately, and face

the fact that it is not just ordinary circumstances, but a designed, well-laid scheme of the enemy to prevent prayer. The enemy, instead of objecting, will promote occupation with a thousand and one things for the Lord if thereby he can crowd out prayer. He does not mind how busy we are in the Lord's work, nor how often we are found preaching, conducting meetings, and doing the many-sided work of the Lord, as we may call it. He knows quite well that all the work for the Lord which is not founded upon triumphant spiritual prayer will count for little or nothing in the long run and will break down. I say that he does not mind you working. Work for the Lord as hard as you can, but if you leave out prayer you will not accomplish very much. One of the subtleties of the enemy is to get us so busy, so occupied, so much on the go and on the rush with—as we think—things for the Lord and the work of the Lord that our prayer is cramped and pushed up into a corner and limited, if not almost entirely ruled out; and the Lord will never accept the excuse: "Lord, I am too much engaged in Your interests to pray." The Lord never favours an attitude like that.

You will remember that when the children of Israel began to talk about and contemplate their exodus from Egypt, the enemy's reaction was to double their labours, that is, to get them so much more deeply occupied with work that there would be no more time for contemplating an exodus. Immediately you begin to contemplate or purpose a fuller prayer-life, the enemy launches a new scheme for keeping you more busy and occupied, heaping up the work and crowding in demands so that you will have no time or opportunity for prayer.

I think that we must face this quite definitely. Of course, there are all the arguments about duty, obligation and responsibility, and it does sometimes look as though to put some things aside for prayer would be neglecting duty, or failing in obligation, or breaking down in responsibility, but there is a place where we have to cast those matters upon the Lord, and pray.

Now, of course, it is very difficult to apply that. There are always dangers about saying a thing like that, because there are always people who are more than ready to let go of their responsibilities, or who do not take their responsi-

bilities seriously. They would be only too ready and glad to
hand over their domestic affairs to someone else while they
cultivate a devotional life. The Lord must safeguard this word.
But we must recognise this: that the enemy will construct
his best arguments about responsibility, duty and conscience
to stop us praying, and there is a place where, if we see prayer
is utterly ruled out, or brought down to such a limited place
that it is completely inadequate for a life of spiritual ascendancy and victory, we have to say: "Lord. I am going to trust
the responsibility with You while I pray, that You will not
allow my breaking away for this time to have detrimental
results, and that You will protect this prayer-time which I
seek for Your glory from the inroads of the enemy."

The principle of the tithe does work, even in this realm.
Give God His portion, His place, and you will find that when
you have given the Lord His one-tenth, you are able to do
more with the nine-tenths than you could do with ten-tenths.
That principle works. But there is a battle *for* prayer, and
the necessity is for a strong, a mighty, a deliberate and a
determined stand in Christ, by the victory of His cross, to
get prayer, to bring in the full weight and the value of the
victory of the cross of the Lord Jesus to secure prayer and
to drive the enemy off the ground of prayer so that that
ground may be held for prayer. It is like Shammah of old,
when he stood in the lentil patch with his sword in his hand
and, single-handed, fought the Philistines and preserved that
lentil patch, and the Lord wrought a great victory. The lentil patch may represent our prayer-ground, which has to be
defended against the enemy in the fullness of Calvary's victory. There is a fight to get prayer and a battle for prayer.
We have, I am afraid, too often accepted the situation that
it is not possible to pray just now, or things are such as to
make if quite out of the question to pray. Yes, they will be
if the devil has his way; they will be always such as to make
prayer out of the question. That is one of his tactics. We have
to clear the ground for prayer in the victory of His Name and
of His Cross. The Cross is just as effectual in securing time
for prayer, if we will apply it and use it, as it is in any other
realm.

But we have to approach prayer on victory-ground. We
have to take up this attitude, and we shall find it more and

more necessary to do so: "Now prayer must be. Everything makes it impossible on the human side, but, Lord, I claim in the victory of Calvary a time of prayer, a clear space for prayer." We have to stand in that victory, and it may mean *standing* before we get through. It is not only the many things that may press in upon us along the line of external circumstances and happenings, to leave no room for a time of prayer. How true it is that when we are actually down on our knees prayer is withstood! It may be nothing on the outside. There may be no doorbells ringing, no telephone going, nor callers coming. We may be shut up in the silence of our own room and be actually on our knees, and then a mighty interfering activity commences. It may be physical. We may suddenly develop a physical consciousness that was not there a little while before, and it will threaten the whole of our prayer-time, so that we find that bodily we have to take up a tremendous burden, a dead-weight. We may even develop positive symptoms of illness of which we were unconscious before. These are facts. And then mental conditions may come in just at that time which were not there before. Oh, immediately, what an inrush of a thousand and one things which have not bothered us up till that moment! The mind becomes occupied by way of reflection and with things we must not forget which have not troubled us until that moment. And what about that sense of numbness, coldness, distance and unreality that descends upon you at such times? If you pray audibly your voice sounds strange and far away, and you seem to be talking into the air. All these things, and many others, come when we purpose prayer. They come on the very threshold, and for a time we meet all manner of discouragements and set-backs to prayer, and if we take the first five, ten or even fifteen minutes as our criterion, we will give it up, close down, get up and get on with something else.

Yes, the enemy is out to prevent prayer, and there is a phase of the battle which has to be gone through in order to get prayer. Again I say, this is nothing strange or foreign to you—unless, of course, you have not had a prayer-life at all, or are one who has never seriously taken up the business of prayer. But I am not saying all this to inform you. I am saying it to you and to myself in order that we may recognise that this is a thing which calls us into battle. It is the warfare of the saints to *get to prayer*, and not only to pray through. There is this aspect of the enemy's activity which is to prevent prayer, and to obtain it is a battle. There has to be a standing, a taking up of a position, and a withstanding in prayer for prayer.

I trust that the saying of all this which is so true to your experiences will nevertheless have the desired effect of making you recognise that in the future your prayer-life is not going to develop if the enemy can prevent it, and if you are going to have it and it is going to develop, then you will have to stand for it. It will not just come. You will not find that you just drift into it. You will never find that you drift into a mighty prayer-life, or that you walk with ease into such a thing. You will find that there is some making and breaking, some conflict and some battle to get it, that every realm of things will be taken hold of by the enemy to prevent it, and all that he has at his command of supernature will be used. You and I, dear friends, have to fight for our prayer-life, and the more we advance with the Lord spiritually, the more we shall find that to be so. It is not that the enemy is out to stop you and me from having a personal prayer-life. That is not what he is against. It is the testimony of the Lord Jesus which is so closely bound up with the prayer-life of the Lord's people that he is out to destroy. You and I, as individuals, as human beings, do not mean anything to the enemy. It is that which is bound up with us, and with which we are bound up in Christ—His sovereignty and His glory.

What Is Involved in Prayer

Now does it occur to you, or even strike you with considerable force, that this resistance to prayer-life on the part of the enemy implies far more than that, it positively declares and proclaims—that the Lord's glory and honour, His Name and His testimony are preeminently secured by prayer? If that is the focal point of the enemy's activity, then it means that the Lord's highest interests are served by prayer. That puts prayer in the first place. That, again, is not new to you, and yet it is a further emphasis upon the fact that the enemy is always trying to get prayer into the last place. He will try to get anything else in relation to the Lord before prayer, and get prayer in the last place. And it does not matter how you

put it, or what you say to Christian people about this, you
cannot get it home to them. "Oh, it is only the prayer meeting tonight!" On Sunday night, when there is ministry of the
Word and preaching, you will have a large gathering, but on
prayer meeting night you go into a side hall which will be
perhaps a little more than half full. And yet on Sunday night
you have said that our main ministry is prayer and everything goes if our prayer-life fails! You may say anything you
like along that line, emphasise it and stress it, but it does
not make any difference. I must confess that I am often bewil-
dered by the fact that so many really spiritual people—for
so I give them credit for being—will crowd to preaching meetings and conferences, but they are rarely seen at a prayer
meeting and leave so few to do the praying in the corporate
prayer-life of the assembly.

Yes, it is just like that, as though listening to an address
were the first and primary thing, and as though getting Bible
teaching and truth were more than anything else. No, dear
friends! Not at all! All that can only become vital, living and
effective in so far as our prayer-life, individually and corporately, is maintained in strength and given the first place.
So suffer whatever there might be of correction in the word,
for it is true, is it not? Oh, we have all been guilty. We all
have to say to ourselves: "Thou art the man!" We do need
so much to get the Lord's estimate of the value of prayer,
and if you go through the Word you will find that He estimates prayer at a higher value than anything else in His people. Look at His own life! Oh, amazement of amazement, that
One such as the Son of God, in all that He was, should yet
maintain such a prayer-life! "A great while before day," or
"continued all night." Yes, He prayed!

And has it occurred to you that some of the most glorious unveilings of truth that we have in the Bible came in
prayers? Read those prayers of Paul in Ephesians and Colos-
sians! "For this cause I bow my knees unto the Father,
. . ." and then he goes on and gives you his prayer, and in that
prayer you have a revelation which is matchless. It has come
in prayer, so that your teaching is based upon the prayer-life
of a man. Your light, in its true value, comes out of prayer,
and there is no light of real value that is not born of prayer.
All the value of truth depends upon the prayer which is

behind it, so that our conferences, our meetings, our addresses, and all the truth that comes just remain so much negative matter if there is not a commensurate prayer-life on our part in relation to it. We have to pray it in and pray it out, and I feel that after a conference the thing to do is to get to prayer more than ever on the ground of what has been said, and take that up before the Lord. If we did that, how much more fruit there would be from our conferences! Instead of having truth in our notebooks we would have it in our lives. Instead of so much more truth that we have now become acquainted with, we would be entering into the working power of that truth if we came back with it to the Lord in prayer. No one is more conscious of the need of having things said to him on this matter than I am at this time, but we are speaking together of these things and I trust that we are all taking them to heart. Oh, for the day when, not for the sake of numbers (for it is not a matter of counting heads) but because of the recognition of the preeminent place of prayer, the prayer meeting will be as crowded as any conference gathering! It only needs the apprehension of God's estimate of prayer, and we shall regard it as at least as important as any conference meeting with a theme and an address. The Lord burn that into our hearts, for that is the preeminent work—prayer.

It is not a great deal that has been said, but it is very important, and let us remember the word in connection with the enemy's determination to prevent prayer. We shall go on to show you that if he cannot prevent it, he will try to interrupt it; and if he cannot interrupt it, he will try to destroy it afterwards. There are other aspects of this thing, but we have perhaps seen enough to get us into some very definite place in relation to our prayer-life in facing it in the Name of the Lord.

CHAPTER THREE

Prayer As Warfare *(continued)*

Reading: I Kings xviii. 30-32, 36-38, 42-45.
James v. 17-18.
Ephesians vi. 18.

We note that what is true of the enemy's activity along the line of prevention of prayer is also true along the line of interruption of prayer. I do not only mean that while you are praying you have interruptions, but he has a subtle way of interfering with the continuity of a prayer-life. You may triumphantly secure seasons of prayer for perhaps a week, or more, and then something is introduced which breaks into that continuity so that you lose it, and you find that after a time a tremendous battle has to be fought to recover that prayer-life. For many of us our history is that of a spasmodic prayer-life which comes in patches, a history fraught with the necessity for every now and then recovering lost ground through having a setback—the interruption of the enemy. So we have to set a watch there, and watch especially against reactions from intensive periods of prayer, slackening off and feeling that now, after that strenuous time, we can take a spiritual holiday. There is always a very great peril there, as David proved. At a time when kings went out to battle, he went up on to the housetop.

Then what the enemy cannot prevent or interrupt, he will seek to destroy afterwards. That is, he will direct his attention to spoiling the prayer-life afterwards. We may have a strong time, or a series of strong times, but if he cannot directly attack our prayer-life, the enemy is always out to spoil it through another angle which does not seem immediately to be related to it, but by which indirectly we are crippled. Our prayer-life may be very strong, good and consistent, but something happens in some other department of our life, perhaps in a relationship somewhere else, and when we come to prayer we find that that thing represents a direct blow at our prayer-life and we cannot go on until that thing has been dealt with.

We must recognise that all these things are just the enemy's efforts, and are a highly organised scheme to destroy, either directly or indirectly, our prayer-life, or to interfere with it. Thus we shall find that our prayer-life is the focal point of everything.

It is when we come really to pray, to the real business of prayer, that we shall discover exactly where we are in all the relationships of our life. The iniquity which we regard in our hearts may not have anything to do directly with our prayer-life, but it comes indirectly as a terrific blow upon us. Things which may be side-shows bear right down upon our prayer-life. The enemy is always putting up these things all round to destroy our prayer-life. We register the state of things when we come to prayer. We may not recognise for the moment what a certain thing means, whatever that thing may be. It may be an interrupted fellowship, a strained relationship, a cross-purpose, or a breach somewhere, and we may not recognise exactly what it does mean until we come to take up our strong prayer-life. Then we find that that thing has struck at the very vitals of prayer and we cannot get on. That thing is out there, and so we are held up here; and then we discover that there has been a subtle working on the circumference of our lives which strikes at the very centre. The enemy would destroy our prayer-life, would, so to speak, throw things at it from the outside to make it impossible. I think you are able to follow what I mean, for experience bears it out.

The Universality of Prayer

Now we come to widen out a little in this spiritual conflict. These passages which we have read present us with a very comprehensive position. In I Kings xviii the account of the battle of Elijah on Carmel is undoubtedly an Old Testament illustration of the New Testament truth, especially of Ephesians vi. These two things go together as type and antitype, as part and counterpart, and what is common to them both is that the sphere of the conflict is the heavenlies. What James says directs the whole of this matter to the heavens: the opening and closing of the heavens, the government of the heavens, the ruling of the heavens. The heavens are the main object in view here, and this conflict relates to the heavens and the heavenlies: "Our wrestling is . . . in the heavenlies." Elijah's conflict was in a very real way a conflict in the heavens where heavenly forces were involved. That, I think, is patent, and that is a common feature in these two portions of the Word.

This particular spiritual conflict in which you and I are found when we have come into God's full purpose and testimony in Christ is, in its ultimate issue, related to the government of the heavens. Who is going to govern in the heavens? There are the principalities, the powers, the world-rulers of this darkness and the spiritual hosts of wickedness who have assumed the place of government. They are in a usurped place, for that is not the eternal thought of God, nor is it His will. Christ is Head, and His Church as His members are, in the intention of God, called to rule in the heavens, to govern as from the heavens. It is a question of what the heavens are in this matter, whether they are to be satanic, or whether they are to be the expression of the absolute lordship of the Lord Jesus in and through the Church, which is His Body. It is the heavenlies, the ruling realities, which are involved, and it is there that our conflict is. That is the sphere of this warfare, and our prayer-life has to do with that. It is not merely to do with the incidents of our lives here on the earth. Oh, that the Lord's people would recognise the immensity of this, for so often the generality of our prayer is in the realm of merely trivial things, and a great deal of time is taken up with telling the Lord all about the little things of our ordinary earthly life which, while they may be important to us and may count in an earthly life, do not touch the ultimate things in God's purpose.

There is such a difference between praying down there and praying against the immense forces of the universe and getting the heavenly things through. The Lord's people want to be lifted in prayer to where the mighty, heavenly, eternal and universal are affected, touched and brought through. There is a great need for us to be brought into our heavenly place in the matter of prayer, where real spiritual matters lying behind the other are touched. Very often the Lord never allows our prayers to be effective in the merely earthly details of our lives because He wants us to see that there is something behind those things which matters a great deal more. You sometimes pray for a thing to happen, a change to take place, or an event to come off, but nothing happens. The Lord seeks—after you have extended yourself as fully as you can on the matter—to show you that there is a spiritual key to that situation, and He cannot do just the earthly thing for you because that would not in any way be to your spiritual increase of intelligence, understanding, knowledge or value, and would only be doing things because you asked Him. He is trying to instruct and teach you so that you come into possession of spiritual situations.

Well, it is the heavens which are the sphere of this conflict.

The Church—the Occasion of the Conflict

What is the occasion of the conflict? What is it for? Well, from the context in both these passages, I Kings xviii and Ephesians vi, you see that the occasion of the conflict is the Church. The Church is the immediate object in view. In I Kings xviii, of course, it is the people of God, and the issue of Elijah's prayer is that their hearts should be turned back. The Lord's people are in view and his prayer is for this people, so he brings them all near and involves them in this issue, and associates them with it, because it is their issue. We know that the thing which is in view right through the letter to the Ephesians is the Church which is His Body, and this is the occasion of the conflict. It is a battle in the heavenlies in relation to the Church, the Body of Christ.

There are two things to be said about that. One, that it is not merely a personal matter, but a collective, corporate matter. This conflict relates to the whole Body of Christ, and the conflict of every individual is a related conflict, relating to all the rest of the saints, so that there is that spiritual relativity which means that if one member is defeated the whole Body suffers spiritually. It may not know why, nor be conscious of its particular suffering, but, registered in the Head and the consciousness of the Head, there is a loss to the whole Body when even one member falls into defeat. The conflict is a related one; and so the enemy seeks to isolate individual members of the Body and bring such pressure upon them as to crush them down, because he knows—not just the value of an isolated member—but the relativity of every member. It is because of this that there is so much spiritual emphasis from the intelligence of the Holy Spirit upon the necessity for praying for all saints, for the fellowship prayer, the corporate prayer of the Lord's people. There is loss to Christ, the Head, if there is not that prayer for all saints.

CHRIST IN GLORY—THE OCCASION OF THE CONFLICT

The other thing to be said about this is that it is not even the Church as the Body which is the ultimate thing, although it is the immediate occasion. We must not put the Church, the Body of Christ, in the preeminent place. It is an occasion, but it is not the final thing. The Church, the Body of Christ, is His instrument, His vessel for His testimony. His testimony is deposited in the Body. It was so in His resurrection, and at Pentecost the testimony of His victory, the testimony of His exaltation, the testimony of His glorification and the testimony of His universal authority in heaven and in earth was deposited in the Church. As the temple in the Old Testament was the shrine of the glory of God, so the Body of Christ in the New Testament is the shrine of His glory, His testimony and His Name, and it is ultimately to strike at that glory, that Name, and that exaltation that the enemy directs his attention to the elect vessel, the Church, the Body of Christ. And so the Church becomes the occasion of the conflict, although not the end, but the enemy gets at the Christ, at the Name and at the glory through the Body. We know that that was true in the Old Testament.

When Israel was in a state of spiritual declension the Lord's glory and honour, His Name, and His majesty were overshadowed, beclouded, and lost to view. When Israel's spiritual life was in the ascendant, then Jehovah's testimony was maintained in full strength. In the New Testament, and in our own time in this New Testament age, the enemy's way of dishonouring the Lord is by destroying the spiritual life of the Lord's people, or by breaking up the fellowship of the saints.

So the Church, the Body, becomes the occasion of the conflict because of what it is in its divinely-appointed vocation, purpose and object. The enemy's bitter hatred and violent opposition are directed against the corporate life of the

Lord's people. He will seek by any means to destroy that, to break up the fellowship of the saints, to set the Lord's people against one another, and to introduce disintegrating things—but, oh, how subtle are his ways in this!

THE STRATEGIC VALUE OF WATCHFULNESS

Here I do feel, dear friends, that you and I will have to do what Nehemiah did, and what the Apostle in this very portion exhorts us to do: "Set a watch"; "watching thereunto," because, as you notice in both connections, it is the wiles of the devil which are in view. They are the subtle activities of the enemy, and to set a watch against the wiles of the devil in practical outworking will, at least in one direction, mean this: that we make *quite sure* that the rumours which we hear and the reports that come to us are absolutely trustworthy. We must make quite sure—"prove all things." We can be divided by a rumour, and split up by a report. We can be set at variance or apart by a mere insinuation. In these days, when the atmosphere is surcharged with fear and suspicion, you have only to hint at the possibility of someone being "unsound" and a spiritual breach of fellowship is created and a gap made. If only we set a watch and made sure, we would find that a great deal of that was unnecessary and unwarranted, and represented a great loss to the Lord Himself and to His people, for when we get really to close grips and sift these things we find there is nothing in them, or, if there is anything in them, they have an explanation and we cannot fail, in all honesty of heart, to accept that as being right. That is very often how it works out.

But, oh! to set a watch against these wiles of the devil! His methods of breaking up the corporate life of the Lord's people are beyond our power to enumerate, and that is where prayer and watching are necessary. Prayer should result in intelligence about the wiles of the enemy, and "watching unto prayer" is watching and praying that you might discover in prayer what it is the enemy is after and how he is working.

We do not want to be obsessed with the enemy, always to have our eyes on him, but we must recognise the facts as they are, and those facts are that throughout these almost two millenniums the enemy has made it his great business unceasingly to destroy the fellowship of the people of God.

Is that true? Is that history? If it is true, what does it signify? That you can never have something that really in any measure represents what is precious to the Lord, something of a spiritual character, embodying some precious element of His testimony, but what it is the object of satanic malignity and cunning which has the one intention of splitting that thing, breaking it up, and getting schism and division there somehow, by truth or by lies. That is history, and surely it gives the whole game away, that a Church in fellowship, a Body rightly adjusted and related, moving together in the will of God, is the greatest menace to the spiritual rule of principalities and powers that there is in the universe.

So it is that to which we should work and direct our attention. Let us lay ourselves out for spiritual fellowship! That does not mean compromising with things which are contrary to the Word of God, and must not mean coming down from any spiritual position to which the Lord has, through cost, brought us. We must be where Nehemiah was when his enemies said, "Come down and let us discuss this matter. We must confer about this." Nehemiah said: "I am doing a great work so that I cannot come down." There must be no coming down to discuss things that are beyond the point of discussion as to spiritual necessity. But, dear friends, any spiritual position arrived at through cost and the deep inworking of the cross must be held only in relation to all the saints. It must not be held out of relation to the saints, nor must those who have it and hold it be made something apart from the rest. No! Whatever may be the difference of spiritual position so far as degree is concerned, fellowship with all saints must be striven after and maintained as far as possible, and it must be reached out for. I do want to urge that upon you more and more, as it is urged upon my own heart, because the Lord's end in giving light and truth may be defeated if the reception of it and the holding of it constitutes those who have it as being something apart from the rest of the saints. He has given it for the Body; if it is held apart, then the end for which He gave it has been missed. Lay that to heart very definitely!

So the occasion of the conflict is the Church, by reason of its heavenly calling and vocation. This is no personal thing, nor local thing: it is universal. The Body of Christ is a universal reality.

THE BASIS OF VICTORY

Just a word or two with regard to the basis of victory
in this conflict. The basis of victory here in I Kings xviii was
undoubtedly the altar, and in Ephesians it is the same. Before
you reach your position in the heavenlies for heavenly conflict and triumph, you have to pass through the earlier chapters of Ephesians and recognise that a death has taken place,
that an altar was there, and that, having died, you have been
"quickened and raised together." All the features of the cross,
the altar, are implied at the beginning of the letter to the
Ephesians, so that both in the representation and in that
which is represented the basis of victory is the cross, the altar.
Elijah took twelve stones, and the constitution of the altar
with twelve stones immediately brings in the administrative
feature in relation to the altar, for twelve is the number of
administration. The altar comprised of twelve stones becomes
the administrative instrument, the governmental principle,
in this conflict in the hands of God. The government is in
the cross, and by the cross, for by His cross He triumphed,
and in His cross He stripped off principalities and powers
and "made a show of them openly." I wonder if, in reading
those fragments of I Kings xviii you were struck with the
terms: ". . . according to the number of the tribes of the sons
of Jacob, unto whom the word of the Lord came, saying, Israel
shall be thy name." What is that? Well, Israel means "a prince
with God," so in that verse 31 we have sons of a prince with
God represented in the altar, in the cross.

Symbolically that speaks to us very clearly of that basis
of our coming into our Prince, our governmental position in
Christ, who is the Prince with God. He is greater than Israel,
for He is *the* Prince with God, and we are sons in Him and
partake of His princeliness. That brings us up into a place
of governmental authority in Christ in the heavenlies, but
it is all bound up with the altar, the cross. The cross is the
basis of victory, and that is borne out again, not only by the
testimony of heaven, the Word of God, but by the testimony
of hell. Satan is an unwonted, unwilling—and I sometimes
wonder whether he is an unconscious—witness to the truth
in this way, for it is perfectly clear that he hated the cross,
and he tried in the first place to keep the Lord Jesus from

it: ". . . this shall not be unto thee. But he turned and said unto Peter, Get thee behind me, Satan." This is Satan try-ing to keep the Lord Jesus from the cross, and then, having failed to keep Him from it, he tried to bring Him off the cross: "If thou be the Son of God, come down from the cross." Those subtle suggestions! ". . . let him now come down from the cross and we will believe him." To be believed in by the world was what He had come for, but, no, the second method of the enemy did not succeed.

The enemy having failed along those lines, and the cross having been accomplished in spite of him, he will seek now to change and alter the preaching of the cross in order to make it of non-effect. He will get people to preach it, and in their very preaching of it make it void. That is extraordinarily sub-tle! It is as well to recognise how far the enemy will go. He will promote the preaching of the cross, and the cross preached by his instigation and under his influence is made non-effective. The Apostle tells us that in his first letter to the Corinthians, that the cross preached in the wisdom of men makes it of non-effect, or void. Men preaching the cross in their wisdom are simply taking the true meaning and power out of the cross. Oh, yes, you hear plenty about the way of the cross, but it is not His way of the cross. The very power of the cross is in its registration against the enemy and all his works, against sin as a principle, and against evil as a state, a nature. The power of the cross is taken out when you speak about the heroics of the cross, and about the way of the cross as, well, any man who denies himself and lays down his life for his country is in the same category as Jesus Christ, who, after all, only laid down His life as any soldier has done. That is the cross in modernism.

Another thing which the enemy seeks to do in relation to the cross is to keep Christians in ignorance of its full mean-ing. It is a great day for the Lord, and a terrible day for the enemy, when a Christian breaks through into the revelation of the full meaning of Calvary. That day marks a new bit of history in the realm of conflict. You may meet a certain kind of opposition on the ground of the substitutionary work of the Lord Jesus, but, believe me, you will meet ten times more when you come on to the ground of the representative work of the Lord Jesus, and when you take up your place in iden-

tification with Christ in death, burial and resurrection in a
spiritual way. Then begins a new history of conflict, of battle, and of satanic antagonism, but you have entered into a
new realm and a new place, and you have new powers at your
command. The enemy has lost his ground. Multitudes believe
in the substitutionary work and rejoice in it, but they are still
going on in the energy of the natural man, even as Christians.
They do not represent a menace to the enemy in those higher
ranges, but when the cross has been so accepted and planted
in our lives that the natural life is set aside—"I have been
crucified with Christ; and it is no longer I that live, but Christ
liveth in me"—then there is a new realm of meaning to the
Lord and of meaning to the enemy, and therefore a new realm
of conflict. The enemy is out to keep that side of the cross
from Christians, and we have said before, and it is true, that
very often you meet your opposition on that line more from
Christians than from any others. It is a strange thing.
Immediately you go on with the Lord into all, the fullness
of the meaning of Calvary you find your chief difficulty is
in the realm of Christians, and, as a rule, "official" Christians.
Leaders will not have it, and you find that your way is made
infinitely more difficult. It is true that the enemy does hate
the fullness of the cross, and he will seek by any means to
destroy its value for believers, to hide its meaning from them,
and if possible to get them to forsake the position and come
down from it, or to persuade them not to accept it.

Well, surely that is his testimony to its value! He is a
witness to its meaning. The cross, then, is the basis of victory, and the enemy knows it very well.

I am not going further than that now. We must take this,
think about it and apply it, but remember this grand, con-
clusive thing Satan is a defeated foe for all who are truly one
with the cross of the Lord Jesus, because Calvary does represent his defeat, and, as we are planted into the death of
Christ, so we stand with Him in that defeat of the enemy,
in that victory of the Lord Jesus. So, however he may rage,
storm, fight, afflict, press, worry, and harass, the fact remains
that for those who are one with Christ in His cross, Satan
is a defeated foe.

CHAPTER FOUR

Some Mental Difficulties in Prayer

Having considered the five phases of prayer, namely, communion, submission, petition, co-operation and conflict, we shall now go on a little further to consider some of the problems which are related to prayer. As we have said, very often an undefined sense of contradiction or uncertainty in the background of our minds has the effect of crippling or paralysing prayer, and we are sometimes hindered by certain mental difficulties which we have never seriously set ourselves to analyse or define. Our object now is to seek to define some of these things, to analyse them, and to nail them down, by way of clearing the ground for prayer in certainty and confidence.

PRAYER AND THE WILL OF GOD

In this connection one of the primary difficulties in prayer arises in relation to the will of God. That, of course, is a very wide sphere of contemplation and consideration, and includes a very large number of different phases, aspects and points, but we shall seek to narrow it down, and as we go on we shall see a great deal more wrapped up in what we say.

As to the will of God, the basic question seems to me to be this: Is it absolute or is it relative? What we are dealing with is that question as to whether the will of God for us is absolute or relative. When it is put like that you may not be helped very much. It sounds very academic, but I will explain what I mean.

Does God permit things because they are His absolute will, or because He would draw us out by them to some position? In the latter case the will of God is relative and not absolute, that is, things do not represent what is absolutely the will of God, but He has permitted them for other purposes, and, therefore, they represent the relative will of God. Now you have your foundation and basis for a very comprehensive consideration of the will of God in relation to prayer.

If we are dealing with the relative will of God, the issue will
be either that those things, having fulfilled their purpose, are
set aside and cease to have any place at all in the will of God,
or they are allowed to remain but we are in a place of ascendancy over them and they become our servants. They are
there, not because God in the fullness of His will and purpose wants them to be there, but because He sees they are
things which are necessary to maintain us in a certain position. If we were perfect creatures the will of God would always
be absolute. There would be no place for the relative will of
God, for it would be unnecessary for Him to permit things
to get us to new positions. But, being imperfect, fallen creatures, the will of God for us is more often relative than
otherwise.

Conflict Between Submission and Importunity

So the problem arises for us along the line of submission and importunity. Those two things seem to be antagonis-
tic to one another, to represent conflict and contradiction.
How can you reconcile importunity with submission? Does
not importunity rule out submission? Does not submission
rule out importunity? These seem mutually against each
other, and yet that is not so. The problem which comes up
in prayer is to keep on hammering at the door, to continue
knocking, and yet to know submission. Does not submission
take the driving force out of your knocking? Does not the
force of your knocking imply that you have not learned submission? It may not always be defined in that way in the
mind, but it creeps in, remaining in the background, and very
often tends to draw that positiveness, certainty and definite-
ness out of prayer so that you find yourself in a no-man's-land.

Well, that is a problem, and we have to settle it as
definitely as we possibly can. The solving of that problem,
I think, is along the line of recognising that the moral element comes in, and God is largely concerned with moral elements and questions. There is something which has to be got
over, or got through, in us, and that means that in the relative will of God there will be many things which are only
allowed, or may even be sent by the Lord, with the object
of, and for the purpose of, getting over certain things in us,
or getting us through certain things in ourselves because

moral factors are in view. (I am using the word "moral" in its broadest sense now, and not in any narrow sense.) We must recognise that the new creation is a moral matter and is not complete so far as we are concerned. It is perfect and complete in itself, but it is not complete in us. The old creation still exists. It is objective and external to the new creation, but it has great influence which it exercises upon the new. Sin is not extinct for the believer, nor is the world as something which registers itself upon the believer. And you do not need me to tell you that the devil is not extinct for the believer! But right at the centre of that old creation is the new creation, which is a moral thing. But it is a moral thing— we may say—in its infancy, and all its moral elements and factors have to be developed to make us moral creatures, in the full sense of the word—that is, responsible creatures, intelligent creatures, and creatures with a new conscience, a new standard of values and a new recognition of principles. A whole new heavenly world has come in, and its knowledge and wisdom have to be possessed intelligently. Its secrets have to be known and its virtues have to be inwrought. By regeneration the Lord has not made us mere automatons or machines, to be acted upon from without, irrespective of our will, our feelings, our desires, our reason or our intelligence, to he carried hither and thither and caused to do things, or made to do things, without reference to ourselves. That is altogether contrary to Scriptures.

But what the Lord has constituted us is moral creatures after a new morality, a new heavenly system and an entirely new intelligence which is not the natural man. We have an entirely new system of judgments, values and appraisements, and in everything the Lord will now refer to us. He will call upon us to exercise ourselves in relation to the new creation impression, consciousness, conviction and intimation from within. Thus the new creation is a moral thing, but because the old creation is still circling and wrapping it round, the new creation will grow by conquest, by conflict, and by strenuous exercise to overcome by subjecting, triumphing over, and by deliberate, strenuous, devoted and persistent application. The renewed will, energised by the Holy Spirit, will not be mechanically operated but will be called to exercise itself in the Lord. Praying in the will of God does not mean that the

Holy Spirit comes and holds your will and your volition and makes you say things without your intelligence. That is an entirely false realm. There is a good deal today where man's intelligence is swept on one side and he begins to flow out with all kinds of things that neither he nor anyone else can understand, but that is not the new creation. The Holy Spirit does not suspend the intelligence and understanding of anyone He uses in this way, but He calls upon the exercise of understanding. "I will pray with the spirit, and 1 will pray with the understanding also," said the Apostle, and prayer in the Holy Spirit is not that we so abandon ourselves to Him that we lose all our own moral life (using that word again in the fullest sense).

Prayer As Educative

Seeing, then, that moral questions are preeminent in the Lord's mind where we are concerned, prayer becomes an education and a training. We speak of "the school of prayer," and that is a very right designation. Education and training are not the same thing. Education has to do with obtaining knowledge, and training has to do with moral worth in practical expression. Get that definition, for it is an important one. We speak of an "educated person," and we mean someone who knows a lot, but speak of a "well-trained person" and we think of someone who is worth something in practical value. There are a lot of educated people who are perfectly useless. We are, therefore, drawn out in prayer, and the Lord sees to it that we are drawn out and extended in prayer, and that represents, on the one hand, the acquiring of spiritual knowledge. We do not get that unless we are drawn out in prayer. It is remarkable how, when there is a full extending in prayer, we learn things, we get secrets and come into knowledge of things. And then, on the other hand, that drawing out in prayer has the effect of training, bringing us into a moral position and on to a higher level morally. We will see what that means presently. Prayerless people will be both ignorant and weak, uneducated and untrained. They will not know God's mind nor be able to do according to His mind.

So we must recognise further that prayer is not merely individual advantage, but it is the prosecuting of a campaign. There is a Divine scheme of things to be entered into. Prayer is not merely for personal and subjective value. It is objective, collective and relative, even in the moral values which result from individual prayer.

THE NATURE OF IMPORTUNITY

Now we will seek to summarise things a little. There are three sides to importunate prayer—but do you see why importunity is demanded, is necessary and is right? And do you see that there is no contradiction between subjection and importunity? Subjection, as we pointed out earlier, is an active thing, a positive thing and not a passive thing. It is coming into line with the Divine mind; and then importunity follows for the development of moral features.

THE MORAL EXCELLENCIES OF CHRIST INWROUGHT

As we have just said, there are three sides to importunate prayer. Firstly, there is the moral side, and that has its own two aspects. We spoke of the ingredients of the incense to be offered upon the golden altar, and we pointed out that these ingredients represented the moral virtues of Christ. On the one hand, these have to be apprehended and appropriated by faith, and that is one aspect of the moral side of importunate prayer: that faith deliberately, persistently, apprehends and appropriates the moral virtues and glories of the Lord Jesus. That is exercise, and it very often represents putting back the intrusion of those arguments which arise from our natural selves and which would discourage prayer. When we come into the presence of the Lord, we should certainly come in with a sense of our own unworthiness, emptiness and weakness, but that is not the ground of our exercise, for that should be settled. Yet often positive, effectual prayer is interfered with, arrested and even checked by persistent obsession with our own sinfulness, weakness and helplessness, and there is a need for positive exercise over the moral virtues and excellencies of Christ in order that we should get them into both of our hands to get before God.

The enemy will thrust in convictions, condemnations and accusations in the presence of God, but we must with both hands lay hold of the excellencies of the Lord Jesus, and until we have done that we shall not get through to the throne, because we cannot get there apart from those excellencies.

There has to be a deliberate refusal to take that condemnation on. We know of some whose prayer-life has become an almost far-off, impossible thing, because immediately they cut themselves off for prayer there is such an inrush of introspection, self-analysis, and consciousness of themselves and the wrong things about themselves that they never get through to anything positive at all.

On the one hand, then, there is faith's exercise, the persistence of faith in the appropriation of those ingredients, those excellencies and virtues of the Lord Jesus, to bring us through to God.

Then there is the other side of the moral factor: those excellencies and virtues have to be wrought in our own souls by the Holy Spirit. The Lord Jesus in the presence of God is the representative Man after God's own heart, but He is not only the representative Man, He is the Man from whom all the members of the new creation in Christ are to take their character, and His full content of virtues and excellencies as perfect Man—and perfected Man—have to be distributed to all His members, so that they take their character from Him and become themselves partakers of His nature in their own souls. These virtues of Christ were tested virtues, tried virtues, proved virtues, and triumphant virtues, and they are now energetic virtues, and not merely passive. The Lord Jesus (may I say this reverently) has not been put in a museum as a model, the supreme specimen just to be looked at and to be admired, but there is generic force and reality in Him. He lives. He is not a model, or a statue. He is the living Christ who imparts Himself, and is ministered by the Holy Spirit, to us, His members. His faith is not just something that has been rounded off, perfected and polished, something to be looked at as we look at a beautiful specimen. It is a faith by which we have to live. His patience is of the same character. We are called to be fellows and partakers in the patience of Christ. As we just mention these things you will have a lot of Scripture rushing into your mind: "Add to your faith. . . ." Add, add, add—and these are virtues of Christ being added to us. We are called, says the Apostle, to be "partakers of Christ." So His faith, His patience, His devotion, His obedience, His suffering and His love have all been tested out, tried, proved, and are triumphant, but not as things apart from us but in relation to us. "He hath granted unto us His precious and exceeding great promises; that through these ye may become *partakers of the divine nature. . . .*"

The moral side of importunate prayer, then, is that the virtues and excellencies of Christ are wrought in us. When importunity represents the demand for patience because God does not answer at once, today, tomorrow, for a week, a month, or a year, what is He doing? He is working into us the moral excellencies of His Son, a perfected and triumphant faith, a perfected and triumphant patience, a perfected and triumphant devotion and an obedience to Him which has no foundation other than that He has required it. Prayer is a training school indeed! These virtues come by exercise. Let us remember that God has an end in view, and that our partnership with Christ to which we are called at length will be moral. It will have to do with character; hence the relative will of God. Sin is not God's absolute will, but He has permitted it. Ah, yes, *but the relationship is with out conquest*, and with the development of the new creation moral life. Suffering is not God's absolute will, but He has permitted it, and He does permit it. It is, therefore, His relative will, which means that His permission and His allowing is for a purpose. When that purpose is reached the suffering may go, or it may still be allowed to remain to keep us in a position, but the position for which it has been permitted has been reached so that the relative will of God has been done. And that applies to everything else. Circumstances, for instance. Many circumstances that come into our lives are not God's absolute will. A breakdown is not God's absolute will, but inasmuch as nothing can come to any child of His without His consent, it is His permissive will.

Spiritual Understanding Secured

Now that raises for us the whole question of seeking, in prayer, to know what God means by things. That is our education. Coming to know what God means by things through deep heart exercise and travail is our training. We have reached a higher standard of life. So the second thing in importunate prayer is knowledge. In the first place the moral life, and knowledge in the second place. There are those who put themselves wholly into God's hands, and they are led into strange experiences of apparent contradiction, There may be a clear sense of what the Lord wants to do, but the absolute impossibility of doing it! No way is open and all the doors are closed. Delay after delay! What is the Lord doing? The first effect should be to draw us out in prayer, fully extend us in importunity. We cannot let it go. We may decide that we will leave it all with the Lord, but we find ourselves coming back to it again and again, and the Lord will not allow us to be indifferent. Well, He is after fuller knowledge and understanding on our part. That is bound up with all the Lord's ways with us, and one thing, which, of course, we know in experience but which perhaps it will be as well for us to have more clearly defined in our minds, is that we cannot learn Divine principles, or obtain spiritual knowledge from books or lectures. They can only be known as they follow the process of generation. First of all there must be conception, which is an inward thing: then there must be formation, and then there must be travail leading to birth. It is a *life* process. We cannot learn Divine and spiritual things from manuals, not even the Bible. We can only learn what is in the Bible along the line of living experience. *The Bible is not a gramophone; it is a microphone.* What is the difference? A gramophone is a thing stored up in itself. A microphone is that which transmits something beyond. The Bible is not a gramophone. There has to come through our reading of the Word something from beyond for our understanding. We can have the gramophone kind of knowledge of the Bible, that is, we may know the Bible as a book through and through, we can have the most wonderful analyses and diagrams. and we may still remain—for all practical and spiritual purposes in a living way—very little use to the Lord.

But if we have a microphone apprehension of the Word, we have the Scriptures, yes, but, more than that, God speaks *through* the Scriptures to us and we have the living thing. We have all, as children on the seashore, taken up shells and put them to our ears to hear the sea roaring. We have brought the shells home to the city, put them to our ears, and have still heard the sea roaring. Is that true? It is a childish delusion. We think when we are children and have the shell in a town that we hear the roaring of the sea, that the roaring of the sea is all stored up in that shell and we have only to put it to our ear and there it is—we hear it. That is a child's thought about that shell, but it is nothing of the kind. That shell is only acting like a funnel which is collecting the vibrations of the atmospheric sounds and causing us to hear what we would not hear with the naked ear. The shell is nothing but a transmitter of the larger thing.

The Word of God taken as a book is just like that shell. If we are in the Spirit it will bring to us the mind of the Lord, but, apart from the Holy Spirit's operation through it to us, it may be just like any other book and we may read it and get no more light from it than we get from any other book. The necessity is for spiritual knowledge, but many make the Bible just a manual.

Now what we are saying is that we cannot know Divine principles or obtain spiritual knowledge from books or from lectures. These principles only come to us along the line of life and experience. Something of a living character is done in us, a life is formed in us and developed, and then it brings us into travail for its full outworking. That is how we get spiritual knowledge. That comes in importunate prayer, and that is why God demands and makes importunate prayer necessary. We get to know spiritual things from the travail of our souls before God, in the long drawn-out experience of anguish. Very often hurry—in the long run—only means loss of time, and we have to come back to get fuller knowledge because we were in too great a hurry. The Lord has to bring many back and tie them up so that they cannot move, and keep them there in deep exercise for an extended period. Then they learn what in the mind of the Lord was indispensable. There are those who are made to know before they go out, but whether it is before you go, or in your having to come back, the same thing is in view with the Lord—that you should *know*.

So the Lord's delays are His times of drawing out in importunate prayer for the sake of spiritual knowledge.

TAKING RESPONSIBILITY IN PRAYER

Then, thirdly, there is the collective aspect. Nehemiah spoke of the prayer which he prayed day and night, but that prayer was relative, for it had to do with the Lord's people. Christ's prayers were of the same character. They were not

just for Himself, but they were related to His own and were
drawn out day and night for them. Paul's prayers were clearly
of the same order: ". . . do not cease to pray for you"; "praying always with all prayer and supplication . . . for all saints."
There is persistence and importunity, but it is a collective,
relative thing. The woman who is in the back of our minds
as we use the word "importunate," or "importunity," is the
one who confronts the unjust judge, and she represents the
Church. Christ's comment upon that word was: "And shall
not God avenge his own elect, which cry day and night unto
him. . . ."

What is the avenging of the saints of their adversary?
Well, it is the great collective thing at the end, the great issue
when the accuser of the brethren is cast down, the one who
accused them before God, day and night. The great Judge
will avenge of the accuser, the harasser of the Church, and
this has its collective aspect. The incident of the friend at mid-
night was again a relative thing, not merely a personal thing.
The man got up because his friend would keep on knocking.
The man was fetched out of bed by his friend's importunity,
but it was in relation to others. All this represents a scheme,
a plan, a campaign, in which all the Lord's people are involved.
God is not only getting us individually to a place, but He
is getting us relatedly to a place with all His people: "till we
all come. . . ." Our travail, our moral training, these contradic-
tions and delays which draw us out and extend us fully are
working in us in relation to the whole Body. It becomes a
relative thing, for it is on behalf of the Body.

The Lord is seeking to have His whole Body perfected,
and every part must have a due working in it in relation to
the whole. One day the cumulative effect of our trials, difficulties and perplexities will be seen in the whole perfect Body,
and we shall see then that when we suffered we did not suffer in isolation, that our sufferings were not detached things
but collective, related, a part of the whole, and they contributed to a much bigger thing than our own personal
interests. We must allow God's full end to give colour to our
personal experience. That which we go through is not simply because the Lord has marked us out to be sufferers alone,
but because the whole Body is His end and we suffer in relation to the Body. For the Body's sake we fill up that which

is lacking of the sufferings of Christ. The sufferings are relative, you see. They are not the absolute will of God, but relative in this further sense that they are moving on to a larger purpose of God. When that larger purpose is reached then that relative will of God in the sufferings will go, and there will be no more pain and no more suffering. We must see the whole plan of God and find that our required, demanded persistence and importunity in prayer affects these three things. The personal moral life of the believer on the heavenly pattern, and the increase of spiritual knowledge are behind the delays which call us out to importunate prayer. There is something that we are going to know that we do not know now. We are going to learn something that we know nothing about, and this drawing of us out is the way by which we come to know what we do not know.

This exercise, this travail, is related to the whole purpose of God and has its place in relation to all His saints. There is no such thing as coercion in God's will. That is foreign to the thought of importunity. Importunity is—although it may not seem like it—co-operation with God. We may think that the effect of it is to coerce God and persuade Him to do things, but God has only drawn us into that way to draw us into cooperation with His will. That is what I meant when I said there were things to be overcome in us, and all kinds of old creation things that have to be got over—our desires, our feelings, our preferences, our judgments, our conceptions, our estimates. In the exercise, activity and travail of prayer we have come into cooperation with God, and we have found that in the long run what we thought was trying to persuade the Lord to do things was His way of getting us to a place where He could do what He wanted. The Lord has strange ways, but in the end He is justified and "Wisdom is justified of her children."

CHAPTER FIVE

The Sword of the Word, and Prayer

Reading: Judges vii. 1-7.
I Samuel xiii. 2-7, 19-23.
Ephesians vi. 17, 18.

As we come to the end of our meditations on prayer there are just one or two further things that need to be said, and these are largely connected with the passages of Scripture given above.

Gathering up the content of chapters xiii and xiv of the First Book of Samuel, the situation is just this: Saul, who officially represents the people, is in a state where faith in God is almost a minus quantity. The result is the domination of fear, and everywhere there is trembling and a tragic absence of cohesion and oneness. The enemy is in the ascendant. The people are unable to do anything because, by a strategic move of the enemy, all the weapons of war have been removed and the forges have been destroyed. In the midst of such a situation there is one man at least who has faith in God, and whose faith sets him in positive opposition to the prevailing conditions. Jonathan still believes profoundly in God, and, therefore, not only denounces the existing state of things, but repudiates it by setting himself positively and actively against it. Thus he becomes God's small instrument for the overthrow of the enemy's power in a day of almost universal declension. He raises a testimony in the midst of very general spiritual weakness and apprehension. Such instances are found scattered through the Scriptures, and through the history of the Church since Bible times. There are two things which are significant and especially to be noted in this story. One is:

THE STRATEGY OF THE ENEMY

This strategy meant that the Lord's people were virtually defeated before there was any battle. Their weapons had been confiscated and the means for producing more had been removed and destroyed.

That was a wily move, and truly one of the master-wiles of the enemy. Can we not see that in this incident in the literal history of God's people there is an indication of how the enemy of God's testimony is always trying to work? And is not this the very thing which obtains very largely today? We have seen in our earlier meditation that the weapons of the people of God are primarily prayer and the Word. Bringing that back to this special connection, it at once becomes clear that a master-stroke of the enemy is to forestall us in that twofold direction. It is of no small importance to us to remember that our adversary does not wait until the hour of battle to set his forces in motion, but is always at work well ahead in anticipation of that hour. For him to do otherwise would be fatal to him. The same applies to us. We have found so often that when we have actually come to deal with a situation we are unequipped, for the essential equipment has been taken from us in advance. In that hour of emergency there is no facility for getting equipment, and we learn a bitter lesson by helplessness in a moment of great need or opportunity. The demand is that we should maintain a steady and strong life of prayer and in the Word when there is no particular call or need, and only thus shall we be on the spot and spiritually equipped when special need arises.

This unequipped condition represents spiritual dishonour and loss of position before God. Have you been struck with the change of title given to the Lord's people in these chapters? Sometimes they are called "the Hebrews"; sometimes "Israel." If you look closely you will find that the Spirit of the Lord calls them "Hebrews" when they are on the side of the Philistines, and "Israel" when they are not. They lose the dignity of that name "Israel"—a prince with God—when they are on the side of the Philistines. When they are not on that side the Lord, in grace, still calls them "Israel," even though they may be in a state of weakness, and far short of what He would have them be. But the Philistines always called them "Hebrews," and the Lord allows that title to stand when they are in Philistine hands. Their dignity as "a prince with God" has gone. What is it that makes us princes with God? It is that prayer-life and that life in the Word. We lose our dignity, our position and our ascendancy if the enemy robs us of our prayer-life and our life in the Word. Is that not true to experience? Of course it is! We were probably taught this when we were first saved, but there is a special and particular activity and determination of the enemy that we shall not pray nor get to God's Word in that larger realm of spiritual conflict and warfare where the whole testimony of the Lord is involved, in that "advance position" of the people of God where they get away from the earthlies as Christians and into the heavenlies as members of Christ's Body. By forestalling, preventing, frustrating and destroying that prayer-life and that life in the Word, he will very soon demoralise the Church and its members spiritually and rob them of their ascendancy.

May the Lord again bring to our hearts the stress and emphasis of the necessity for standing against the wiles of the devil! For they are directed, not only to oppose the prayer-life that we have, but to prevent us from having more of a prayer-life and a life in God's Word. Do suffer this repetition, for I am certain that it is needed. You realise that if the enemy can have his way you will not have a prayer-life. He will put anything and everything conceivable, natural and supernatural, in the way of prayer to prevent it, and in the way of your life in God's Word. These are the two mighty weapons of our warfare. There needs to be that aliveness and awakeness to the enemy's devices which put us also in the place of being able to forestall. The Apostle said, "We are not ignorant of his devices," and to be aware of what the enemy is out to do is half the battle. Oh! things come along so often to hinder prayer and our life in the Word! They come along in such a natural way, in such an unassuming and unpretentious way that they seem to be just the sort of things that would naturally happen and we expect them as the natural and, perhaps, to-be-expected things of our lives, but when we have gone on a few weeks we have found that our prayer-life has gone. How did it go? The enemy did not make a demonstration, nor come in some obvious way and announce that he was going to destroy our prayer-life with this or that, but it just happened.

WATCHING UNTO PRAYER

Watch *unto* prayer! Watching and praying in this sense is watching that you may pray, and watching against things that would stop you praying. And there must be a "lest" in us: ". . . lest Satan should get an advantage." You see, there is forestalling, prevention on our part, a standing against the wiles of the devil. We must have a fresh question about very ordinary, natural occurrences to see if there is not some weapon in them, some subtle device of the enemy to rob us of prayer. What is it that prevents the necessary, the essential prayer-life? Let us ask whether, after all, this is a thing about which we have to take a stand. Let us interrogate the thing. There has to be a greater watchfulness on our part against the strategic movements of the enemy in this direction lest we have our weapons stolen, or unsharpened. Well, I am sure that that is a note that needs to be rung out more and more. Do watch against the wiles of the enemy which are directed to take away your weapons of warfare, your prayer-life, and your life in the Word!

THE PLACE OF THE WORD IN PRAYER

These two things are joined together by the Holy Spirit: ". . . the sword of the Spirit which is the word of God; praying. . . ." The Holy Spirit has linked these two things closely. He might have put the sword in the beginning, or He might have put it somewhere else. You would have thought that the Apostle, taking in the Roman soldier as he stood there, seeing the girdle and the sword attached to the girdle, would have put the sword next to the girdle and said: "Having on the girdle of truth and the sword of the Spirit." But no. he has taken the girdle apart from the sword, and he gets on with the other parts of the panoply which are protective and defensive, and then he brings the two offensive things together at the end: the Word and prayer. They are both basic to a life, not only of being able to resist and have the defensive, but of actual victory, of overcoming, a life which is progressively aggressive. That is what comes out in I Samuel xiv. There was a sword with Jonathan, and there was a going up on his hands and feet. There was the activity of faith with the weapons of warfare on his part, and he overcame. We have said that it is a tremendous thing to be able to come with the Word of God backing up your prayer and to be able to say to the Lord: ". . . according to Thy Word." It is a great strength to be able to give the Lord His Word.

Let us take Psalm cxix by way of illustration and point out how frequently the Psalmist used that very phrase: "Quicken thou me according to thy word" . . . "Strengthen thou me according unto thy word." Then let us go on to fill in the word that corresponds with the petition: "But if the Spirit of him that raised up Jesus from the dead dwell in you, he that raised up Christ from the dead shall also quicken your mortal bodies by his Spirit that dwelleth in you." That is God's Word. It is a great thing to have the Word of God with you in prayer so that you may take it before the Lord. It gives you a place of strength. And it is also a great thing to be able to meet the enemy with the Word of God. The Lord Himself went into the wilderness and was tempted of the devil forty days. How did He meet the devil? Just with the Word of God! The Word of God was His weapon, and in the end He went through and overcame with that weapon. It is not that we meet the enemy objectively and begin to quote Scripture audibly to him. That may be necessary sometimes, and it may sometimes be good exercise to meet the enemy with an audible declaration of what God said, but, dear friends, it is necessary to have God's Word in our hearts so that we stand on the promises at all times of temptation and pressure and inward spiritual assault. We cannot stand on them if we do not know them. There is a great strengthening of position when you have the Word of God under your feet. A life in the Word is a very necessary thing for effectual prayer, and these two things go together in a positive, aggressive overcoming of the enemy.

PRAYER AND THE OVERCOMERS

Then this further thing comes out in this portion: That it is a small company which is there in that position. Jonathan says: "There is no restraint to Jehovah to save by many or by few" (I Samuel xiv. 6). It is a comparatively small company, but they represent the key to the whole situation for the Lord. They stand for the others in a relative position, and the Lord knows that the others would be hard put to it were it not for this small company. The Lord must have them for the sake of the rest. In the final issue the others come into the good which this small company has secured for them. It is what we have so often called "the overcomer company," a little group—comparatively speaking—who are standing their ground and maintaining their prayer-life and their life in the Word. These are the hope of the Lord's people, and the Lord's people have no hope apart from them. They are the Lord's key to the larger situation, and He must have them there for the sake of the rest. It is Benjamin, the link between the alienated and distant brethren and the one who is by the throne. It is the little one who is the occasion of their being brought into the full blessing. It is a privileged position, although it is difficult, costly and fraught with much travail and suffering. I must say more to myself, and you must say more to yourself, about the privilege of being an overcomer. I am afraid we are very much impressed with the suffering, the cost and the strenuousness of it, but it is the privilege of standing in a position which is going to mean much to the Lord in a great number of others who may not be in that position at present which ought to impress us.

If the Lord is to bring them, He does not do it, nor can He do it, directly. He does it through the ministration of those who are in that close fellowship with Him which represents a mighty victory over the strategy of the devil. It is a position of privilege, and that is why those who are going that way with the Lord become the central object of the devil's hate and malice, and why it is such a battle for them to maintain the position to which the Lord has called them. So much hangs upon them because of the responsibility which is theirs by reason of the link, and the value of that link, between them and—perhaps—multitudes of others. So Jonathan and his armour bearer (and this is the part of the story that I like so much) had a secret understanding. There were those two massive, forbidding crags on either side, and the Philistines were up there in the place of advantage. Their secret understanding was this: "If they say that they will come down to us, all right, we will wait for them. But if they say: 'Come up to us,' then we shall know that the Lord has delivered them into our hands." You would have thought that they would have put it the other way round, for then they would have had all the advantage and it would have been comparatively easy. But to believe that being called upon to scale those difficult, forbidding crags was the Lord's sign of victory, well, that makes the situation a very strong one, does it not? And the Philistines said: "Come up to us!" So Jonathan said: "The Lord hath delivered them into the hand of Israel," and as they advanced on hands and feet, which was very difficult climbing, they said: "The victory is ours." They were climbing in a victory, not for one. They had their weapons, they had faith in God, they stood in a victory and went on in that victory. And Jonathan hewed the Philistines down. They fell before him and his armour bearer slew them. Then the Lord sent an earthquake. When faith had gone as far as it could go, He co-operated and sent consternation among the Philistines. Then the poor, weak Hebrews saw their chance and turned on the Philistines. That was not very noble, nor very honourable, but Jonathan had been the instrument to bring them out of their weakness into strength, out of their indistinctiveness into a clear testimony, and out from the place where the clearness of their testimony was lost into a place where now they could take their stand. And a lot of people just need a Jonathan activity to bring them into a clear place. They will come in if the Lord has an instrument strong enough to meet the enemy on their behalf, but they will not come in until there is something that begins to smite the Philistines for them. Are you going to be one of these?

THE SIFTED COMPANY

I must close, but I do want to say just a word about the Lord sifting down until He gets something like that, about the necessity for reducing unto effectiveness. Jonathan, his armour bearer and a little company represented a sifted people. They were sifted down on this matter of faith in the Lord, and they were sifted right down to the ground where prayer and the Word were their very life. Gideon's company represented that: a sifted company brought down to a position of absolute faith in God, for that was what God was after— "Lest Israel vaunt themselves against me saying, Mine own hand hath saved me." They had to be right down to a place where God was their only estate, and faith in Him was the ground upon which they stood. Then every man had to put his sword on his side and stand in his place. You have a very good picture in Gideon's "three hundred" of a sifted company standing in prayer and the Word of God: "The Sword of the Lord"—the Word of the Lord. The Lord saw to it that all who had heart trouble went home, for a fearful heart is useless. Faith is necessary here. A divided heart is no use and disqualifies its owner. A fearful heart was the first test, and a great host went home because they were fearful-hearted. A divided heart was the next test, and those who went down on their hands and knees to drink the water showed that they were not wholly ready for this business. Those who stood and lapped out of their hands were eager, for they kept on their feet, and this drinking was only done because it was necessary.

Those who lapped were of undivided heart and were wholly in this business. A divided heart disqualifies, and the Lord sees to it that divided hearts are sifted out. At last He gets His company, and they are all with Him in the faith of the Son of God, having a life of deep fellowship with Him in prayer and in the Word. That will always be a sifted company, and we should not be discouraged or think that a strange thing has happened when the Lord begins to sift out and many go home. That is the Lord's way of getting effectiveness. He must sift. He Himself, while here on the earth, gave us very much in His personal teaching in this very connection. He calls, and the reactions to His call are: "Lord, suffer me first to go and bury my father." Then there are other interests: "I have bought five yoke of oxen and I go to prove them"; "I have married a wife"; "I have bought a piece of ground, and I must needs go and see it." That is a divided heart! And then we have His own word: "If any man cometh unto me, and hateth not his own father, and mother, and wife, and children, and brethren, and sisters, yea and his own life also, he cannot be my disciple"; "Whosoever doth not bear his own cross, and come after me, cannot be my disciple." That is no faint heart! The Lord calls for that, and by the three hundred He delivers the Midianites into our hands, and He saves Israel. They are the salvation of the rest.

OUR WARFARE

T. Austin-Sparks

Our Warfare

PREFACE

THE following chapters were given as messages in conference at Honor Oak, London. Whilst a considerable background of spiritual experience in the service of God lies behind them, the form in which the messages were given was prompted by a reading of that great volume by Field-Marshal Sir William Slim—*Defeat into Victory*. Every chapter really needs a book to itself, as there is far more unwritten than is contained in this small book.

At the present time, as the consummation of the age draws nearer and the final settlement is in view, the battle which divides the universe into only two contending kingdoms is raging fiercely and relentlessly. It is therefore necessary that everything possible be done to inform, instruct, counsel, warn, encourage, and support those who are involved and affected. We appeal to all who read these pages, not to approach their message in any attitude of mere interest or theory, but to study them as though they themselves were directly involved in the tremendous issues at stake.

To leaders, and others in responsibility, we especially appeal, that they would consider what is here in the light of their own present experience of a " great warfare " (Dan. x. 1). If leaders would but get together to review this whole matter of the spiritual conflict, more might be accomplished in the direction of turning Defeat into Victory.

Should Field-Marshal Slim's eye ever catch sight of this volume, I hope that—rather than resenting it—he will be glad that his great reversal in the earthly realm may serve, even in a small way, to affect the so-much-greater realm of the eternal and heavenly.

T. AUSTIN-SPARKS

FOREST HILL,
LONDON,
1960.

CONTENTS

CHAPTER 1

SUPREME COMMAND

*"For though we walk in the flesh, we do not war ac-
cording to the flesh (for the weapons of* OUR WARFARE
*are not of the flesh, but mighty before God to the cast-
ing down of strong holds)"* (II Corinthians x. 3, 4).

ALTHOUGH the Bible contains so much about the
warfare of God's people, and although we as His people
may have had much teaching on the subject, it would
probably be true to say that we have largely failed to
apply the instruction we have received—to situations,
to circumstances, to happenings ; and that this accounts
for many of our troubles, individually and collectively.
While there is much for which the enemy is not to be
blamed as the first cause, but which is due rather to our
own foolishness or unguardedness—our *own* faults—
yet there is still very much more that is attributable to
his interest, to his interference, to his action. Our need
to-day is not so much to be informed as to the reality of
spiritual conflict—we know that to be a fact!—as to
be more alive to the extra factor lying behind situations, the situations with which we are trying, with so
little success, to cope. We try to cope with *things*, as
though they were everything, and so often we miss their
real underlying significance.

9

What we need, therefore, is understanding and wisdom—for wisdom means the ability to apply knowledge —wisdom as to this whole spiritual campaign, our warfare and its principles. But let me say at once: we are not embarking upon a study of Satan, or demons, or demonology! It is a very favourite trap of the enemy to get people occupied and obsessed with himself, and, by the help of God, we are not going to fall into that. Our object is to study spiritual warfare itself, as viewed mainly from the Lord's side.

Let me here put in a brief word as to the origin, or occasion, of the messages here presented. Not having a great deal of time for general reading, I make it a matter of prayer that all my serious reading may be spiritually profitable and of value—whether it be reading a spiritual book or not. Just before leaving on a recent voyage to the United States, I was exercised in this manner, when a book came to my notice, and an extract from it arrested me. It was the record of the great South-East Asia campaign in the second World War, and was entitled: *Defeat into Victory*. It is a heavy volume of 550 closely printed pages, with an added 23 for index. But having been arrested by this extract, I took the book with me and read it on the voyage, making careful notes. And as I read, I was more and more impressed that through it the Lord was leading me to something—that He had a message in it for His people.

There is enough in this volume to provide material for lengthy meditation. Much of it could be of real value, in this day particularly, to the people of God, and especially to those who have a sense of responsibility for the Lord's interests. For our present consideration we shall only pick out a few of the most vital and essential points; but, when I mention a few of the subjects covered in that volume, you will recognise its very great possibilities. Here are some examples: Supreme Command; Staff and Personnel—with all the order flowing therefrom; Loyalty Upward to the Top and Downward to the Bottom; Training; Provisioning; Diversity of Function in Unity of Object; Intelligence; Morale; Flexibility; The Great Objective—on the one side, of the Supreme Command, on the other side, of the enemy. The discerning will recognise that these ten points could provide scope for valuable consideration for a long time. If all that were translated and interpreted into spiritual terms, and the Lord's people were in possession of such strategy spiritually, what a tremendously efficient people they would be!

Now, it must be remembered that this is a volume of lessons learned, and that most of these great lessons were learned through defeat. That is, that the terrible story of the first South-East Asia campaign—with its devastation, retreat, loss of tens of thousands of lives, and all that goes with that—became history because the vital factors mentioned were either absent or inadequate or in disorder. Surely this provides us with a field for instruction. Should not the people of God and their leaders learn from their defeats and their set-backs at least as quickly and thoroughly?

HIGHER DIRECTION

We begin with the main thing: 'Supreme Command'. And here the writer of this book uses an expression which I like very much. He calls it: 'Higher Direction'. That is fine! That gets us there! 'Supreme Command'—'Higher Direction'. In that connection there occurs the following sentence: 'The first step towards ultimate victory was the setting up of the Supreme Command, controlling all allied forces of land, sea and air.' What a statement that is when we carry it into the spiritual realm! The turning of a terrible catastrophe, tragedy, defeat into a glorious and consummate victory is here said to have had as its first step—perhaps its main step—the setting up of the Supreme Command. This will resolve itself into several quite distinct matters for our recognition. But this document proves in itself (of course in its own realm, here on the earth), beyond any question or room for doubt, that everything centres in and hangs upon Supreme Command, or Higher Direction.

This was something that seemed to have been overlooked, or had at most been regarded as optional; but now, here is this overwhelming weight of evidence and proof which says that it is absolutely essential. This Higher Direction, this Supreme Command, is not mere idealism, it is not just something official—it is vital. In this case it was clearly demonstrated that the saving of multitudes of lives, of months and years of time, of honour, liberty, and victory, all hung upon this one matter. Lives were lost, time was thrown away, honour besmirched, liberty sacrificed, victory turned to defeat, and possession turned to loss and nothing, because of the absence of this Supreme Command, this Higher Direction.

And in the light of two thousand years of history, no one will think it exaggeration to say that that is largely the story of the Church: lives, souls, lost; time given away; the honour of the Lord and His Church dragged in the mud. Liberty, victory, fulness?—no, there has not been a great deal of these. And may it not be traceable to this same thing: an undervaluing of, or maladjustment to, the Higher Direction, the Supreme Command? It proved, in the war, to be essential and vital and not open to any option; and in the Church there must be One over all, above all, in all, and through all, and *only* One in that position.

MUTUALITY OF UNDERSTANDING

The matter of the necessity for Supreme Command is analysed, and one thing that comes out of that analysis is this: there must be mutual knowledge and understanding between the Supreme Command and the Forces. Here is a quotation: ' A Supreme Commander, if he is wise, will see that his troops know him '. Much is said about that. The Supreme Commander is not just a name, a figurehead; some remote person somewhere, with his hands upon everything, someone talked about. He is personally known. This book shows how the

Supreme Commander made it his business to get down among and be known to his troops, to have a personal touch ; he knew his people and they knew him.

This is a simple but profoundly wise statement. What does it carry with it? It carries with it the basic principle that the Lord's first need is to bring us to know Him. Before we can do anything, we must *know* the Lord. There is no victory without that. Our knowledge of the Lord will determine the measure of our progress in this warfare. The fact is that it is so often for want of that knowledge that we are held up or defeated. To put that the other way round : it is so often just when we come into a new knowledge of the Lord that we go on in a new way of victory. The Lord takes infinite pains to get His people to know Him.

This takes us back into the New Testament. In his letter to the Ephesians—that great battle letter (for such it is)—Paul puts tremendous weight upon the word ' *know* '. Right at the beginning, he prays : " that ye may know what is the hope of his calling " ; " that ye may know . . . the riches . . . of his inheritance in the saints " ; " that ye may know . . . the exceeding greatness of his power " (i. 18, 19). " That ye may *know* . . . " ! That word ' know ' is a governing word in this whole matter of our warfare. Tried warrior that he was, Paul laid the greatest stress on knowing the Lord. " That I may know him . . . ", he wrote elsewhere (Phil. iii. 10). He said that that was far more important than all the other things that are regarded as important by men. He contrasts that knowledge with all that he had had previously—a great world-wealth of inheritance. ' But ', said he, ' I count all that as nothing—as refuse—*that I may know Him* '. That made Paul the warrior he was, and from him has come so much for the Church militant.

' The Commander, if he is wise, will see that his own troops know him.' If that could be said of a mortal man here on this earth, *our* Supreme Commander is no less wise. It is the utmost wisdom—we say it reverently—on the part of the Lord to ensure that our knowledge of Him is ever on the increase.

The Marks of a Supreme Commander

In the next place, let us look at the characteristics required of a Supreme Commander, and their effect upon his forces.

(a) HE HAS A CLEARLY DEFINED OBJECTIVE

Firstly, the Supreme Commander should have a clearly defined objective. We ought to know, from the New Testament, that *our* Supreme Commander has that ; but it is of infinite importance that we know also, with Him, what that clearly defined objective is. That this is not so, accounts for so much of our weakness, resulting in such loss and delay. How many of God's people could express in a few words, from the New Testament, exactly what is the supreme objective of the Lord? Let us challenge ourselves: could we do that? On half a sheet of notepaper, could we put down what the Lord's supreme objective is? If not, we are at a loss, in limitation, in this battle. Think what it would mean if a sufficient number of the Lord's people were solidly bound together by a clear and unquestioning apprehension of the Lord's ultimate objective! He has made this known to His forces; we have it in His Word: " To make all men see . . . " (Eph. iii. 9). Do you remember what it is they are to see?

(b)   HE HAS A CLEAR PLAN FOR REACHING HIS OBJECTIVE

Secondly, the Supreme Commander should have a comprehensive and detailed vision of how he will reach that objective. Our Supreme Commander, without any doubt, has a detailed vision of how He will reach His objective, and therefore we need to be instructed in that in like manner. In other words, we should know, with the Lord, where we are going and what we are after. Are we ' beating about the bush ', as we say ; are we going round in circles ; are we just experimenting? What proportion of all our efforts and expenditure is achieving anything really effective? It is the need of the people of God to be moving together in the integration of a single vision—the vision of the objective and of how God intends to reach it. This is not knowledge beyond our possessing. We have the documents in our hands, if only we would study them and pray for spiritual illumination on this matter. As God's people, we need to be deeply exercised as to how the battle is going. We must first of all know what is God's supreme object-

ive—not just what is incidental or subsidiary ; and then,
if God has given any light in His Word as to the principles, the ways, the means, by which He intends to
reach that end, we must make it our business to know
these things also.

(c) HE HAS COMMAND OF ADEQUATE RESOURCES

Thirdly, a Supreme Commander must have command
of adequate resources to carry the campaign through.
That is searching. We need, of course, have no question on that score so far as *our* Supreme Commander is
concerned. We can and must be perfectly at rest on that
matter, deeply and quietly and finally assured that He
has all the resources at His command for seeing this
through. The book to which I have been referring has
a long and terrible story to tell of disaster resulting from
inadequacy and insufficiency of available resources.
There is, as we have said, no question about the adequacy of our Lord's resources, but we surely need to
come into the good of that. Again we refer to this great
battle document, the letter to the Ephesians: " Blessed
be the God and Father of our Lord Jesus Christ, who
hath blessed us with every spiritual blessing in the
heavenly places in Christ" (i. 3). Paul had a wonderful
apprehension of the resources available for himself and
the Church in Christ. It was that apprehension that
called forth some of his most joyful superlatives: " O
the depth of the riches " (Rom. xi. 33) ; " the unsearch-
able riches " (Eph. iii. 8) ; and others.

B

A further point of vital importance is this: that, while the Commander may have all these resources at his disposal, it is a terrible thing if something gets in between the Commander and the Army, so that the supplies for the latter are not forthcoming. Of course, that opens up another great subject—that of Communications. But for our warfare there must be no gap whatever, whether of doubt, misapprehension, distance, or anything else, between what is there with Him and in Him for us, and what we are knowing of these resources. Again I say that much weakness and defeat, individually and collectively, is due to the needless poverty of God's people, who seem to be drawing upon and enjoying so little of their inheritance. Many do not know of the resources available. No wonder the enemy is having so much of his own way!

(d)   HE HAS THE CONFIDENCE OF HIS FORCES

Fourthly, the Commander must have—' A staff and Army having implicit confidence in him, and willing to subordinate all personal and sectional considerations to him—absolute confidence in his judgment, his wisdom, his generalship, even when his ways are not understood.' If men can talk like that about one another, when stating the essentials of a victorious campaign on this earth level, surely that is something that we ought to understand and carry over into the spiritual—' A staff ' (what is the spiritual equivalent of this?) ' and Army, having implicit confidence in the Supreme Command, in His understanding, in His wisdom, in His judgment, in His generalship, even when His ways are not understood.'

Sometimes He commands and His commands are difficult to understand; sometimes His ways are really "past finding out"; sometimes it almost seems that what He is doing, or essaying to do, will prove completely disastrous. Nevertheless, when we cannot or do not understand, when His ways run counter to our best natural judgment, then is the test: have we implicit confidence in Him? When He seems to be doing nothing, when He seems to be absent from the field, when His ways are so strange and mysterious, have we implicit confidence in His judgment, His wisdom? It is a test, is it not?

But remember again, that that whole campaign, both in its first phase of disaster and defeat and in its second phase of glorious full victory, hung upon that—a willingness in all concerned to subordinate all personal and sectional interests to the Supreme Command and give him unquestioned leadership. And a like unquestioned devotion on our part is surely called for. Nothing could serve the enemy's purposes better than for us to have a question about our Commander's leadership, a doubt about His generalship, His wisdom; that would just sabotage the whole campaign. They are words easily said, perhaps, but that is the subtlety of the battle we are in. Very often the battle has to be won inwardly before it can be won outwardly, and the inward battle circles around this question of implicit confidence in our

Lord, unquestioning devotion to Him, the subduing of everything to His Lordship. Until we are settled on this point, we are a weakness in the Army, and we shall not be in the way of victory.

(e)   HE HAS THE LOYALTY OF HIS FORCES

Fifth, the Supreme Commander must have the absolute loyalty of all concerned. Much is made of that. Moreover, there must be not only loyalty to the Supreme Command, but loyalty also to all appointed by the Supreme Command, and loyalty amongst all ranks— loyalty, in fact, to the whole ' outfit '. What a vital matter this is! May not the explanation of a great deal of painful history be traced to some measure of disloyalty on our part—if not to our Lord, then to one another, to the Lord's people? There needs to be a new loyalty all round, upward and downward, and a committal to the Lord's supreme purpose: which means that anybody and everybody in that purpose is our comrade, and we are committed to him and to her.

THE SPIRITUAL PARALLEL AND APPLICATION

Now these five characteristics of a Commander, embodying as they do the great strategic principles of this campaign, must be interpreted and translated into spiritual strategy. There must be the supreme value of a focal point of confidence and co-ordination. This is exactly what was established in the resurrection, ascension, and exaltation of the Lord Jesus: " . . . made him to sit at his right hand . . . far above all rule, and authority . . . and every name that is named " (Eph. i. 20, 21). There is the Supreme Command, the Higher Direction, the focal point of all confidence and co-ordination. Paul said much about this matter of co-ordination in the Head. Everything is " fitly framed " ; every joint ' makes supply ' (Eph. iv. 16) ; everything works harmoniously together and makes its contribution, when it is focused in the Head, and when He is " head over all things to the church " (Eph. i. 22, 23). I know I have changed the metaphor from the Army to the Body, but the principle is the same.

But although it was in the ascension and exaltation of the Lord Jesus that this focal point of all confidence and relatedness was established, it only came into operation on the day of Pentecost. The ascension and exaltation of Jesus is, in fact, the explanation of the presence of the Holy Spirit (John vii. 39). Pentecost, after all, is the counterpart of Joshua's experience before Jericho. Joshua, lifting up his eyes, saw a man standing with his sword drawn, and he "went unto him, and said unto him, Art thou for us, or for our adversaries? And he said, Nay ; but as captain of the host of the Lord am I now come " (Josh. v. 13, 14). Joshua prostrated himself, took off his shoes, and worshipped—he went down before that One. That represents Pentecost in its outworking. The Captain of the hosts of the Lord has come to take over. The Holy Spirit is here in the Name and function of the exalted Lord. Which raises the whole

question of how far the Church and every individual—
the Army and every member of it—is under that one
government of the Holy Spirit. That, and that only,
will ensure a victorious campaign, a turning of defeat
into victory.

THE CHALLENGE OF 'THE SUPREME COMMAND'

This matter of the Lord being in His place has a very
wide application. There are quite a number of people
who recognise and accept the leadership of the Lord
Jesus, in name and phraseology and profession, but who
in themselves are a definite contradiction to it. There
are quite a lot of 'free-lances' in this war—people moving on their own in an unrelated way—who strongly,
yes, vehemently declare, 'Jesus is Lord': but, if they
only knew their own hearts, *they* are lord of their lives,
of their ways; *their* likes and dislikes and preferences
govern. Yes, there are those who, while acclaiming
Jesus 'Lord' and speaking about 'surrender' (a great
word, 'surrender'!), are nevertheless strong objectors
to any kind of discipline, any kind of government, control or direction. They repudiate all that sort of thing;
they say: 'I am *free* in the Lord!' The Lord's own
appointed under-officers are either ignored or insulted,
or at least not honoured.

This is just playing into the hands of the enemy. All
wisdom is against it, and we have a mighty weight of
evidence in the Word of God that it is not God's mind.
God has, first of all, His Supreme Command, His

Higher Direction, but He has also under that Command His ' subordinate staff ', if we may use the term—His ordered system of delegated spiritual responsibility ; and this must be recognised. If it is not, the Army is held up, and the enemy is given just what he wants. Moreover, there is complete confusion and frustration in the ranks.

There are, on the other hand, those people who have put legalism in the place of the Holy Spirit, who have substituted legality for light and love, made *it* the Supreme Command, constituted a system the final authority. As we know, Paul encountered this legalism in the battle ; and, if we may judge from the letter to the Galatians, it was this that drew out his fighting spirit more than anything else. ' Let him be anathema ! I repeat : Let him be anathema !' (Gal. i. 8, 9). This was directed against anyone who would put a system in the place of the Holy Spirit.

Others are like the Corinthians who, in their spiritual disorder and weakness and defeat, were actuated solely by natural preferences, natural judgment and natural choices amongst men and things. Their selection and allegiance is according to human thoughts and judgments, likes and dislikes. If such considerations get their way, ' Corinthian ' conditions will prevail. And let us remember that Paul headed up the whole Corinthian situation into the threat of a repetition of what happened to Israel in the wilderness, with all those armies of the first generation (I Cor. x. 1 — 11). They perished there ; ' and ', says Paul, ' that is the way you are going, unless you see to this one thing, that Jesus Christ is Lord. You must not be governed by your own preferences, your likes and your dislikes, your judgments and your choices. Unless you give the Holy Spirit His rightful place, in charge of your soul with all its activities, that is the end to which you will come—you will perish in the wilderness!'

May the Lord find us recognising the "Supreme Command": obedient to Him, and loyal both to Him and to one another.

THE TWOFOLD MAIN OBJECTIVE

" For though we walk in the flesh, we do not war according to the flesh (for the weapons of our warfare are not of the flesh, but mighty before God to the casting down of strong holds) ; casting down imaginations, and every high thing that is exalted against the knowledge of God, and bringing every thought into captivity to the obedience of Christ " (II Corinthians x. 3 — 5).

WE pass now to the next of the vital things in the warfare—The Twofold Main Objective : the twofold main objective of God, the twofold main objective of the enemy. This great campaign has two aspects : one is primary ; the other is secondary. One is the final supreme issue ; the other is the means or instrument for its attainment. We shall consider both of these things, but mainly the second.

First of all, the supreme objective of God—and therefore of Satan—in its primary aspect, may be summed up in what is meant by 'the Throne'. The rights, the claims, and the aims of the Throne ; the sphere and range of its influence ; the honour that is bound up with it ; the government that it implies ; the prosperity and well-being of the people over whom it is set : all these things go to make up what is meant by the Throne. That,

supremely and finally, is God's objective. All those
things are but aspects of God's interests and activities
and concern in this great campaign. The Throne, with
all that meaning, is involved in this tremendous conflict.

It is, therefore, easy to see what is the enemy's objective : it is the reverse or contrary of what we have just
stated. He aims at the repudiation of the rights and
claims and interests of that Throne ; the curtailment,
and, if possible, the complete removal, of the influence
of that Throne ; the depriving of the people under it of
their prosperity and well-being. All this is what the
enemy is set upon ; and his consummate object, along all
those lines, is himself to take over everything—even the
very Throne itself.

In making these statements, I am, of course, keeping
close to the Scriptures and close to history. We ought to
realise what it is that we are involved in and what we are
up against.

THE CHURCH THE INSTRUMENT OF THE THRONE

With that brief word on the primary aspect of the
supreme objective, we pass to what I have called the
secondary aspect : but it is only secondary in that it is
dependent upon the primary. This—the means for the
attainment of the supreme objective—is the instrument
in which all those features and factors of the Throne are
vested, to which they are committed and entrusted. In
order to repudiate the rights, the claims, and the interests of the Throne ; to bring dishonour and reproach

upon it; to curtail or wipe out the sphere of its influence; to rob its subjects of their prosperity and well-
being: in order to do all this, the enemy must destroy
or put out of action the whole force in the field—the
vehicle and means of operation of that Throne, the
instrumentality of its effectiveness. That vehicle is the
Church. It is to the Church that all those interests of the
Throne are committed; it is in the Church that they are
vested.

But let us not consider that word 'Church' objectively: let us bring it right to ourselves, and apply every
word personally. In this matter we need not fear that we
shall be too subjective, too self-occupied or introspective.
Our conception of 'the Church' must not be of something vague or mystical. Wherever even two or three
are gathered into the Name, there is the Church in real,
though minute, representation, and everything begins
there. And so it is that these tremendous things in relation to the Throne, as the supreme and ultimate objective of God and the enemy, are focused upon us as a part
of the Church.

THE GROANING OF THE CREATION RELATED TO THE CHURCH

There is a sense in which it can be said that all the
trouble centres in the Church. Like the prophets, one of
whom was addressed as the "troubler of Israel" (I Kings
xviii. 17), the Church is the 'troubler', not only of
Israel, but of all the nations and of the kingdom of

Satan. Even in our own day, there is a great deal that
corresponds to those tremendous convulsions in Egypt
that led up to the ejection of Israel. That is the explanation of much that is taking place in the nations to-day.
Convulsions in the nations—what for? Well, Paul says
that "the whole creation groaneth and travaileth "—
why? It is waiting for "the revealing of the sons of
God " (Rom. viii. 22, 19). It is toward the birth, the
manifestation, the precipitation, of that which God has
ultimately in view, that there are these convulsions in
the nations. That may seem a big thing to say, and
indeed, if we had not Bible ground for saying it, we
should be saying something too big. But all those convulsions in Egypt were because of a people in their
midst who had to be got out—and the power behind
that kingdom was not prepared to let them out! The
hierarchy of wicked spirits that were the real rulers of
the land of Egypt did not want that people out, because
they knew that the emancipation of Israel would constitute the greatest possible menace to their hold upon
Egypt and other nations of the earth.

Centuries later, when Israel was again in captivity,
there were upheavals in Babylon. Through the prophet
the Lord said : " I have sent to Babylon, and will bring
down all their nobles " (Is. xliii. 14, marg.)—what for?
To get the people out. Convulsions in Babylon! And
there are plenty of convulsions in the nations of the
world just now. I believe that the trouble is largely
because of the Church. Once the Church is extricated
and out, while there will be disintegration, judgment

and so on, Satan will breathe more freely here. But, whether this be a right interpretation or not concerning national and international upheavals and tumults—and I think it is—there is no question whatever as to whether or not it is true about the kingdom of Satan. The cause of the trouble, disturbance and upheaval *there* is this other force that is in the field. *It* is the troubler.

THE CONFLICT FOCUSED UPON A TRUE EXPRESSION OF CHRIST

Now, immediately there is a movement towards the practical expression of anything approximating to the Church as it is revealed in the New Testament—especially as revealed in such fullness through the letters of the Apostle Paul—disturbances take place which are more than human, for which there seems to be no rational explanation. This should give food for thought. It is profoundly significant that no comparable spiritual disturbance arises when Christianity is anything short of this. There may be a presentation of doctrine without organic expression: that does not worry Satan very much. We may be orthodox and as sound as it is possible to be, and still not meet the full force of Satan's objection. But let an organic expression of the Church for practical purposes be brought into view, and you will find trouble coming from everywhere and nowhere!

Again, when Christianity is a formal, ecclesiastical system, without spiritual power, Satan does not trouble either himself or it one little bit. When Christianity is a mystical, aesthetic, artistic, soulish imitation of spirituality, Satan is not at all troubled—rather very pleased. He is delighted when mysticism is interpreted as spirituality, and multitudes are held in the illusion. When there is profession without organic reality, there is no trouble. When there is but a name, a title, a designation, without correspondence to the Divine pattern, it is left to go on its way unchallenged. When there is an organization, an institution, without a heavenly nature and spiritual character, its course is more or less unchecked. But let the Lord bring into view something that really sets forth Christ corporately, and then there is trouble—trouble, such as we have said, that cannot be explained along any natural, human lines at all.

The enemy is, in fact, bitterly opposed to any real, living, organic expression of Christ in his territory. For such an expression really represents the Throne of God, in effect and in impact, and therefore there will be trouble. The forces of Satan in any and every way are set against the realisation of that. From apostolic times until now, there never was an expression, however small, of the Church in its heavenly, spiritual and eternal character, that was not the object of the most determined and many-sided effort of Satan to destroy it. There is a great deal of history bound up in that statement. This is, after all, just the meaning of Ephesians vi. 12 and onward, is it not? "Our wrestling is not against flesh and blood, but against the principalities . . . powers . . . world-rulers of this darkness . . . spiritual hosts of wickedness in the heavenly places." But long before Paul wrote those words, Paul's Master, the Lord Jesus Himself, had spoken about this great Satanic opposition. He spoke of " the gates of Hades "—which I understand to mean ' the councils of death '—as being active with the determination to prevail against the Church.

Now it would be far too big a matter for us to try to range the strategies and tactics of the enemy in this connection. But let us note two things.

The first is that the Throne—with all that that implies—is most closely affected by the representation of Christ—whether good, or bad—that is found in the Church ; that is, according to whether Christ is, in fact, represented or *mis*represented. The Throne is affected more directly and immediately by the Church than by anything else. That is the fact.

Secondly, we need always to remember that secondary causes are not primary causes. Would that we might be more alive and alert to that ! We are caught almost every time on that matter. Things happen : people behave in such and such a way ; circumstances arise ; there is strain, tumult, tension and what not ; and we attribute everything to the secondary cause—to the person or the persons concerned, to the circumstances, the conditions, or whatever it might be. We do not go straight to the first cause. We fail to recognise that behind everything is this sinister force ; behind that person's behaviour there is something more ; behind all this there is something at work with no less an objective than the undermining of that Throne—its honour, its

glory, its range and sphere of influence, its rights and its
claims and the well-being of its people. In many a little,
seemingly casual, ' happening ', it is nothing less than
that which is involved : but we take it on as something
in itself, and wrongly make the secondary cause the first.

In the previous chapter I said that there are many
things that we should attribute to our own foolishness,
rather than to the Devil. But there is this other realm,
and lest you think I am exaggerating, let me bring you
to the Word. Some of these so-called secondary causes
—failure to recognise which leads to the defeat of the
Church, or the set-back of the Army—are actually
found in this letter to the Ephesians, the great warfare
letter of the Church.

' EPHESIANS '—THE WARFARE LETTER
" THE EXCEEDING GREATNESS OF THE REVELATION "

In the three great chapters at the beginning of this
letter, we have presented the Church of God ; that
marvellous vessel, that Divine masterpiece, born in the
counsels of God in eternity past. I fear that the chapter
divisions sometimes prevent us from recognising the
continuity, the unity of the whole document, and from
passing naturally from one stage to another. But here
we have the presentation of this great thing—it is as it
were brought out from eternity and shown to us. And
this presentation, comprehended in a few hundred
words of human language, is something which for well-
nigh twenty centuries has defeated and defied every

attempt to fathom it, and to-day it is drawing out and extending men more than ever before. That is not exaggeration. Can *you* fathom it? Look again at some of the shortest sentences in those first three chapters—they will defeat you!

Now, the subject-matter contained in the second half (chapters iv — vi) of the letter ranges itself into four sections, the first two short, the last two long. Whilst we shall review them very brieflly, let us not fail to apply them.

(a) "WALKING WORTHILY OF THE CALLING"

Paul, having thus presented the Church, now, by a perfectly natural movement, passes to a consideration of the practical consequences. His opening words are full of challenge and test. " I . . . beseech you to walk worthily of the calling wherewith ye were called, with all lowliness and meekness, with patience, forbearing one another in love, eager to maintain the unity of the Spirit . . . " (Eph. iv. 1 — 3 ; vs. 3 R.S.V.). Now, these are things that are directly related to certain very common ' secondary causes '. But this whole immense purpose, that has been unveiled, divulged, as out from eternity, rests for its true expression, for the proof that it is no mere vision, no mere idea or ideal, but a reality—it all rests upon our ' walking worthily '. It rests upon our walk. Everything depends upon our lowliness, meekness, patience, our forbearing one another in love, our eagerness to keep the unity. Does that challenge us? But

C

those are our spiritual weapons in the field, and much grace and faith is needed if they are to be used effectively.

Oh, the provocations, the annoyances, the irritations! —all that comes upon us in the course of a day to make our life a contradiction and our walk unworthy! The challenge to lowliness! The snare of self-assertiveness, loudness, occupying the limelight, bringing ourselves into view, drawing attention to ourselves, wanting people to take note of us—all that and a thousand other things contrary to lowliness and meekness! "With patience, forbearing one another, giving diligence to keep the unity"—so our Revised Version; the Revised Standard Version has: "eager to maintain the unity" —eager, *eager* to maintain the unity! Ah, that is a battle, a tremendous battle, a desperate part of the conflict. The enemy is particularly persistent and persevering with things like these, because they make a caricature of the Church, and they touch the Throne.

But every one of those things can be carried into the realm of what we call 'secondary causes'. 'But *he* did so and so . . . *she* said so and so . . . and I got upset . . . and I have a right to be upset!' That is looking at things as they appear on the surface, instead of looking right through the things and seeing something else. Ah, yes ; if we look deeper, we shall find that there is a primary cause. Often the very timing of the thing proves that— it is so sinister and so uncanny. Or a consideration of where the attack comes from, or the why of it, may reveal its true source. But we are not always alive to that.

We get caught in the thing and defeated, and all our wonderful conceptions of this marvellous Church count for nothing—they just go to pieces.

(b) "THE UNITY OF THE FAITH"

We turn to the second section, chapter iv. 4—6. Here, quite briefly, the thing challenged is the peril of making something extra to Christ the basis of unity. "There is . . . one Lord, one faith, one baptism, one God and Father of all". That is the basis of unity. But it is possible to make a division by means of that, if you are so minded. I have heard people ask, 'What does the "one baptism" mean?' Some say: 'Of course it means the baptism of the Holy Spirit', and others: 'Of course it means the baptism of water'—and at once there is a division on the very fundamentals of unity! I do not think that either of those interpretations necessarily applies here. What it does mean, I believe, is this: that 'we were all baptized in one Spirit into one Body' (I Cor. xii. 13), and the "one baptism" is baptism into Christ. You can say that it is by the Holy Spirit, if you like. I challenge you to say that it is by water. No one is baptized into Christ by water. They may testify to baptism into Christ by means of water, but that is another thing. The one baptism is that, when we believed, we were all baptized in one Spirit into one Body.

The issue, then, is: Are you in Christ? Have you been baptized into Christ? That is fundamental to unity. If we make something more to be a basis of unity, then

we split the unity, we destroy it, we contradict the truth
of the oneness. This foundation is sufficient. If we knew
all that is included in this " one Lord, one faith, one
baptism, one God and Father ", we should have enough.
If we live according to that, we take a lot of ground
from under the enemy. Immediately we begin to add to
that, as the basis of unity, then we begin to give the
whole position away. Our special interpretations and
teachings and doctrines have no value whatsoever as a
basis of unity. All that matters is the foundation, and
that is sufficient.

(c) HOLINESS OF LIFE

The third section, chapter iv. 17 – v. 20, is a long
section, containing a great many things and covering
much ground. But if you read the section through, you
will find that it all amounts to this: holiness of living,
personally and relatedly. And remember that the enemy
is against that. He triumphed in the greater part of the
churches in Asia along that line. The chief thing that the
Lord had to lay at their door, in His messages through
the Apostle John, was corruption, defilement, wrong in
the moral life. Paul, here, has much to say on this matter
of holiness, first in ourselves individually and then between us and others. For if the enemy can touch us and
spoil us on that ground, he has struck at the Throne: he
has brought reproach upon it, he has limited the sphere
of its influence, he has robbed us and others of our
inheritance. And that is searching!

(d) HUMAN RELATIONSHIPS

Finally, we have the fourth section: chapter v. 21 —
vi. 9. This section deals, in the main, with domestic relationships—husbands to wives; wives to husbands;
children to parents; parents to children; servants to
masters; masters to servants. And these relationships
present peculiarly good opportunities for enemy activity.
But here, again, we are so insensible to reality that we
habitually make these secondary causes the primary
ones. How often it is that provocations and strains and
difficulties in these family and social relationships have
the effect of putting us spiritually right out of action, of
crippling or even nullifying our spiritual life. And,
again, these things often come up in such an uncanny
way. Can we not learn this lesson from our defeats? So
often the enemy comes along, either through the wife
or the husband, in relation to something of very great
spiritual interest that is about to emerge. We may know
nothing of this—but he knows! The same thing may
happen with regard to the children; the Devil can play
many tricks through them.

So the whole range of these relationships is brought
in here. The point is: we must not always lose our heads
and straightaway blame the persons concerned. If we do,
we have lost the battle. Let us first of all, if opportunity
offers, go quietly away and say: 'Now, what is the
enemy up to—what is he after? There is probably something more here than just this upset, however real and
justified it may seem. It is quite true that this and that

has happened ; it is not imagination : but is this the beginning and the end of it? Cannot this be completely
destroyed from behind? Cannot this be dealt with at
Headquarters?' You see what I mean. On a hasty and
superficial view, we might take all these things for
primary causes. But quiet and prayerful reflection will
enable us to recognise them as in all probability only
secondary ones. We must not make secondary causes the
criterion, but must get behind them to the hidden primary cause—in this case the activity of the great enemy.

REVELATION AND WARFARE RELATED

Now you will notice that the four passages, or sections, that we have just considered are placed between
Paul's mighty unveiling and presentation of the Church
and his great *exposé* of the spiritual warfare over it. A
significant position! Here is this matchless thought of
God, the Church, presented. Here, at the other end, is
the warfare with myriads of evil spirits. And, sand-
wiched right in between, we find husband and wife, and
wife and husband ; children and parents, and so on. Do
you protest that there is no connection ! ? I submit, in
reply, that the " therefore " of chapter iv, verse 1, holds
this middle section, concerning our conduct and behaviour, in direct relation to the preceding revelation ;
saying in effect : ' *Therefore,* unless you watch these
relationships, all that revelation counts for nothing !'

And the " Finally " of chapter vi (which word does
not mean ' Last of all ' ; it means ' Now, taking every-

thing up from this point onward ', ' Gathering everything up to go on ')—that " Finally " gathers into the
battle both the revelation and the conduct. " Finally, be
strong in the Lord . . . For *our wrestling* . . . " This is *all*
part of a tremendous fight. It is as much a part of spiritual warfare to deal with all the things which you may
regard as the trivial commonplaces of everyday life—as
much a part of the great spiritual warfare and the great
issue of the Throne, as to be right out in the naked battle
with the enemy himself.

In closing, we note that all this that we have seen
carries with it certain serious implications. It says this, to
begin with: that the holding of the doctrine of the
Church, as in Ephesians i — iii, without corresponding
life and walk, may sabotage the whole issue. We may
have the conception of the Church—wonderful terms,
wonderful ideas ; we may talk endlessly about it, because
it is so marvellous, so fascinating—*but is it working?* Is
it really working? Are we truly in it? The answer will
only be found in our daily walk and conduct, in all the
so-called ' commonplace ' relationships that we have
mentioned. That is the answer. It is really a matter of
how much we are in this with all that we are and all
that we have.

I remember hearing Dr. Campbell Morgan make a
very challenging remark. He said: ' Allow me an impossible proposition : Supposing Christ is to be defeated,
what do you stand to lose? How much of you is invested
in this matter? Do you stand to lose everything if Christ
is defeated?' Yes, it is an impossible proposition, because

He never can be defeated. But supposing that in some way or other He is defeated *in us*, what do we stand to lose?

AT THE HEART OF THE CONFLICT IS THE THRONE

Again, to divorce all these practical matters from the interests of the Church and from spiritual conflict is to have no dynamic with which to deal with them. Do you grasp that? If you cannot deal with these domestic situations effectively : if you are just struggling with them— ' he is such an awkward husband ', ' she is such a difficult wife ', ' those children are such a handful '—if you are struggling to cope with them, and you know that you are not getting very far, may it not, after all, be a Church matter, that you have not an adequate background for dealing with the situations? May it not be that you are trying to deal with it as something in itself, instead of bringing it into relation with the Lord's testimony? that you are not recognising that this discord, this disagreement between you and your husband or your wife *touches the Throne*, touches the Lord's honour, and must be dealt with on no lesser ground than *that*? It is not merely a matter of settling our little domestic problem —we must have a dynamic for dealing with situations in general. And it may be that, when we bring these things into the right realm, recognising that they are a part of the great spiritual conflict in which the Throne is involved, we shall find things happening surprisingly.

But we come back at length to where we started.

Beyond and above all this detail, the dominant issue is that of the Throne: its honour and glory ; its sphere and range of influence ; the rights and claims and interests of the Throne, and the well-being of the people under it. Everything comes back to that, for that is the object of the conflict. In our homes, and in our local companies, let us cease to criticize, to judge, to condemn, looking at one another, and laying the blame at the door of things and people ; and let us see if our problem ought not to be dealt with from behind. And let the Church deal with it so, in any locality. Let the Church face the situation squarely: ' Look here, the Lord's Throne and the Lord's honour are touched by this. We believe that God raised up this instrument and vessel: if so, it was in relation to the Throne. It is necessary, therefore, that this vessel be a true representation of the Church, according to the Word of God ; and hence we realise that all Hell will be out to spoil it, to mar it, to wreck it, to destroy it.'

Why is this so? Not because the enemy cares anything about you or me, as individuals, or about any little local group or company, as something in itself ; but he has his eye on that Throne, and our situation—either in the home or in the church—is touching that. Let us adjust to this reality—for it is all here in the Word, it is true ; let us deal with matters in that way. Let our attitude be: ' This situation must not proceed any further ; because of what is involved, it must not remain another day. The enemy must at all costs be spoiled in this!'

CHAPTER 3

MORALE

Reading : Judges vii. 1 — 7

ONE of the most important aspects of the whole
subject treated in our book, *Defeat into Victory*, was the
question of ' Morale '. A very great deal of space is given
in that record to this matter of morale: for its lack on
some occasions, and its collapse on others, were responsible for what was little less than a complete rout ;
conversely, its recovery played a very large part in the
glorious consummation.

THE REDUCING OF GIDEON'S ARMY

That word ' morale ', of course, lies right at the heart
of the story of Gideon. It sums up the whole matter,
does it not? First of all, there is an elimination of everyone who is fearful and trembling ; in the second stage,
everyone who has interests which are personal and
which, standing to suffer, would cause the breakdown of
morale, is bidden to go home. This great reducing movement was called for by the Lord in order to get a certain
quality. Of course, as regards numbers, this is no kind of
argument either for one thing or the other : it is not an
argument for large numbers and it is not an argument

for small numbers. Nor, let us be clear, has this anything to do with salvation. The *redeemed* are to be ' a great multitude which no man can number ' (Rev. vii. 9). " The Lord is . . . longsuffering . . . not wishing that any should perish, but that *all* should come to repentance " (II Pet. iii. 9). The Lord has no reservations in that sphere ; He never says that *that* number is too great. But here it is a question of service—specific service and responsibility for the interests of the Lord amongst His own people. It is a matter of the Lord's honour.

To get the real value of this story, we need to remember the situation which obtained at that time amongst the people of God. For the issue was indeed the honour of the Name of the Lord, as deposited with His own people ; and for the deliverance of that Name from reproach and dishonour among His people a certain quality of fighting force is required. That is the heart of the story, and that is what we are considering at this point.

THE CHALLENGE OF ACTIVE SERVICE

Now before we go further with the matter of morale, may I come back to the general matter of our warfare. We may have had much teaching on various aspects of Divine truth and revelation, such as the Church, the Body of Christ, and other matters, and it may be that the teaching has not been without value—it may even have been quite profitable. But I wonder whether we have made enough of this matter of our being, as the Lord's

people, really *on a war footing*. Has it really come home
to us that we, the people of God, are supposed to be in
the field under *war* conditions? Is there the mentality
and consciousness in every section and in every individual that we are in a great campaign ; that there is no
let up in this matter, and that we are in it up to the hilt?
There may be, and indeed often is, a real gap between
our teaching, instruction, information, on the subject of
Christian soldiering, and the assured conviction of being
actually in a war—on active service. So many of the
Lord's people listen to the teaching, and are interested in
it, but they are not really in the fight, not really counting in the battle. To sing ' Onward, Christian Soldiers!'
and to do no fighting, is silly.

Surely, at such a time as this, the Lord would challenge us all, young and old alike : ' Are you really alive
to the fact that you are out in active warfare, in a great
campaign? that you are a part of something tremendous
that is going on in this universe, and that you have a
personal and quite definite place in it?' It is a matter of
urgency that this should be brought home to us definitely and clearly. It may be that much of our defeat, many
of the casualties amongst us, are largely due to the fact
that we have not been on the war-path with the enemy :
we have been letting him have his way far too much, we
have been giving him ground, we have been letting him
play around with us and do as he likes. If only we had
been standing on our feet in this matter, perhaps some
casualties might have been avoided. We have just accepted circumstances—including physical weaknesses—

as unrelated things in themselves, instead of standing up and at least raising the question : ' How much is there of the enemy behind this?' Of course, it may not be that in every case of physical or other limitation the enemy is having the ascendency, but in a great many cases he is, and the way of deliverance is to recognise that we must " lay hold on eternal life " and " fight the good fight of faith " (I Tim. vi. 12, A.V.). " *Lay hold* on eternal *life* "!

THE FOUNDATIONS OF MORALE

Now, on this matter of morale, I want to quote an excellent passage from the book of which I have spoken. Says the writer, the great Field Marshal who made this report : ' Morale is a state of mind, it is that intangible force which will move a whole group of men to give their last ounce to achieve something without counting the cost to themselves, that makes them feel that they are part of something greater than themselves. If they are to feel that, their morale—if it is to endure, and the essence of morale is that it should endure—their morale must have certain foundations. These foundations are spiritual, intellectual, material, and that is the order of their importance. Spiritual first, because only spiritual foundations can stand the real strain.' (Is that not fine? Of course there may be varying conceptions of the meaning of the word ' spiritual ', but when one interprets this in the realm of heavenly things, the principle is so sound, the wisdom so profound.) ' Intellectual next, because men are swayed by reason as well as feel-

ing. Material last—important but last—because the
very highest kinds of morale are often when men's
material conditions are at their lowest.' (What a great
deal of spiritual profit could be drawn from that!)

He goes on to say: ' I remember sitting down in my
office and tabulating these foundations something like
this:

' I.   The Spiritual:
   (a)   There must be a great and noble object ;
   (b)   Its achievement must be absolutely vital ;
   (c)   The method of its achievement must be
         active, aggressive ;
   (d)   The man must feel that what he is and what
         he does matters directly towards the attain-
         ment of the object.'

(How full that is of vital and necessary lessons when
translated into the realm of things heavenly!)

' 2.   The Intellectual:
   (a)   He must be convinced in his mind that the
         object can be attained' (that is searching!) ;
 ' (b)   He must see, too, that the organisation to
         which he belongs, and which is striving to
         obtain the object, is sound and efficient ; '

(Perhaps we could interpret that as meaning that we
must believe in our cause and recognise the adequacy of
the Church's spiritual equipment for gaining the object
in view.)

 ' (c)   He must have confidence in his leaders and
         know that, whatever dangers and hardships

he is called upon to suffer, his life will not be thrown away for nothing.

'3.   The Material:

(a)   The man must feel that he will get a fair deal from his commander and from the Army;'

(We have no fear about getting a fair deal from *our* Commander! We know He will give us a fair deal. But perhaps we cannot always be so certain of getting a fair deal from the Army, either individually or as a whole. To be certain of the support of the rest of the Army is an important factor in morale.)

'(b)   He must, as far as possible, be given the best weapons and equipment for his task;'

(That throws us back, does it not, upon the responsibility of 'under-shepherds' to give instruction in "the whole counsel of God", that the Church may be 'throughly furnished' for her warfare?)

'(c)   His working conditions must be made as good as can be.'

Having thus analysed and summarised what he means by foundations of morale, the writer next adds a classic sentence, which I have doubly underlined. Note, this is a Field Marshal of the Army speaking. He dares to say:

'The Christian religion is above all others a source of that enduring courage which is the most valued of all the components of morale'!

And the book contains much more like that. This

matter of morale is of the greatest importance. It was
against the possible lack or breakdown of such morale
that the Lord took those very serious precautions with
Gideon ; when He said: "By the three hundred men
that lapped will I save you, and deliver the Midianites
into thine hand " (Judges vii. 7).

THE ENEMY'S ASSAULTS UPON MORALE

Now, if we think about it for a few moments, we cannot fail to realise what a great deal our New Testament
has to say about morale. For, after all, such admonitions
and entreaties as: "Be strong in the grace that is in
Christ Jesus " (II Tim. ii. 1) ; "Be strong in the Lord,
and in the strength of his might" (Eph. vi. 10) ; "Quit
you like men, be strong " (I Cor. xvi. 13) ; all such ex-
hortations have to do with this strategic matter of spiritual morale—spiritual stamina to go on and to keep going on. I want to stress the importance that the Lord
attaches to this. Let me refer for a moment to what we
were saying in the previous chapter. The great objective
of the enemy is to bring reproach upon the Crown, upon
the Throne ; to repudiate its rights, its claims, its interests ; to rob the people of the Crown, of their heritage.
And if that is to be met and countered and overcome,
this matter of spiritual stamina that we are calling
'morale' is of tremendous importance.

The writer from whom we are quoting makes some
sorry comparisons of conditions in the opposing sides at
the beginning of the campaign. Speaking about the

enemy's morale, he says that for a long time it was almost impossible to break it, and he puts it down to one thing. He says: ' The enemy fought his battle as though upon every individual there rested the whole interest, the whole issue.' For instance, if 500 men were told off to hold a position, ' we had to kill 495 before we got that position and the remaining five killed themselves. Not one man would surrender.' In every individual there was this consciousness that the whole war-issue rested upon him and his life: he was in this thing without any reserve or question, or other interest. That was the secret of his morale, and that lies behind, on the one hand, the great story of the enemy's long-continued victory, and, on the other hand, our defeat.

That is the key to the whole matter, is it not? " Whosoever is fearful and trembling . . ." Why should we be fearful and trembling—why? Why should we be afraid? Is there something in our life for which we care more than for this great issue—that of the Throne and the Crown, the government and our fellow-countrymen's heritage of heavenly citizenship? Is there something that to us is of greater importance? Then that is the root of the fear and trembling. The very presence of fear indicates that there is some other interest. If the interests and honour of the Throne are our only concern, it means that all other things have been set aside and we are in this battle to the death. That, clearly, underlay the strength of morale in the story of Gideon ; these people had no alternatives, no secondary considerations.

Says our writer: ' The fighting soldier facing such an

D

enemy must see that what he does, whether he is brave
or craven, matters to all his comrades, and directly influences the result of the whole battle.' It is this personal
aspect to which everything is headed up in this seventh
chapter of the book of Judges. This is clearly brought
out in the more modern translation given in the Revised
Standard Version : " He of whom I say to you, ' This
man shall go with you,' shall go with you ; and any of
whom I say to you, ' This man shall not go with you,'
shall not go " (vs. 4). God was dealing with thousands,
yet He would not handle them as it were ' in bulk '. He
dealt with them man by man ; He made it a personal
matter with each man individually. And so it was—
' *This* man shall go with you . . .', and, ' *This* man shall
not go with you . . .' The whole thing was made
personal.

THE CORPORATE EFFECT OF MORALE

But—" none of us liveth to himself, and none dieth
to himself " (Rom. xiv. 7). That is to say, the way you
and I individually stand up in this battle affects the
whole issue. Did we but believe it, what a wonderful
source of support and strength this is ! But whether we
believe it or not, that is a statement of fact. It is recognised in the natural world, and it is just as true, if not
more so, in the spiritual realm. " Now *we* live, if *ye*
stand fast in the Lord " ! (I Thess. iii. 8). Your behaviour
and mine in the battle—whether we stand up or give up
—profoundly affects other people. It surely does ! We
need to lay hold of that and to say : ' The issue, after all,

does not begin and end with me. My conduct, my spirit, my attitude affects others. If I am weakening in the fight; if I am an unreliable soldier; if I cannot be trusted from one day to another as to how I shall be and where I shall be: if I am like that, it affects the whole situation. It is a cause of weakness in the whole Body corporate, in the whole constitution.' It must be our constant motive for girding ourselves and being strong, that our brothers and sisters need us so—the whole battle needs us to be like that. We dare not be weak and give up, for in this business we just cannot isolate ourselves.

The Lord was acting on this ground with Gideon's army. He said, in effect: ' If I were to allow any one man, fearful and trembling, to come into this undertaking, he would affect all the others, and I cannot afford that: let every such man go. And if I allowed any man to come in who had personal interests to serve, whose natural pride and conceit would take some glory to himself, that would be disastrous for the whole issue: let all such go home. The men who are to be here, who are to be the instrument of this deliverance, must be men who have been reduced to sheer, intrinsic worth.' That, surely, explains much of the Lord's dealings with us— reducing, emptying, weakening, breaking down, scattering. What is God doing? Just making way for intrinsic values, the values which are to be found when our objective is the Lord, and only the Lord. The issue for us must be the Lord—His glory, His honour.

That, in a few words, is morale. Much more could, of course, be said on this vital matter. Let me close with one other short extract. Says the writer:

'We had the advantage of our enemies in that our cause was based on real, not false, spiritual values. We fought only because the powers of evil' (what a phrase!) 'had attacked those real spiritual values.'

Now we know that he was referring to the values of 'life worth living' (he uses that phrase later), those things which really make life worth living; but let us interpret this in the realm of heavenly things. The passage will bear repeated reading. He proceeds:

'The man must feel this, feel that indeed he has a worthy cause and that, if he did not defend it, life would not be worth the living. Nor was it enough to have a worthy cause—it must be positive, aggressive; not a mere passive, defensive and 'anti-something' feeling, but positive and aggressive.'

All that is the foundation of morale. We need to lay it deeply to heart, for we are in something far bigger than the South-East Asia Campaign. Far, far greater issues are at stake; a far greater Crown and Throne and Name and Government and Country are involved; a far greater enemy is in the field. And so Paul makes his appeal: "I therefore . . . beseech you . . .", and brings the whole matter of the battle for the Church's glorious consummation to this: "Finally, be strong in the Lord, and in the strength of his might. Put on the whole armour of God, that ye may be able to stand . . . Take up the whole armour of God, that ye may be able to withstand in the evil day".

"Be strong in the Lord"! May the Lord help us!

CHAPTER 4

INTELLIGENCE
AND
DIVERSITY IN UNITY AND UNITY IN DIVERSITY

"That no advantage may be gained over us by Satan : for we are not ignorant of his devices" (II Corinthians ii. 11).

A.   INTELLIGENCE

THE next of the vital factors in our spiritual warfare that we are to consider is the matter of Intelligence. The above fragment of Scripture is quoted, not as a peg upon which to hang something, but as a key to very much more than its own context from which we may seem to be separating it. We refer again to the book from which many extracts have already been cited, the great record of the campaign that was conducted in South-East Asia during the last war. Under the heading of ' Defeat '—to which subject, half of that long account is devoted, a sad and tragic part—there occur these words:

' Our Intelligence was extremely bad. We were like a blind boxer trying to strike an unseen opponent and to parry blows we did not know were coming until they hit us. The extreme inefficiency of our whole Intelligence system was probably our greatest single handicap.'

You will weigh all this, because it is most significant in the spiritual realm. The writer continues:

' The first thing to get right was the Intelligence organization. Until we could rely upon a reasonable degree of information we could not hope successfully to hold the enemy. We never made up for the absence of methodically collected Intelligence, which should have been available to us when the war began.'

Now these few extracts, if we carry them over into *our* warfare, are most enlightening, instructive and important. Spiritual intelligence for spiritual warfare : that covers a very great deal of ground. As is so emphatically pointed out here, it is fundamental to the whole campaign. If we are lacking in spiritual intelligence, we shall be lacking in one of the vital requirements for victory. That is a well-informed and considered judgment in the earthly realm ; and, as we have repeatedly said, if it is true, as it has been proved to be, in the natural, how much more true it is in the spiritual—how much more is involved in this matter of intelligence in spiritual warfare !

SPIRITUAL INTELLIGENCE COUNTERS THE BLINDING WORK OF THE ENEMY

And so we pass from the natural warfare to the spiritual, the warfare in which you and I are, or should be, engaged.

We note, firstly, that God's whole scheme for our deliverance from Satan is based upon, or made effective by, spiritual intelligence, or spiritual enlightenment. We are told that, at the conversion of the Apostle Paul, in indicating his life-work, his commission, the Lord said : *" I send thee, to open their eyes, that they may turn from . . . the power of Satan unto God " (Acts xxvi. 17, 18).* Here it is clearly assumed that, by nature, all men are in the power of Satan ; and it is implied that they are there by reason of blindness. The nature of their bondage, of their captivity to Satan, and of his sway over them, that which gives it its power, its strength, is spiritual blindness. The way out, therefore, is not by means of an objective, external drive upon their captor, by trying to deal smashing blows at some imaginary spiritual force called ' Satan '. It is by means of an inward operation whereby spiritually blind eyes are opened, made to see. I repeat, therefore, that the whole scheme of man's deliverance from the enemy is based upon, and made effective by, spiritual enlightenment—that is, by spiritual intelligence.

(a) HIS CONCEALMENT OF HIMSELF AND OF MAN'S CONDITION

The enemy's supreme tactic in maintaining his power and his sway over mankind is along this line of keeping them in ignorance. One of his most successful devices is that of concealing himself—keeping man in ignorance of himself and of his work—and also of concealing from man his own condition. Man, of course, will not credit himself with blindness. It is a very difficult thing to make man believe that he is blind. Has he not intelligence, has he not common sense, has he not education,

has he not many things, all of which he regards as enlightenment? The most difficult thing is to make him
believe that he is blind ; and that is a sure and certain
proof that Satan has marvellously triumphed. He has
hidden from man his own real condition, and has made
him blind to his own blindness.

(b)   HIS INTERCEPTION OF KNOWLEDGE

Another of the enemy's great tactics is to intercept all
knowledge. There is a great deal in this book about reconnaissance, and the interception of reconnaissance : of
how the enemy gained the upper hand, and secured his
tremendous victory in the first campaign, very largely by
completely crippling the reconnaissance arm of the opposing forces. The writer makes constant complaint and
remonstrance about the absence or the failure of reconnaissance, and what it cost. In this matter of interception, of cutting off every agent and instrumentality that
would bring intelligence to the opposing side, the enemy
was in the unquestioned ascendant.

I do not propose to say much on the subject of our
knowledge of the enemy, our information concerning
him and his ways ; I want to get on to something more
profitable, more positive, than that. But this concern of
the enemy to intercept intelligence, to cut it off, to make
it impossible, to keep the Forces in ignorance, is an
important factor, and we shall have to underline it as
we go on.

The Apostle Paul, who, as we have already said, was a

great fighter, a great warrior, was very much alive to this matter. He himself was up against this problem all the time. It would be a profitable line of study to collect all that Paul has written on the matter of enlightenment, of revelation, of intelligence, of spiritual understanding. For instance, it is impressive to realise that six times over, in different places and in different connections, Paul uses the phrase: " I would not have you ignorant . . . " (Rom. i. 13, xi. 25 ; I Cor. x. 1, xii. 1 ; II Cor. i. 8 ; I Thess. iv. 13). If you take up the context of each of those six occasions, you will find that there is something of great significance bound up with each. " Brethren, I would not have you ignorant . . . ", he says ; and then follows something of vital importance.

Spiritual intelligence, then, is related in the first place to man's deliverance from the blinding and befogging activity of Satan.

THE INHERITANCE SECURED THROUGH INTELLIGENCE

In the second place, the whole basis of securing the inheritance of the people of God is that of spiritual intelligence. It is something more than being just saved. Salvation begins with spiritual enlightenment, the opening of the inward eyes. But thereafter, the pursuit of salvation to its ultimate objective, the fulness of Christ, is along the line of spiritual intelligence, illumination, understanding, knowledge. It matters not whether those words mean different things, or are inflections of the same thing ; the issue is the same.

We know, for instance, that the book of Joshua is the book of the inheritance. The people are going in to possess, to occupy, to exploit, to *inherit*. But what was the very first move, when Israel had come to the borders of the land, forty years previously? The setting up of Intelligence. Spies were sent to spy out the land. Joshua sent over intelligence officers, his Intelligence Corps. Intelligence was a tremendously important thing here. We might say that Joshua and Caleb were themselves the very embodiment of the principle of Intelligence. It was they who brought the report which, in the long run, resulted in a people going in and possessing. But note at this point an interesting and impressive and significant thing. *The people thought to stone them! (Num. xiv. 10).* You see, the enemy is not only over there in the land—he is entrenched in the very hearts of the people themselves, he has got a footing there. How true that is to principle and to history! Let any of the people of God begin to get some new light, and, as the Lord's instrument, they will become the object of Satan's hatred: he will stir up forces to stone that instrument. He hates instruments of spiritual enlightenment.

We pointed out, in chapter 2, that the Letter to the Ephesians is all of a piece: that, although there are progressive movements, it is nevertheless concerned with one thing—it concerns the Church coming into her inheritance. For the realisation of that there is tremendous conflict. 'Principalities and powers and hosts of wicked spirits in the heavenlies' are arrayed against that, so it says. But what is it that precipitates the conflict, that makes it active, that brings us up against the evil forces? Paul is praying ' that the eyes of your heart may be enlightened, that you may know ... that you may know ... that you may know ... ' *Therein* is the explanation of the conflict. It all circles round this—' that the people of God may *know* '. We do well to ask ourselves if we have really grasped that—if we are sufficiently alive to that.

Conclusions

(1) PROGRESSIVE INTELLIGENCE ESSENTIAL TO VICTORY

What are the conclusions, then? Firstly, that intelligence, spiritual knowledge and understanding, are a very great factor for victory in this whole spiritual warfare. Do let us lay that to heart. We shall find it out and prove it sooner or later. The ' sooner ' or ' later ' depends upon whether we really grasp this fact. We shall not come through into full victory without spiritual understanding: we shall not get there willy-nilly, just anyhow: we shall not drift into it: we shall not just find ourselves there. All along the way we shall find ourselves up against situations with which we shall be unable to cope, demanding a spiritual understanding and knowledge from the Lord without which we shall be unable to get through. The key to every further advance is more spiritual knowledge, more spiritual understanding. Without it, we shall be held up indefinitely.

Is that not true to experience? We come to an impasse, and have to go to the Lord ; and, until the Lord gives light, we are locked up in that impasse. Once the light flashes; once we see; once we are able to say, 'Now I understand the meaning of this thing!'—the Devil's hold is broken, and we are released. If only we realised the background of situations, being quick on the scent to get the significance of happenings and not just taking them at their face value ; if we were to say, ' Well, it all looks so natural, it all seems to have a very natural explanation of human fault and circumstance and what not, but there may be something else behind this ' ; if only we were more on the alert, it might be that we should not ourselves be knocked out of the fight, and other people who sadly needed our help would not be deprived of it. Satan lays his schemes very deeply, and covers them up so cunningly, does he not? He argues, ' Well, you see, it was this and that and some other thing.' Oh, no, it was not ! —and even if it was, it should not have had this effect upon us.

Spiritual intelligence, then, is a tremendous factor in spiritual warfare and in spiritual growth and progress. ' That we may know . . . that we may know . . . '—and therein is a great battle !

(2) INTELLIGENCE MUST LEAD TO ACTION

The second thing in our conclusions is that our intelligence, our knowledge, must be followed by action. It must be *practical* knowledge, not merely theory. We have all the theory of spiritual warfare in the Bible, have we not? we have the whole scheme from Genesis to

Revelation! But are we applying it? Is it applied knowledge, or is it only theoretical? Is it followed by action? Or, when a situation arises, does all the theory we possess fail to serve any useful purpose? does it fail to come to our rescue? Our knowledge must be applied and practical knowledge. It must lead to action.

(3) THE NEED FOR WATCHFULNESS AGAINST ENEMY-INDUCED INERTIA

Thirdly, the enemy's special concern is to keep God's people from increased spiritual knowledge: and that statement covers a great deal of ground. So often, when the Lord is purposing to impart to His children some particular spiritual knowledge, there comes over them a strange inertia: and that kind of inertia can sometimes be sinister. It is something more than mere tiredness or weariness; it seems to come over us suddenly, for no apparent reason. I have often, during a long experience, seen the children of God robbed of something vital through succumbing to that feeling of inertia and staying at home at such a time.

We need to weigh up our inclinations to stay at home, and judge them. There are times when it may be of the Lord that we remain quiet and alone at home, but let us be careful that we are not just being smothered by the enemy, in order that we may be robbed of something. Oh, the unwatchfulness of God's people! What loss it leads to! Yes, the Devil will create an inertia, or raise up some difficulty, some impediment, some circumstance,

just to intercept—just to make sure that you are not there
on some occasion; and then, like Thomas, when the Lord
comes in you are absent. You know, that is a loss which
is not easily recovered, and it may lead to some very real
defeat in coming days. The very thing that you needed
for a coming situation may have been there, provided by
the Lord. Because you were not alive to the meaning of
what was happening, and accepted the circumstance or
the event at its face value, you missed some spiritual
gain. How important this is! How very much alive we
must be, ' intelligent unto intelligence '! As Paul says,
" with all prayer and supplication praying . . . and *watching* thereunto . . . " (Eph. vi. 18).

(4)   THE ENEMY'S OPPOSITION TO AN ENLIGHTENING MINISTRY

Finally, opposition to a ministry which would make
God's people spiritually strong is one of Satan's very
definite activities. There is much history behind that
statement. If there is a ministry—I am not thinking only
of personal ministry—or any other instrumentality
which can minister to a fuller knowledge of the Lord
and to an understanding of His purposes concerning
His Church, then not only the ministry itself, but the
instrument of that ministry, the vehicle and the vessel
of that ministry, and the place of that ministry, will all
be an object against which Satan will be determinedly
set—for its undoing, for its breaking down, for its disintegration, for its paralysis ; somehow—anyhow—to

destroy that instrument of ministry. Would that we might be fully alive to this!

B.   DIVERSITY IN UNITY AND UNITY IN DIVERSITY

What an immense variety of functions go to make up an efficient and effective fighting force! Almost endless are the auxiliaries and the complementaries, both of activities and of means. In an army, you have a large number of definite ' sub-forces ', or contributing forces. Think of some of the main branches known to us: the Army Service Corps, for supplies; the Engineers, electrical and mechanical, for all installations and repairs and construction; the Ordnance Corps, for a large variety of things such as surveying, mapping, routeing, and so on; the Pay Corps, which is quite an important one, to see that men get their due and their rights (and it is strategic to do that: if there is a grumble in that realm you may upset the whole organization!); the Intelligence Corps, of which we have just spoken; and the Medical Corps, dealing with the whole matter of health and healing and care, and numerous other duties. Here are many, many functions; and yet, both within these main branches and without, there are almost countless details, committed to different people, all of which are essential.

And here is a really magnificent little paragraph from the book. What it says is good, but that it should be said by a Field Marshal is almost better, for it indicates that right at the top, notwithstanding all the great responsi-

bilities and the important position and the name, the
smallest detail was not overlooked. He has been speaking about the man right up in the battle-front, who is
aware of his responsibility, aware of the effect and influence of his behaviour and his demeanour ; and he
goes on :

'But it is harder for the man working on the road, far
behind, the clerk checking stores in a dump, the telephone operator monotonously plugging through his
calls, the sweeper carrying out his menial tasks, the
quartermaster's orderly issuing boot-laces. I say it is
harder for these and a thousand others to see that they,
too, matter. You may be one of the half million in the
Army, but you have to be made to see where your
menial task fits into the whole scheme of things, and to
realise what depends on it and on you, and, moreover,
to feel pride and satisfaction in doing it.'

You see what I mean? Diversity in unity—unity in
diversity. Many Scriptures will come to mind : " There
are diversities of gifts, but the same Spirit . . . all these
worketh the one and the same Spirit " (I Cor. xii. 4, 11).
Paul has a great deal to say about this matter of diversity
in unity and unity in diversity. And the Lord would have
it to be found in the Church.

THE HOLY SPIRIT: SUFFICIENT, INDISPENSABLE, SOVEREIGN

Now, let us seek to realise, first of all, that the Holy
Spirit is comprehensive of all needs for this great cam-

paign ; that is, He covers the whole ground of what is required. He Himself is the supply and the dynamic, the ability for every section and every department and every function. He comprehends the whole and leaves out nothing that is essential. He covers everything. To put that round the other way : in the Holy Spirit there is everything that is required of ability, of faculty, of gift, of enablement, for this whole campaign, in all its departments and details. He is given to the Church to be all that.

But the next step is to realise that the Holy Spirit is given to each one, personally, with the object of making each one a functioning factor in the great campaign. There ought not to be a single individual in Christ who is not counting in this battle, who is not a vital factor in it, who is not really telling, who is not in some way making a contribution. If such ' non-functioning members ' should exist, there is something wrong, because the manifestations of the Spirit are given to us " to profit withal ", says the Word (I Cor. xii. 7). " Given to each for the profit of all ", is Conybeare's rendering : that is, to make us a part of the inclusive profit and gain. And if we are not a vital factor in this warfare, it means that the Holy Spirit is somehow being hindered, checked, thwarted, frustrated in us. There is something wrong in our relationship to the Holy Spirit.

Thirdly, the Holy Spirit gives gifts as He will : that is, He is sovereign. It is not for you or for me to say what we are going to do in the Army, what place we are going to hold, what work we are going to do. That is the pre-

E

rogative of the Holy Spirit. We have only to recall Paul's words, at the conclusion of the passage we have already quoted (I Cor. xii. 11), about the gifts of the Holy Spirit being distributed as He wills. You and I, therefore, should claim, as our very birthright, that the Holy Spirit should qualify us in some way to be a functioning member of this great Army—whether it be as ' the quartermaster's orderly distributing bootlaces', or whether it be something that we might think far more important: although it would certainly be a serious matter if a fighting soldier had not got his bootlaces!

What I mean, of course, is this. All these things are necessary ; they are essential to the whole. It is not for us to say that ours is too little a job—that it does not matter. It does matter : yes, right down to a ' bootlace' it matters in this whole. And it is not just the *nature* of the job that you and I may be doing, or be given to do, that makes it important. Its importance lies in its relationship to the whole. Nor is it a question of *personal* importance—it is not that *you* or *I* are so important ; any importance we may have comes from our relationship to the whole. And so we need to seek adjustment in this matter.

It is my firm belief that the Holy Spirit would in some way qualify, for quite definite functioning in this warfare, every member, every individual. For, in this ' unity in diversity ', where everything is so related, every member is significant.

The Incentive of a Sense of Vocation and a Spirit of Service

I close with a word about the saving value of a sense of vocation, of service. If only we had this awareness of the greatness of the thing that we are in! If only we had a new sense that, as recipients of the Holy Spirit, we are those who should *count*, should *signify*: for that is why we have received the Holy Spirit—to make us count. And it *matters* about us. It does not matter *to us* about ourselves, but it does matter to the whole order of things. If only we had a due sense of that, what a great deal we should be saved! If our attitude is: 'I don't matter, I don't count', what is the result before long? A miserable life!

I recently read an article about self-pity, in which the story was told of how the help of a psychiatrist was sought by a woman who said that she had a nervous breakdown coming on. She evidently expected him to take a lot of trouble and analyse her history and give her some comforting words of advice. But he said: 'My dear woman, go home, turn the key in your front door, make your way to that poor district down there across the railway, find somebody who is in need of help, and get busy, and your nervous breakdown will never come off!'

There is much good, Divine common sense in that. We are enlarged by giving. We lose nothing by giving; our increase comes along the line of giving, of turning outward. Yes, " always abounding in the work of the

Lord ", always turned outward ; animated by a spirit of
service, seeking to be useful or helpful wherever we can;
not just with a Bible under our arm, ready to go and
speak at a meeting, but in all sorts of practical ways
being a spiritual and physical help to the Lord's children.
That is the way, not only of saving us from a miserable
existence, but of bringing ourselves enlargement.

That is very practical, but it is very true. The Spirit is
given to us "to profit withal"! The Holy Spirit can
enable us to be of value in ways that we cannot be
naturally. Where would most of us be if we were left to
ourselves, to our own natural resources, gifts and abilities—or lack of them? We should be of no use at all, for
we have nothing. But the Spirit makes up wonderfully
for our deficiencies; He really does make good our
short-comings. By the Spirit's aid, every one of us can
and should and must be counting in the battle.

CHAPTER 5

MENTALITY, OR ATTITUDE OF MIND

" For though we walk in the flesh, we do not war accord-
ing to the flesh (for the weapons of our warfare are not
of the flesh, but mighty before God to the casting down
of strong holds) ; casting down imaginations, and every
high thing that is exalted against the knowledge of God,
and bringing every thought into captivity to the obedi-
ence of Christ " (II Corinthians x. 3 — 5).

TAKING the latter part of the above passage :
" Casting down imaginations " (the margin gives as an
alternative " reasonings ") ". . . and bringing every
thought into captivity to the obedience of Christ ", we
will now look together at the matter of mentality in
relation to this great spiritual warfare. The perils and
threats to victory of a wrong mentality ; the tremendous
advantage of a right mentality. I am again drawing upon
the book to which reference has been made throughout
these chapters. Although, in that book, the word ' mentality ' is not specifically employed, what I am saying is
certainly found there in substance.

A WRONG MENTALITY AS TO THE HIGHER COMMAND

Returning to the subject of our first consideration—
that of the Supreme Command—let us state at once that

69

there exist perils of a wrong mentality concerning the
Lord Jesus, the Supreme Commander of all the Forces in
the field which go by the name of the Church. The
wrong mentality concerning Him is this: that He is One
from whom to *get* everything, instead of the One *to*
whom to *give* everything. There is a great danger of
always thinking in terms of what we are to get from
Headquarters, of what advantages are to accrue to us, of
drawing toward ourselves: in effect—although we
should never admit this—really putting ourselves, our
interests, in the place of those of the Supreme Command; for that is how it works out.

It is just at this point that 'popular' Christianity has
done a great deal of harm. Christianity has been put
upon a wrong basis, or perhaps, to be a little more charitable, upon an inadequate basis, and the preaching is
almost exclusively in terms of what we are to *get*. We
are to get salvation; we are to get eternal life, peace, joy
and satisfaction—all this and Heaven as well! But the
emphasis is so largely upon what *we* are to get from the
Lord Jesus, our Supreme Commander. It is at least an inadequate mentality, if not an altogether wrong one when
it is a made a principle; it is a misinterpretation of the
whole Christian life. We will come back to that in a
moment. The right mentality—and, mark you, the only
one that is going to serve the great purpose and to
minister to the great objective—is the mentality that is
governed by the principle: 'Give everything to the
Lord'; not 'Get everything from the Lord.'

This is the governing principle of the Godhead, the

principle that to give is the way of fulfilment. In the case of the Lord Jesus, that is made very clear in one classic passage of the Apostle Paul. We are told that He " emptied himself . . . becoming obedient even unto death, yea, the death of the cross. Wherefore also God highly exalted him, and gave unto him the name which is above every name " (Phil. ii. 7 — 9). Fulfilment, the restoration of His voluntarily laid aside fulness, came to Him along the line of emptying, giving, pouring out. For that is, I repeat, the principle of the Godhead, and it is to be the mentality of all those who are engaged in this great warfare. We shall be knocked about, brought up short, arrested, defeated, just in so far as we are all the time thinking in terms of what should come to us. Let us make no mistake about it : it will be like that. The self-centred life is always the discontented life. The possessive life is the circumscribed life.

But the out-going life is the life of abundant return— it all comes back. " Give, and it shall be given unto you ; good measure, pressed down, shaken together, running over " (Luke vi. 38). Those are the words of the Lord Jesus. Do you want eternal possessions? The way to re-ceive—but don't do it with this motive—is to *give.* That is the principle. You see the wrongness of the kind of mentality about the Lord Jesus that feels He should all the time be giving, giving : that we must more and more receive from Him : that He is only there for our benefit! You see how false that is, how unsound and how danger-ous : because, immediately we find that He is not giving like that and things are becoming a little difficult, we lose interest in the whole matter, and become paralysed in battle, helpless as fighters, impotent in service. It is due to a wrong mentality about the Supreme Command. He is there to receive the honour and the glory and the riches, and the dominion and the power, and everything. And while He *will* give and give and give, eternally give, our relationship to Him must be on the basis, not of how much *we* are going to get, but of how much He is going to get from us.

A WRONG MENTALITY AS TO THE CHRISTIAN LIFE

Secondly, there are the perils of wrong ideas about the Christian life. There is the prevalent idea that the Christian life is merely a matter of being saved and being blessed; salvation and blessing, and all that goes with salvation. For many, this is the sum of the Christian life; this is how it is put by many Christian preachers and leaders, and this is the mentality which is encouraged. But the Word of God makes it perfectly clear that the Christian life is something far more than that. Our mentality, or ' mindedness ', concerning it, should be that of being involved in, and a part of, the great conflict of the ultimate elemental forces of this universe.

For that is the issue. Long, long ago, something tremendous was set in motion; and ever since then, down through the centuries, the great purpose of God has been challenged and disputed. All through these generations the people of God, men of God, have given themselves in relation to that one great battle in the universe; and it still goes on—it is not at an end yet. The real nature of the Christian life is that you and I, immediately we become related to the Lord Jesus Christ, are called into *that*, involved in *that*. We are involved in what I have called the ultimate elemental forces of this universe in conflict: no less than the whole hosts of the Kingdom of God and of Heaven, on the one side, and, on the other side, this vast and vicious kingdom of Satan.

That is the Christian life! Do not have any illusions about it! The Lord Jesus allowed no one to have illusions about it : " Whosoever doth not bear his own cross, and come after me, cannot be my disciple " (Luke xiv. 27). " Whosoever would save his life shall lose it ; but whosoever shall lose his life for my sake, the same shall save it " (Luke ix. 24). You see, that is straight, frank, candid and honest. This is what we are in ! It is a great privilege to be in it, a great honour to be in it, but that is it. Let us have no wrong mentality about this. Through getting a wrong mentality about it, many people have become disappointed. They wonder, sometimes ; they say : ' Well, I did not bargain for this ; this is not what I expected, this is not what I became a Christian for. They told me that my life was going to be full of joy and happiness and peace, that everything was going to be beautiful and lovely, and that I would have a wonderful time —but now what have I landed into?' Well, there *is* joy and there *is* peace ; there is *all* that, thank God ; but we have to recognise and to adjust to the fact that we are in a battle, a fierce, unrelenting battle ; and there is no discharge from the battle in this life.

A Wrong Mentality as to the Church

Thirdly, there can be wrong ideas about the Army
itself—that is, the Church: the Church is the Army. It
is possible to have a wrong mentality about this. The
wrong mentality that is possible—and I would say this
with emphasis—is that the Army, the Church, is the end
and the object of everything. Now, we say much about
the greatness of the Church, and we in no way exaggerate in so doing. We speak of it in superlative terms, as
'God's masterpiece', and so on. We are encouraged by
the Word of God to think of it as something great and
wonderful, even magnificent. Yes, the Church is a very
wonderful conception in the mind of God from eternity;
the Church has a very large place in the Divine counsels;
it is to be presented at last to the Lord Jesus as a glorious
Church. I will not recount all the great things that have
been or could be said about it.

But, when all has been said that could be said, we
have still to say: The Church is not *the* object, it is not
the end; the Church is not the *ultimate*! The Church is,
after all, no more than the instrument; it is but the vessel, it is but the agent. There is something beyond the
Church—the Church only exists for something else.
Perhaps its greatness in fact derives from the 'super-
greatness' of the object which it is to serve. Let us, then,
not make the Church the end, the 'everything'; let us
not think that we have to live only and utterly and ultimately for the Church. We have to remember that, just
as the Army does not exist for itself, does not go out in

the campaign, into the field, for itself, but in the interests of the sovereign and his kingdom, so the Church exists and engages in warfare solely for the glory of the Throne, for the glory of the One on the Throne, for the glory of the Kingdom. That is the object of the Church's existence.

If we have faulty ideas here, we shall find that they constitute a weakness. If we put the Church in the place of Jesus Christ, we shall find ourselves in trouble with the Holy Spirit. That is not in any way to displace or to belittle the Church: but the Church exists for Christ. All our Church conceptions, all our relationships in that connection, indeed everything to do with that, should be governed by the fact that everything is for Christ—it is for Christ's sake. Why the Church, and why all that is said about the Church and related life? It is for Christ's sake! We must regard them as being, not ends in themselves, but for the satisfaction of Christ. We must have a clear mentality on this matter, and put Him in His rightful place.

A WRONG MENTALITY AS TO MINISTRIES

We come next to the matter of functioning in the Army, or, to speak in spiritual terms, the ministries, the functions. Here again we can have wrong, defective, faulty ideas and mentality, and it may be that we need to make a little adjustment over this matter. What is the real meaning and value of ministries? Is ministry just a question of imparting knowledge and information? A great amount of that is, of course, done, in and by ministry. But is that what it is for—just teaching? No, the function of this ministry is something more than the imparting of knowledge and information. We are an Army in the field, and what is needed in a day of battle is not lectures—it is provision for the actual need in which we are found. If we come to the ministry provided in a condition of conscious need, we are in a way of getting real value. But if we are only coming for the sake of attending meetings and hearing addresses and receiving more and more knowledge and information, we shall never thereby be qualified for this battle.

Do you see the point? Here is this background of conflict. From time to time the Supreme Command visits the various positions, gathers the staff together and reviews the situation: he assembles all his men and talks to them. But the scene is a scene of battle. It is a time of war, not of peace; the conditions prevailing are war conditions; the scene and circumstances are those of actual war. Why does he gather the men around? To give them lectures on the theory of military life? Not a bit of it! He calls them together in order to give help and instruction on how to meet the existing and immediate situation; to direct as to how to cope with that which confronts them, with that which they are up against right there and then.

And that ought to be the nature of all our meetings and our ministry. We ought all the time to be a people on a war footing, right up against emergencies, threats, perils and dangers. If we had that mentality, that we

really are so engaged ; that we are right up against a very
persistent and cunning enemy ; that we are in truth in
the thick of the battle—our meetings would serve
much greater purposes, our ministry would be of far
greater value. Suffer this emphasis and stress. Our meetings must at all costs be redeemed from being just
sessions of theory. We can reach saturation point in that
way, so that we are unable to take any more. But if we
are right in this battle, and really meaning business, if
we are up against things and want help, we shall go
where help is to be found. We ought to be at our meetings on this footing: ' I need it, I cannot do without
it, my situation demands it.' But if there is no demand,
how valueless will be the supply! We need to get
our mentality adjusted over this. Our meetings and
ministry must represent a provision for immediate,
actual need.

And if we really are in the business, the Lord will see
to it that we are in need, all right! He will make things
very practical, very real. He will see to it that our Christian lives are constantly brought up against new needs.
Do not worry, do not think things have gone wrong, if
you find yourself up against a situation for which you
have no answer! The Lord is doing that to keep you
moving on. Our progress is only along that line, on the
basis of growing need. Immediately that stops, we stop.
We go no further than our sense of need—and our very
acute sense of need. The Lord keeps most of us there,
does He not?—in a way of very real, practical need :
more need, and ever more need. Blessed be God! He

only does it in order that the need may be supplied. But
when things become a matter of course, a matter of
habit, a matter of—'Well, we are going along to the
meeting because it is meeting night'—then we simply
make every supply dead. May the Lord bring us together
every time as in uniform, that is, on a war footing, as in
a council of war.

All ministry must have a practical background, both
for giving and for receiving. God save those of us who
minister from ministering just theories and material!
The Lord keep all who minister on the basis of a very
practical background, so that what is ministered is born
out of experience and actuality in life. The ministry
must not consist in searching out matter and putting it
together and retailing it as addresses. Not at all! It must
be born out of life, right up to date. And there must be
active exercise on both sides—in those who minister and
in those who receive. It must be a practical matter : there
must be action about it. There must be, on the part of
all, a very serious quest, the seriousness of which is born
of the desperateness of the situation : the situation being
that, unless we have this knowledge from the Lord, unless we have life from the Lord, we are going under in
the battle, the enemy is going to gain. That is the nature
of those councils of war, those 'conferences', those
meetings with our Supreme Commander, to which we
sometimes gather. They are just that we may be equipped
for our job—and our job is fighting. Our object at all
such meetings should be to get equipment for our very
life-work, which is now on hand.

A Wrong Mentality as to Others

Lastly, we come to wrong ideas concerning the other personnel in the Army—the other people in the Church. We have many wrong ideas about one another. Some of them are hardly worthy of mention. You know how easy it is to be selective, to look at the other man or woman and write them off as not counting for much, saying, ' Now this one, you know, this one counts for something, means something ; this one has got measure. But that other one, well—no.' Be very careful! That is dangerous. Our kind of selectiveness, our judgment of people, may sabotage the whole movement. And, after all, what about ourselves? Where would you be, where would I be, if the Lord had been very particular, very particular *indeed*, to have the right measure and stature and quality? Where would *I* be? where would *you* be? I know where I would be : I would not be in this warfare or ministry ! I settled it with the Lord, long ago, that *He* must provide all the qualifications to keep me in. But, you see, He has to do that with the others as well, and He can. We must be very careful about this matter.

We must be very careful, too, that we do not, as is sometimes done, contemplate others as competitors and rivals who are seeking to get an advantage over us. We must not be ' touchy ' about our own position and our own rights and prerogatives ; be very touchy and explosive if someone else is put before us, or seems to have been put in our place, given a favour, and so on. It is a horrible thing to think of such an attitude amongst

Christians, but it can happen only too easily. By taking personal offence, because of something that has been done that seems to be placing us at a disadvantage, we can be put out of the fight at once—put right out of the battle! In such a situation, whether we judge it to be right or wrong, our attitude must be this: 'Lord, I am *Yours*, I am *Your* man, I am in this for *You*. Men can do what they like—put me out, put others over my head; they can do what they like. That is between You and me, Lord, and between You and them.' You see, if you allow yourself to take offence, be hurt and grieved because of others, the enemy can come in on that ground, and you will become a casualty—you may as well be carried out on a stretcher straight away! If you are going down in that way you are no use to the fight. Be careful! Let us be careful of our attitudes, of our mentality, when it involves other people.

That could be enlarged upon, but we leave it there, with just the reminder that a favourite manœuvre of our enemy is to get amongst us and make us look at one another and misjudge one another, misinterpret one another, get us mistrusting one another. And what is the good of an Army like that—all looking at one another with questions or suspicions or hurt feelings! What a state of mind! The word is: " Casting down imaginations "—and, if we only knew all the truth, we should discover that a great deal of it is imagination; it is not real. We should find that, after all, that was not meant, that was not the implication at all; it was our imagination—it was how it came to us and our imagination got busy on it. And we are put out!

Clever manœuvre of the enemy! The counter to that is found in our passage: " our warfare . . . casting down imaginations . . . and bringing every thought into captivity to . . . Christ ". Do it now! Lay hold of those thoughts that have done you injury and perhaps done someone else injury. Lay hold of them! They will make you unfit for battle; they will affect the whole issue; they will touch others in the Army. There is a great deal of Scripture behind that, if we like to call it up. Lay hold of those thoughts and bring them into captivity to Christ. Make sure that you are right, and, even if you are right, be prepared to forgive, to be charitable, and at any rate not to make a personal issue of it.

A Wrong Mentality as to Ourselves

How prone we are to have wrong ideas about ourselves! Paul said: " I say . . . to every man that is among you, not to think of himself more highly than he ought to think " (Rom. xii. 3a). What ought you to think of yourself, what ought I to think of myself? In the light of God's grace, of God's mercy, of God's love, in the light of God's holiness, what ought we to think of ourselves? " . . . Not to think of himself more highly than he ought to think; but ", continues Paul, " so to think as to think soberly, *according as* God hath dealt to each man a *measure of faith* " (vs. 3b); that is, if we may take another word of Paul's out of its context, " *according to the measure* of the gift of Christ " (Eph. iv. 7). The

F

measure of our self-esteem will be in inverse proportion
to the measure of Christ that we have. How much of
Christ have we received? Well, if we have a super-
abundance of Christ, if we have more of Christ than anyone else, we shall not think highly of ourselves at all.
The more we have of Christ, the less we shall think of
ourselves, the less we shall want to talk about ourselves,
the less we shall be in view, the less we shall want to be
in the limelight.

"Every man . . . not to think of himself more highly
. . .". What ravages such a wrong mentality could make
in an Army! Just imagine what would happen if men
behaved like that—thinking more highly of themselves
than they ought to think, ' throwing their weight about ',
as we say. No, that will not do ; that is only playing into
the hands of the enemy. Our safety lies in ' thinking
soberly ', according as each of us has received of the
measure of Christ. In this great battle, it matters greatly
what kind of mind we have. " Have this mind in you,
which was also in Christ Jesus . . . " In an earlier chapter
we have urged that every one should realise that, in a
related way, the army depends upon the units : that the
whole can suffer through the weakness of the individual.
Thus it works both ways. We can overestimate our personal importance, or we can underestimate our related
significance. To think of ourselves as we ought to think
will mean that we do not err in either direction : we
shall recognise that it *does* matter about us, but that it
matters relatively, and not just personally—that is,
independently.

Chapter 6

DISCIPLINE, PROVISIONING, AND FLEXIBILITY

" Suffer hardship with me, as a good soldier of Christ Jesus. No soldier on service entangleth himself in the affairs of this life ; that he may please him who enrolled him as a soldier " (II Timothy ii. 3, 4).

(A)   Discipline

IN these well-known words of Paul, we are introduced to the most important matter of discipline. What is discipline? It could be described as the steadying effect, the girding power, of purposefulness, as opposed to looseness and carelessness and slackness. It is what the Apostle Peter calls " girding up the loins of your mind " (I Pet. i. 13). Now, in that great South-East Asia Campaign to which we have been referring, discipline had, naturally, a very large place. We will consider it in its connection with five different, though related, things.

(1)   AS TO BEHAVIOUR

In the first place, discipline is related to behaviour. I am not quoting from the volume, but there is a great deal said about this matter of behaviour. It is so easy to accept the subtle idea that, when you are on a war footing (especially under conditions such as obtained in that campaign), discipline does not matter so much: you can throw off the restraints of the parade ground and need not bother about the strict rules and regulations of training; you are free from all that and can just plunge straight into the battle. But the writer of this book makes much of the importance of bringing into the battle all those rules of training and discipline and behaviour. And you will at once see that our behaviour as the Lord's people is a most vital factor in the campaign. The New Testament, as we know, has a great deal to say about Christian behaviour, and it is not without very real purpose that the Lord makes such large mention of it in His inspired volume. He knows the importance of our conduct, our demeanour—of how we behave. With Him it is a vital part of the battle. It matters; it makes a great deal of difference. We are not to be slack, loose, careless, in our way and manner of life. The enemy makes great gain out of that sort of thing; it puts a most effective weapon into his hand against the Lord's interests, against the whole object to which we are called.

You and I, as Christians, have got to watch our behaviour: not only before the world, but—as we shall emphasize again presently—even in secret. It matters whether we are disciplined in the matter of behaviour. The great point that this book makes of behaviour is that discipline should have become second nature: it should not merely be something put on for the occasion, when it is expected and when eyes are on us, when we are more or less on parade before the officers. We should not need to be told or pulled up. Disciplined behaviour should become second nature ; it should just be *us*—we *are* that. Our behaviour should betoken what we are.

A simple point is made by the Supreme Command in that connection. Soldiers, when they are on the parade ground or in training, are, of course, very careful about their saluting of officers ; it is a part of their discipline. But it was noticed that, when they were all mixed up in battle conditions, officers and men together under actual war conditions, they became very slack, very careless and loose, in this seemingly small matter. And the Supreme Command said : This is something that shows whether men are really trained men or not ; it gives them away. If they were really disciplined men, the conditions under which they live would make no difference at all : they would carry out the rules and regulations of their training under all circumstances, for it would have become second nature. They would salute an officer just as much in those active service conditions, even in jungle warfare, as they would on the parade ground cr in training.

This illustration should impress upon us the importance of realising that discipline is not just something artificial, something that we assume ; it is not just the behaviour that we put on when we are being watched and when it is expected of us. It is how we behave when we are caught off our guard that reveals what we are. While that may sound very simple and elementary, it is a very important thing in the Christian life. The discipline of the Holy Spirit in our lives will show itself

under all conditions: we act so, because we *are* that—
that is what we *are*. When we are in public, where we
know that it matters what people think of us, we can put
on mannerisms, assume an artificial voice, pose, effect.
But when we are with a few, for whom we have not a
great deal of respect, we can put off the guise and really
show our true nature. This is fatal to reality!

(2) AS TO CARE FOR HEALTH

Then there was the matter of discipline in regard to
health. It was of the utmost importance that every care
and precaution related to health should be most carefully, most meticulously observed. But terrible havoc
was wrought in that campaign by disease; many thousands of men were lost to the fighting forces through
carelessness in the matter of health.

How much more urgent, then, is care of health in the
spiritual realm! It is very important that you and I
should be disciplined in the matter of spiritual health. In
Latin, the word for ' health ' is cognate with our word
' salvation '; and salvation connotes ' preservation ', ' deliverance '. Discipline in spiritual health means to be
alive to the perils to spiritual life, the threatening inroads to the spiritual condition. Very much could be
said on the matter of spiritual maladies, spiritual diseases,
spiritual infirmities. Many of them overcome us because
we are not disciplined, we are not careful, we are not
watchful; we are not alive to things that can undermine
our spiritual health. It is of great importance for the

battle that we should be spiritually healthy, be in good health and strength. This is something of which to take real account. The question on any given issue should be —not: Is it right or wrong? (in a permissive sense)— but: Will this unfit me for the battle? will this in any way weaken me in the great campaign in which I am engaged?

You see, it is fitness for the fight that matters, but the peril of carelessness over it is ever present. So, to the man to whom the Apostle says: " Suffer hardship as a good soldier of Jesus Christ ", he will also say: " Lay hold on eternal life " (I Tim. vi. 12, A.V.). There are times when we are slack in this matter: we need life, and there is life available, but we do not lay hold of it as we should —we just let go. A disciplined Christian is one who will say in the time of threatening or actual weakness: ' This is the time for me to lay hold on life, not to give way, not to let go. If I let go, I shall be put out of the fight. I must put up my defences against these things that would weaken ; I must react to this situation ; I must resist ; I must lay hold on life.'

I can but hint at what I mean, but if you had read the terrible account of the decimation of the forces in this campaign by disease, through carelessness as to health, you would see that there is point in this. And we have an enemy who, in a spiritual sense, is constantly sending germs our way, with the object of putting us out; but there is such a thing as really laying hold on life, being strong to resist, and maintaining our spiritual strength by the grace of God.

(3) AS TO SELFLESSNESS

A further aspect of discipline relates to the need of being always alive to the fact that what we do or fail to do involves others. An illustration is given in this book of how that worked out in the case of one particular man (and maybe of others through his example), who was on sentry duty under war conditions. He was extremely, desperately tired, almost exhausted, and yet he had a very important point to guard. Many lives were involved in the matter of his alertness. So, having to stand on guard in one place, quietly and alone, for long hours of the night, what did he do? He put his rifle in front of him with the bayonet fixed, and he put his chin on the point of the bayonet, so that if he nodded—well, he knew what would happen. Because of others! That was something the Commander-in-chief took note of, that the man should do a thing like that because of his sense of responsibility. To have nodded, to have gone off to sleep at that moment, would maybe have given the enemy the advantage. We know what the New Testament says about Satan getting an advantage (II Cor. ii. 11).

But here again, the point of discipline is the realisation that we do not live to ourselves or die to ourselves (Rom. xiv. 7); that in what we do we involve others. That has already been said in an earlier chapter; but let us hear the added emphasis as it comes up again in this connection. 'Now then, I must—or I must not—and not only because of myself. If it were only myself, well, what matter?' If it just began and ended with ourselves, we would sometimes perhaps let our lives go and our testimony go. But there is very much more in it. ' I dare not, I must not—or I must—because . . .'—because of others and because of the battle. Discipline calls for selflessness.

(4) AS TO LOSING HEART

How great is the constant temptation, under the long-drawn-out wear and tear of the campaign, to weaken, to lose heart, just to drop out, or to cease to be a positive factor. How often we have to pull ourselves up, do we not, under discouraging conditions, when we are inclined to feel it is not worth it, when inertia comes over us and we fall into a state of despondency and depression. That is the time when discipline is tested. The undisciplined just give way ; the disciplined do not. Our reaction to the temptation to give up will be according to whether we have or have not been thoroughly disciplined. We are tested then ; we are found out.

(5) AS TO SERVICE

Finally, discipline is related to service. That was involved in what we said just now, but it is particularly so in regard to the *spirit* of service. In the book that we have been considering, it is made very much of that there should be a *spirit* of service. I think that spirit is leaving the world, is being very largely lost to the world to-day. There are very few left who have a spirit of service— shall I say, of *servanthood*. But the Lord Jesus said : " I

G

am in the midst of you as he that serveth " (Luke xxii. 27). " The Son of man came not to be ministered unto, but to minister " (Mark x. 45). It is not difficult to see the connection between service and discipline. Evidence of it is, indeed, provided by the association of the contrary conditions to these in the world to-day. The opposites go together : the loss of the spirit of service goes hand in hand with the loss of discipline.

THE LORD'S CONCERN FOR DISCIPLINE

Let us now bring this matter right over to our own lives as the Lord's people. It is very important for us to realise that the Lord Himself is most particular on this question of discipline. Perhaps we know it, in a way ; perhaps we have come up against it ; and yet maybe we have not given it much thought—we have not looked it straight in the eyes and recognised it. The Lord Himself is very particular about discipline. Whether we do or not, the Lord views everything from the standpoint of the war. He has filled the Bible with this matter of warfare. He Himself is declared to be " a man of war " (Ex. xv. 3). The Lord knows that there is a war on, and He knows everything about it. We may think we know a little about it, but He has complete cognisance of the full extent and range of this spiritual war that is in progress. For it is a terrific conflict that is raging between these two great kingdoms and powers and systems. And so He views everything from the standpoint of the war, and deals with us on the basis of war conditions. He is therefore most particular about this matter of discipline.

Now, let your imagination rove over such a point of view, and at once you will see why the Lord is very strict with us. He would say to us, in effect: 'Do you not realise that you are in a great conflict? Do you not realise that you are—or at any rate are supposed to be— a soldier on active service, under war conditions, and subject to all the rigours of such conditions? In the light of this, what kind of Christian are you?' The Lord does not let us off; He pulls us up, He really keeps us on a basis of discipline, because He views everything from the standpoint of the war and its issue, whether we are effectives or not. Perhaps that is why He was seemingly a little unkind to Elijah under the juniper tree. 'What are you doing here? You are supposed to be in the battle! What are you doing here? The battle is on! We have just had one tremendous set-to on the mount, but we are not through with this yet. What are you doing here?' But whether that be the right interpretation of the story or not, I find that very often the Lord challenges me like that: 'What are you doing here, what do you mean by this? What are you down there for? Are you forgetting that there is a war on and that you are in it?' So the Lord is careful, particular; He deals with us from that standpoint and on that basis.

And, as we said earlier, do not forget that the Lord takes account of us in secret. The parade ground is one thing, when everybody is looking on and we know what is expected of us before all eyes. But the Lord takes account of us in secret. He did of David. David was

God's choice because He had watched him in secret—in secret responsibility. You and I must remember that God chooses and uses, promotes and advances, those who remain true without the incentive of publicity. Have you grasped that? Do you want the Lord to choose you, to use you, to advance you, to give you more responsibility, to promote you? He will do it, not by what you are in the public eye, but by what you are in secret: for it is there that discipline counts most—when there is nothing whatever to give us an incentive, other than, ' Well, there is a battle on, and we must count in it!'

This covers, of course, a lot of ground. It explains so much of the Lord's dealings with us, does it not? That is why we have such discipline, why we are put into positions where it is so hard, where there is seemingly no inspiration, no encouragement, no incentive at all. We are brought into situations where we are either going to stand or fall, and sometimes the testing is the more intense because it seems to us not to matter which we do. That is a real test of discipline!

(B) PROVISIONING

We come now to a factor that will sooner or later vitally affect an Army and all the units which make up the Army—the matter of provisioning. There may be much enthusiasm at the setting out, a good deal of abandonment. There may be a great deal of initial good spirit and good intention. But the things that count in the long run are constitution and stamina and endurance, and those things depend upon provisioning, on supplies, on food. You know Napoleon's statement, do you not, about that on which an Army advances? It is very true! And if it is true in the natural, it is equally, if not more, true in the spiritual. It is a very great mistake, indeed it positively imperils the Forces, to send them into the field on a hand-to-mouth basis of supply, without adequate support in resources. And in the story of which we are thinking, thinning ranks, disaffection, disintegration, and many other troubles arose because the men were not being properly fed, because adequate provisions were not available.

PROVISIONING A VITAL FACTOR IN ENDURANCE

Food, then, is a vital factor in the whole strategy of war. Provisioning is, indeed, not a luxury—it is an absolute necessity; and that is true spiritually. You and I must put from our minds any idea that the obtaining of spiritual food is something optional, governed by whether we feel inclined for it or not. To have adequate resources available, and to make good use of them, is an essential part of the whole campaign. And so our attitude toward this matter has to be quite a serious one. The war depends upon our spiritual constitution, our powers of endurance, our stamina, and these in turn depend upon our feeding, upon the provision made. Fighting forces cannot continue indefinitely on stimulants, certainly not on 'dopes'; they need *feeding*.

But in the Christian world there is a lot of 'stimulat-

ing ' and ' doping ' going on that is not feeding. It is an
endeavour to work something up, to get people going
for a while ; but it will not work when they come into
situations where real endurance is called for. And so the
Supreme Command takes account of this—it makes provision for a long-term conflict ; and the sooner we get
adjusted to that, the better. There are those who may
fight pretty well if they think it is all going to be over
soon. But we know quite well, do we not, from history
that it is those who can hold out the longest who win the
day. How much there is in the New Testament about
this whole matter of spiritual stamina, and endurance,
and steadfastness ! " He that endureth to the end, the
same shall be saved " (Matt. x. 22, xxiv. 13). (Compare
Heb. iii. 6, 14 ; vi. 11 ; Rev. ii. 26.)

Now, there is far more in this matter of the Lord pro-
viding spiritual food for us than perhaps we realise. Let
us make no mistake about it : sooner or later we shall be
found out over this. It will be those who have been
nourished in spiritual things, built up in spiritual things ;
who have made good use of all the possibilities of spiritual food available : it will be they who will stand when
the real test comes. Is it not true to our experience, even
in quite a simple way, that very often when we are up
against things we are able to draw upon what the Lord
has taught us in the past? Without that reserve, we
should be at a loss—we could not get through ; but now
we are all the time able to draw upon what the Lord has
given us. How wonderfully it rises up, again and again,
just as He promised (John xiv. 26), to save us in a criti-

cal hour and situation! We remember His word and His way in the past: and it counts, it amounts to something. But on the other hand, how many there are who just go out under the pressure, because they have no background—they have not that knowledge of the Lord which the occasion demands.

THE NEED FOR CONCERN REGARDING GOD'S PROVISION

But we need to remember that, while the Lord is only too willing and ready to make provision, He does demand that there be a concern for it on the part of those for whom the provision is to be made. I think that this goes to the heart of a great deal. There is, as you know, a widespread complaint about this matter of spiritual food: a complaint that there is so little available, so little real teaching, so little strong meat. However it may be put, there is quite a complaint about this food shortage. But may not the existence of the condition complained of be very largely due to an insufficient concern for spiritual food on the part of either the officers or the people? They have not been careful over the matter, not really concerned about it. They have been content to live upon a light diet of Christian things. The Lord will make resources available for those who really mean business. For those who are really right in the battle, who are really concerned about His honour and about the victory, the Lord will see that adequate supplies are there. If you and I are not of that mind and dis-

position, the Lord Himself will not 'cast His pearls
before swine '—He will not give His spiritual riches to
those who are not greatly concerned. But, if we are, then
He will make the provision.

You see, the Lord always aims to make His provision
profitable, by giving it over against a practical background. There has to be a practical background before
we can profit by the provision the Lord makes. That is
why He is constantly precipitating us into situations that
make it necessary for us to know Him in some deeper
way. Is it not a very familiar fact that what we have in
the whole of the New Testament is given to us over
against a very practical background? Men did not sit
down to write essays and treatises, and that sort of thing.
They were facing extremely critical situations, and they
wrote to meet those situations. It was matters of life or
death that drew out all these writings. That was the
background ; and what was true then is still true in our
lives, that we shall never profit by the Lord's provision
unless we have a practical background.

The Divine Provision—" The Bread of Life "

What we need to grasp is that the principle of food is
life. It is not a matter of whether we like or dislike,
whether we fancy or do not fancy—whether we are
' finicky '—it is not that at all. It is simply and entirely a
matter of life—LIFE ! That is why the Lord Jesus said :
" I am the bread of *life* " (John vi. 35). And if we are
to profit by that Bread, there must be the same life in us

as is in the Bread. There must be a correspondence of life—life taking hold of life and life ministering to life. It has to be a *vital* matter, not just interest.

It is a solemn fact that you can have a thorough-going acquaintance with the Bible as a book, and you can attend all the Bible lectures that are going, and still not grow spiritually. I know that to be true. For some years I was closely associated with Dr. Campbell Morgan, as one of the members of his Bible Teachers' Association, the whole method of which was the analytical teaching of the Bible. But with all that, and years of it, many of the people who attended the Bible lectures showed little or no spiritual growth. Very few of them came to anything like spiritual maturity ; they were still babes after they had heard it all. They had it all stored in their notebooks—they knew it in that way ; but as for being vital factors in the great campaign, they counted for little or nothing.

No : it is not merely a question of knowing the Bible in that way, although that may be a useful thing as a foundation. The essential thing is that it should be a matter of life—indeed of life or death. Those are the two alternatives. Our very survival depends upon this matter of food.

And the food is Christ. The Lord Jesus did not say, ' I give you a volume of teaching to feed upon.' He said : ' *I* am the bread of life "—' I, *personally*, am the bread of life '. And so before we can profit by the bread we must know a vital, practical relationship with Him. There has to be a *life*-relationship between the feeder and the food.

It is really a question of the *kind* of food. Different species require different kinds of food: the food of one class of creation differs from that of another. You and I could not live on the food of certain species of animal; they probably could not live on our kind of food. A spiritual person (which is to say a *normal Christian*) belongs to a species whose need can only be met by spiritual feeding: that is, by a real, living knowledge of the Lord; and it is that alone that will make for triumphant warfare. A 'natural', intellectual acquisition of knowledge of the Bible is no substitute for spiritual food.

Let us, then, seek to draw the important lessons from all this. Let us not think of spiritual provision as something that we can take or leave. Such an attitude will find us out in the battle, sooner or later. I believe that there are many in this world who are now discovering the tremendous value of all that they have been taught and have learnt of the Lord in the past, while others are finding that they have not the resource for going through.

(C) FLEXIBILITY

I quote again from the book: 'The hardest test of generalship is to hold the balance between determination and flexibility. In this the enemy failed. He scored highly by determination; he paid heavily for lack of flexibility.'

In case this word ' flexibility ' should occasion difficulty, let us suggest some alternatives. For instance : adjustableness ; adaptability ; teachableness, or ' teachability ' ; resourcefulness ; originality. These are all side-lights on the word ' flexibility '. In the South-East Asia campaign, the quotation that I have given meant just this : that the enemy had got so much into a rut ; he was so decided on a certain course, and was so rigidly bound by it, that if anything upset it he was completely de-moralised. He had no alternative; he had no resourceful-ness with which to meet a surprise, to meet something that was outside of his programme. If things went off his set course, he was just thrown into confusion. As this quotation says, ' he paid heavily for his lack of flexi-bility '. Here we really have something to learn.

Perhaps we cannot make too much of the quality of *determination*. The New Testament is so full of the matter of steadfast endurance : being set on going on : not being turned aside ; and this is right—we should be people like that. But you see what is said here : ' The hardest test of generalship is to hold the balance between determination and flexibility.' When you get down to it, you find that that really is a hard lesson : it is a hard thing to learn how to adjust yourself to new situations, and yet remain steadfast. Happily, we have some illustra-tions of this in the New Testament, and we do not go very far into the history of the Church before we come on them.

(1)   PETER AND CORNELIUS

Now Peter had got his fixed way, his fixed position, according to the Old Testament and his interpretation of it. And from his fixed position, his rigid, static position, he would argue with the Lord: "Not so, Lord"! Until he had "thought on the vision" (Acts x. 19), and got through with the Lord on the matter, he was not flexible, he was not adjustable, he was not even teachable. But what a tremendous advance, not only for Peter, but for the whole Church, when, without giving away any steadfastness or determination, he adjusted to the new light that the Lord gave, to a new knowing of the Lord, and the way of the Lord. And yet many people cannot do that; they just cannot do it.

(2) PHILIP AND THE ETHIOPIAN EUNUCH

Take the incident of Philip and the eunuch. It is just the same principle. Philip was down at Samaria, and under the blessing of the Lord wonderful things were happening. Philip could easily have said, 'The Lord is blessing me, the Lord is doing a great thing: I ought therefore not to leave this—this is where the Lord is working, this is what the Lord is doing', and so on. Well, of course it depends upon whether the Lord tells you to or not. But it also depends on whether you are open to the Lord: upon your having no fixity or finality about your position, but being ready to be moved by the Lord—even though it may seem a strange kind of move to be transferred from a revival centre, with many coming to the Lord, to an almost empty desert.

Nevertheless, it meant no small advance for the Church that Philip was flexible. For the matter did not end with a desert. From that point there opened up for Philip a long story of ministry. We are not now dealing with New Testament development or history; but you will find, if you look into it, that, after this contact with the Ethiopian, some very vital things came into being through the ministry of Philip. And it all hung upon this matter of flexibility, adjustableness; on whether the Lord was free to have His way in that life, or whether Philip would say, ' No: this is where I am and this is how things are ; this is what the Lord is doing and where He is doing it; and here I stay ' ! It may be that comparable issues are in the balance in the lives of many servants of the Lord to-day.

(3) PAUL AND MACEDONIA

One more illustration—and it is a very great one, is it not?—Paul and Macedonia. Paul was set on going to Asia and Bithynia. But he came to the point where he was brought up short—"forbidden of the Holy Ghost": "the Spirit of Jesus suffered them not" (Acts xvi. 6, 7). But Paul was adjustable, that is the point; he was flexible. And so—Macedonia and Europe! and how much more! !

These three examples illustrate the principle of being open to the Lord: of being in the Lord's hands and not in your own: of not being under any fixed mind as to what the Lord should do, and where He should do it, or how He should do it—that is with Him. It is one of the most important principles that the Lord would teach us.

GOD'S UNCHANGING TRUTHS AND CHANGING METHODS

We have to recognise that there are two sets of things. On the one side there is fundamental truth, about which we are never flexible and from which we never depart. There can be no question of giving up fundamental truth, or of changing our foundations. They remain : on that we are—or should be—inflexible. We ought to be immovable, too, on the matter of the all-governing object of God : as to that, we are set, and nothing will move us. And it is also required that we be found with steadfastness of spirit.

But, on the other side, we have to recognise that God changes His methods. While He does not change His truths and His foundations and His object, He changes His methods. He has in His own sovereign right the pre-rogative to do as He will, and to do a new thing that was never heard of before. But that is something that Christianity to-day, for the greater part, just will not allow ! It will not even allow God Almighty to do something that He has never done before ! The lines are set, the whole compass of truth is boxed ; the methods are so-and-so, the recognised ways and means are these. Depart from these, and—well, you are unsafe, you are dangerous. There is no room allowed for the Holy Spirit to do new things. But herein is the balance : with the unchanging foundations of truth, unchanging object of God, un-changing steadfastness of spirit, on the one side, there is yet, with all that, a balance to be kept, on the other side,

with God's changing methods, God's sovereign right to
' go off the lines ' if He wills : for the lines may not be
His lines at all—they may be man's lines. God says, " I
will do a new thing ", and His absolute right to do a new
thing must be recognised.

So much, then, for flexibility. It is a very important
thing. Fixity in tradition, immovability in certain doctrinal positions, is resulting in great misunderstanding
and confusion, arrest and disintegration. Through this
limiting of the Holy Spirit, much is being lost.

Now, even if we do not grasp or appreciate much of
the details, there are simple lessons lying on the surface
of these three things that we have considered.

(a) *Discipline.* The Lord must have a disciplined
people, and He is very particular about our discipline in
all its connections—behaviour, spiritual health, and
so on.

(b) *Provisioning.* The Lord would have a well-nour-
ished people, and He would have us careful about our
spiritual food, to guard it. The enemy has a real eye to
business on the food of God's people, as Gideon will tell
us (Judges vi. 3, 4, 11).

(c) *Flexibility.* The Lord's desire is that, while we
should be very steadfast and immovable as to those
things which are fundamental to the faith, and in spirit,
and in relation to His ultimate end, we should yet be so
open to Him, so teachable, as to be, in a right way,
pliable ; in a right way, yes, changeable. There is much
paradox about all these things, is there not? It is wrong

to be changeable in some ways, but when it is the Lord calling for this adjustableness to Himself and what He would do, it is certainly right, and our response may, indeed, affect the whole issue of the war.

These things, presented to us in the Word by illustration and incident, embody very important principles. But when all is said, it comes back to this—everything strengthens this matter : *We are in a war*—a war that is no mere vague, abstract, ' airy-fairy ' kind of thing, but is very real, with many practical matters relating to the issue. These practical matters of behaviour, of provisioning, and of adjustability, all relate to the issue of this war.

The Lord teach us, then, the laws of—

OUR WARFARE !

SeedSowers
P.O. Box 3317
Jacksonville, FL 32206
800-228-2665

904-598-3456 (fax)   www.seedsowers.com

THE CHRONICLES OF THE DOOR *(Edwards)*

The Beginning 8.99
The Escape 8.99
The Birth 8.99
The Triumph 8.99
The Return 8.99

THE WORKS OF T. AUSTIN-SPARKS

The Centrality of Jesus Christ 19.95
The House of God 29.95
Ministry 29.95
Service 19.95

COMFORT AND HEALING

A Tale of Three Kings *(Edwards)* 8.99
The Prisoner in the Third Cell *(Edwards)* 5.99
Letters to a Devastated Christian *(Edwards)* 5.95
Healing for those who have been Crucified by Christians *(Edwards)* 8.95
Dear Lillian *(Edwards)* 5.95

OTHER BOOKS ON CHURCH LIFE

Climb the Highest Mountain *(Edwards)* 9.95
The Torch of the Testimony *(Kennedy)* 14.95
The Passing of the Torch *(Chen)* 9.95
Going to Church in the First Century *(Banks)* 5.95
When the Church was Young *(Loosley)* 14.95
Church Unity *(Litzman, Nee, Edwards)* 14.95
Let's Return to Christian Unity *(Kurosaki)* 14.95

CHRISTIAN LIVING

Final Steps in Christian Maturity *(Guyon)* 12.95
Turkeys and Eagles *(Lord)* 8.95
Beholding and Becoming *(Coulter)* 8.95
Life's Ultimate Privilege *(Fromke)* 7.00
Unto Full Stature *(Fromke)* 7.00
All and Only *(Kilpatrick)* 7.95
Adoration *(Kilpatrick)* 8.95
Release of the Spirit *(Nee)* 5.00
Bone of His Bone *(Huegel)* 8.95
Christ as All in All *(Haller)* 9.95

* call for a free catalog 800-228-2665